HISTORY OF THE
ANGLO-SAXONS

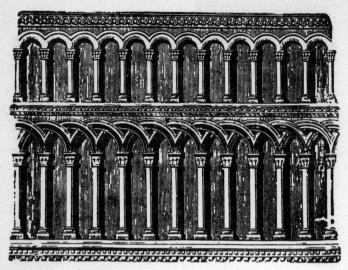

Intersecting Norman Arches, Lincoln.

St. Cuthbert's Cross.

HISTORY OF THE
ANGLO-SAXONS

SIR FRANCIS PALGRAVE

SENATE

History of the Anglo-Saxons

Previously published in 1876 by
William Tegg & Co., London

This edition published in 1995 by Senate, an imprint of
Studio Editions Ltd, Princess House, 50 Eastcastle Street,
London W1N 7AP, England

ISBN 1 85958 177 3
Printed and bound in Guernsey by
The Guernsey Press Co. Ltd

PREFACE.

My dear Friend,

The volume which I have now the satisfaction
of transmitting and inscribing to you, as a sincere,
though very inadequate, testimony of my respect and
regard, has been much altered in plan, since I was
employed upon it at your residence.

The chapters which you then perused, were intended to constitute a selection of incidents and
passages from English history, in professed imitation
of the admirable model furnished by the " Tales of a
Grandfather." As I proceeded, however, I became
more and more inclined to complete the annals of our
country. One chasm in the series was filled up after
another, and the narrative, having been composed,
de-composed, and re-composed, assumed the shape
in which it is now offered to you. That a work,
originating under such circumstances, should present
some variations of style and manner in its different
parts may, perhaps, be anticipated by the reader, and

pardoned by the critic; nor am I, on the whole, inclined to regret them.   All the merit of a volume of such humble pretensions as the present, consists in its utility.   It is my business to teach, and not to seek applause; and, considering that the "History of the Anglo-Saxons" may possibly fall into the hands of individuals of very unequal ages, I am not entirely sure whether even a greater inequality of treatment might not tend to render the lessons more generally intelligible and useful.

There are matters relating to ancient times, which, at least as far as my ability extends, cannot be distinctly brought before the consideration of a reader who is strange to the subject, without employing the most familiar and colloquial expressions.   As an example, I will instance the details of the difficulties attending ancient travelling, in the ninth chapter. The main incident of the little picture which I have introduced, were suggested by passages in the dialogues of St. Gregory; and after sedulously labouring to give a more elevated tone to the relation, I was compelled to strike out all my amendments, and to write *stet* in the margin of every line of the original text.   Other topics there are, on the contrary, which cannot be satisfactorily brought down to such a level. Explanations of the technical forms of government— the tenures of land—the principles of public policy

—delineations of character,— all come under this category ; and, therefore, in a work which can only be considered as elementary, or as a help to those who have not the leisure or the inclination to consult multifarious and diversified sources of information, the irregular contexture of the parts may, perhaps, contribute to adapt the whole of the purposes for which it is designed.

"Books," says Dr. Johnson, in the well-chosen quotation by which Mr. Murray recommends me to his customers, "that you may carry to the fire, and hold readily in your hand, are the most useful after all. A man will often look at them, and be tempted to go on, when he would have been frightened at books of a larger size or a more erudite appearance." Let me hope, then, that occasionally, whilst the younger branches find some amusement in the tales and adventures here brought together, some of the older folks may not be unwilling to take this little summary in hand, as a temporary substitute for the unmanageable folios produced by the unwearied industry of Saville, and Twysden, and Warton, and Wilkins, and which have so often descended to the floor from the desks, on which they surround me.

Upon the original sources whence the volume is derived, I will not at present enlarge; it being my intention, on a future occasion, to discuss the origin,

character, and merits of our ancient chronicles. It is
sufficient to observe, that the authorities for all the
more material facts are given in the larger work, in
which I have attempted to deduce the " rise and progress of the English Commonwealth" by and through
the history of the legal and political institutions of
our country. You will, perhaps, miss some of the
transactions noticed in that invaluable record, the
Saxon Chronicle, which you first rendered in our
vernacular language,—and you will see that I have
not attempted to enter into any details of the earlier
succession of those monarchies which finally acknowledged the supremacy of the sons of Cerdic. Yet I
hope that no fact which can fairly be considered as
tending to develop the main *epos* of Anglo-Saxon
history, has been excluded from the pages which I
have compiled.

I have attempted to direct the attention of the
student to the connexion between the states of modern
Christendom and the fourth great monarchy, the Roman empire. By some of our most popular historians,
Robertson, for instance, this fact has been entirely
forgotten or denied ; nor does the relative position of
ancient and modern Europe appear to have been
clearly understood even by Gibbon,—though the
main views have been established with singular
acuteness by Dubos, in his " Histoire critique de

l'Etablissement de la Monarchie Françoise dans les Gaules," one of the most valuable historical essays in the whole compass of literature.

Our contemporaries have done much for the elucidation of this question. Savigny has demonstrated the continuance of Roman policy and a Roman people far into the middle ages. The rise of the royal prerogatives of the English kings out of the principles of the Roman jurisprudence, has been traced, with profound learning, by Mr. Allen. And, after having long investigated the subject, I may, perhaps, be allowed to add my opinion, that there is no possible mode of exhibiting the states of western Christendom in their true aspect, unless we consider them as arising out of the dominion of the Cæsars.

In our own English history, it is also equally important that the inquirer should keep in mind the distinct and separate political existence of the different Anglo-Saxon states, after they became subject to the supremacy of one monarch. No opinion is more prevalent, and at the same time more entirely unfounded, than that which presupposes that the conquests of Egbert, so erroneously styled the " first sole monarch " of the English, incorporated the various states and communities of the Anglo-Saxon empire. This union was effected by very slow degrees. Long after the conquest, we may discern vestiges of the earlier state of government. Perhaps it was not until the reign of Edward I. that England became one commonwealth, under one king; and, from the federative spirit of our ancient constitution, some of its best and most important characteristics were derived.

I shall not be obstinate in defending the few etymologies which I have introduced. Let them be taken as helps to the memory—such I have found them—and as such they may be useful. Most of the disputes arising out of the origin of words, are literally *verbal* disputes; and, taken in connexion with history, the material points are, not so much the remote origin of a term, as the immediate source from which the sign passed into the speech of the people, and its primary application in their nomenclature. But before I dismiss this topic, let me observe that a considerable portion of the repute into which the science of etymology has fallen, in consequence of conjectures, which, to a superficial examiner, may appear overstrained, will, in great measure, be removed by deliberate inquiry. To omit more familiar examples—who would, at first sight, imagine that "*Bet*" and "*Wager*" are plants springing from the same root, only varied by the soils in which they have been planted?

In the Latin VAD-*iare* and the Anglo-Saxon

Wæd-*ian*, we find the same verb, differing only by the termination of the infinitive ; or, to speak more correctly, by the verb abbreviated and suffixed, which has converted the noun, or radical syllable, into a word of action. In the *Romance* dialects of the Latin, the transitions from "*Vadiare*" into "*Guadiare*," "*Guatgiare*," "*Guagiare*," "*Gaggier*," "*Gageure*,"—only require to be pointed out as the intermediate shades of pronunciation and inflection. From "*Gageure*" our "*Wager*" is formed : this being the shape in which we derived the term for *pledge* from our Norman conquerors. But "*Bet*" is our own, and of direct Teutonic or Anglo-Saxon lineage. "*Wæd*" or "*Wed*," in our ancient speech, is a thing pledged—the root of the verb,—and "*Bad*," whence our "*Bet*," *i. e.,* a *pledge*, or engagement that you will pay the sum you venture,—is merely a dialectical inflection of the root, used anciently in Damnonia, occurring in the compact between the English and Britons of the west. "Gif *bad* genumen sy on monnes orfe." "If a *pledge* be taken from a man's chattels." In the Danish and Belgic tongue the word is almost as near to our common term, being "*Ved*" and "*Wette ;*" and you will recollect the many derivatives, such as "*Wadset*," "*Wedding*," &c., which are all grounded upon the primary idea of "*Pledge*" or compact.

As a further help to the memory, I have also endeavoured to connect the facts of our annals with British topography, and for that purpose I have sometimes deviated a little from my direct path. Amongst the many causes which have contributed to render our Anglo-Saxon history unpopular, is the extreme difficulty of forming any definite idea of the obscure and shadowy personages who figure in its pages. But by associating their names with familiar localities, we obtain a better acquaintance with them. I am sure that Sir Walter Scott's verses, describing "King Ida's castle huge and square," have, in the present generation, done more for that same King Ida, than Nennius and Malmesbury, and all the chroniclers put together : and I have brought "Tamworth town" forward as much as I could, in order that the recollection of "Tamworth Tower" may aid to impress my readers with the remembrance of Offa, the Mercian King.

The primary purposes of this little work forbid my entering into regular discussion upon the Anglo-Saxon laws. Nor could I venture into any lengthened investigation concerning the nature of our Saxon legislature : but as you may possibly think that this subject requires some explanation, we will suppose ourselves placed in the Hall of Edward the Confessor, he who, like his predecessors, held the state of

" King of the English—Basileus of Britain—Emperor and ruler of all the sovereigns and nations who inhabit the Island—Lord Paramount of the sceptres of the Cumbrians, the Scots, and the Britons,"—and suppose yourself to be Haco, a Norwegian stranger, introduced by an Anglo-Saxon friend, and listening to his explanations of the assembly which you behold :—

" Those persons who are sitting and standing nighest to the king, are his chief officers of state. That tall, thin, rough-looking man is Algar, the *Stallere*, whom the Franks call the Constable of the Host ; and great as he is, I assure you, Haco, that not one of the king's horses is sent to grass without his special order. The portly nobleman, with the huge knife and wooden trencher, is Æthelmar, the *Dish Thane* —he carves the meat for royalty. Hugoline, that cautious, sly-looking clerk, is the *Bower Thane*, or Chamberlain ; he keeps the key of the king's *Hoard*. You would be astonished to see the heaps of treasure in the low, vaulted chamber ; and yet there is not quite so much in the Hoard as there used to be. After we had driven out your countrymen, the usurper Hardacnute, and restored our darling, King Edward, the true and legitimate heir of the right royal line of Cerdic, the *Huscarls* of the Palace still continued to collect the *Danegeld* as rigidly as before ; and many

an honest husbandman had his house and land sold
over his head, within three days after the tax became
due, to pay the arrears which he had incurred. Not
that our worthy king was ever a penny the better for
the Danegeld. Good man, he never troubles himself
about money, he leaves all that charge to Hugoline.
If you were to empty King Edward's purse before his
face he would not bid you stay your hand; he would
only say—Take care, friend, that you are not found
out by Hugoline. Though the king was so little
benefited by the taxes, I suppose that others fared
better; and the Danegeld was levied as rigidly as
ever—until one day, the king rose from his bed, asked
Hugoline for the key, and went alone into the Hoard.
And when he came out again, he told us all, with
looks of the utmost horror, that he had seen the foul
fiend dancing upon the money-bags containing the
gold which had been wrung from his suffering people,
and grinning with delight. Whether the king had
really seen anything, or whether we inconsiderately
took as a fact, what he intended merely as a parable,
denoting his opinion of the iniquity of the taxation,
I cannot tell, but from that day the Danegeld was
levied no more.

" Those quiet, shrewd-looking men, with shaven
crowns, are Osbern, Peter, Robert, Gyso, and the rest
of the clerks of the King's Chapel.   He who sits at

the head of the bench, is Reinbaldus, the Chancellor.
These venerable persons have been gradually gaining
more and more influence in the Witenagemot ; though
anciently they were only appointed for the purpose
of celebrating mass and singing in the king's chapel ;
and Reinbaldus, the Chancellor, holds merely the
place of the Arch-Chaplain of the French kings ; he
is a kind of dean, the king's confessor, who takes care
of the king's conscience, and imposes very hard pen-
ances upon him when he has sinned.   But for some
time past, our kings have been accustomed to turn
their chaplains really to good use, by employing
them constantly as their writing clerks.   In this
capacity the most important matters of public business must pass through their hands.   Hence they
have much power, and a power which was totally
unknown to our ancestors ; and in this innovating
age, their influence has been greatly increased by a
fashion which our good King Edward has brought
from France. He has caused a great seal to be made,
on which you may see his effigy, in his imperial
robes ; and to all the *writs* or written letters, which
issue in his name, an impression from that seal is
appended.

   " It is by such writs that our king signifies his
commands.   If a question of great importance is to
be decided before the thanes of the shire, in a manner

out of the ordinary course, it is heard before certain
clerks, and others, named by the king's writ. If a
clerk is promoted to a bishopric, he must have a writ
before he can be placed in his chair or throne. If
you wish to obtain the king's protection, or his
'peace,' you had best obtain a writ, by which this
favour is testified. For this purpose you must apply
to the clerks of the chapel. Whether issued by the
king's special direction or not, the writ is often a
long time in making its appearance. And suitors
find that a golden cup placed in the king's wardrobe,
or a bay stallion sent to the royal stable, has a great
effect in driving the chaplain's quill. At present,
great part of our law business is cheaply, expe-
ditiously, and equitably despatched in the ordinary
folk-moots, or courts of the hundred, or of the shire,
which go on regularly, by immemorial usage, without
any writ, or other sanction from the king. These
tribunals we derive from our remotest ancestors. We
had law before we had prerogative, and folk-moots
long before we had kings; and in your country,
Haco, they exist in great measure unimpaired. But
if, from any cause whatever, these popular courts
should decline amongst us, and the pleas which are
now decided before them, be transferred to the king's
court, it is easy to see that the whole management of
the law will fall into the hands of the chancellor and

his clerks, and of those whom the king may depute to administer justice in his name.

"So much for those who are about the king. With respect to the Witenagemot itself, you will observe, that it is divided into three orders or estates. The mitres and cowls of those who are nearest to the king, sufficiently point out that the 'lewed-folk,' or laymen, have yielded the place of honour to the clergy. The prelates, howeves, have a double right to be present, not only as teachers of the people, but as landlords. Our government, Haco, is founded upon the principle, that, in all matters concerning the commonweal, the king ought to take the advice and opinion of the principal owners of the soil. We allow only of two qualifications for a seat in this assembly : either such a station as, in itself, is an undeniable voucher for the character and respectability of the individual ; or such a share of real property as may be considered a permanent security for his good behaviour. Noble birth alone, much as we respect ancient lineage, tells for nothing whatever in our English Witenagemot, if unaccompanied by the qualification of *clerkship* or property.

"You see that near the bishops and abbots are many clergy of inferior degree. Every bishop brings with him a certain number of priests elected or selected from his own diocese. Learned clerks have told me, that this is in compliance with the canon of an ancient council; and they believe that this deputation from the dioceses has in some measure contributed to shape our temporal legislature. Others think that some such councils as the Witenagemots were held even when the Romans governed this island, and built those stately towns and palaces, of which you have seen the ruins. If Bishop Aldhelm, he who was so well read in the old Roman law books, still lived, perhaps he could give you further explanations. But the history of the past is of less consequence than the business of the present day.

"The dignified clergy, as they sit in a double right, act to a certain degree in a double capacity. In all matters of general legislation, they vote with the laymen; but if business more particularly relating to the church is discussed, they retire, and settle the affairs amongst themselves. They frequently present their 'canons' to the king and to the secular members of the Witenagemot, for the approbation and sanction of the laity. I doubt whether such sanction is strictly necessary for the validity of the ecclesiastical canons, but so long as a good understanding prevails between our clergy and our laity, it will not be necessary to define the exact boundaries of the temporal and ecclesiastical jurisdictions.

"Beneath the clergy, sit the lay peers and other

rulers, who are bound by homage to the Crown.
That vacant seat belongs to Malcolm, King of the
Scots, or, as some begin to call him, the King of
Scotland. The wicked usurper Macbeth had possession of his throne, and of those dominions in
Lothian, in respect of which the homage of the King
of Scots is more particularly rendered. Malcolm,
the vassal of our King Edward, had a full right to
claim the aid of his superior, and it was granted
right nobly. By King Edward's command, the stout
Earl Siward marched all his forces across the Tweed,
with a mighty army. Macbeth had called the Northmen—your countrymen, Haco—to his aid ; but his
resistance was hopeless : he was expelled, and Malcolm, as King Edward had commanded, was restored
to the inheritance of his ancestors. Malcolm ought
to be here in person. When he comes up, he is
escorted from shire to shire, by earls and bishops ;
and, at convenient distances, mansions and townships
have been assigned to him, where he and his attendants may abide and rest. Yet, with all these aids,
the journey is most tedious, and not unfrequently
accompanied by danger; besides which, it is not
altogether safe for Malcolm to leave the wild Scots,
his turbulent subjects, uncontrolled during the very
long space of time—seldom so little as half-a-year,
which he must pass upon the road ; Watling-street

is much out of repair; it has not had a stone laid upon it since the arrival of Hengist and Horsa; and the top of the Roman fosse-way is worse than the bottom of a ditch; and, therefore, the attendance of the King of Scots is generally excused.

" The King of Cumbria, and the kings or ' under kings ' of the Welsh, sit nigh unto the King of Scots. The two latter, Blethyn and Rhivallon, have just now sworn oaths to King Edward, and given hostages, that they will be faithful to him in all things, and everywhere ready to serve him by sea and land, and that they will perform all such obligations, in respect of the country, as ever their predecessors had done to his predecessors. But the Welsh are an unfaithful nation, untrue even to themselves. Griffith, the brother of the Welsh kings, to whom they succeed, was slain by his own men, and his bloody head was sent by Earl Harold to King Edward, at London. The Welsh are constantly rebelling against us; but we keep a firm hold upon them, and compel them, upon every needful occasion, to acknowledge our supremacy. To do them justice, though they rebel, they are truth-tellers, and never deny the fact of their legal subjection. In their triads, as well as in their laws, they commemorate the sum paid by Wales, when their kings receive the seizin or possession of their country from the King of London.

And in the very register-book of their cathedral of Landaff, have they recorded how Howell the Good submitted to the judgment of the Witenagemot held by Edward the Elder, the son of the Great Alfred, and was compelled to restore to Morgan-hên and his son Owen, the rich commots or lordships of Ystradwy and Ewyas, which he had appropriated to himself, contrary to conscience and equity.

"On the same bench with these vassal kings, sit the great earls of the realm, distinguished by the golden collars and caps of maintenance which they wear. These marks of honour have, however, long belonged to them; for it is thus that the effigy of the venerable Aylwine of East Anglia is adorned, as you may see upon his tomb at Ramsey minster. He who looks so fell and grim is Siward, the son of Beorn, Earl of Northumbria. The good people in the north, who give credit to all the sagas, or lying tales of your scallds, actually believe that Siward's grandfather was a bear in the forests of Norway, and that when his father, Beorn, lifted up his uncombed locks, the two pointed shaggy ears, which he had inherited from the bear, testified the nature of his sire. Siward himself takes no pains to contradict this story. On the contrary, I rather think that he considers it as a piece of good policy to encourage any report which may add to the terror inspired by his name. He has declared that he will never die, except in full armour.

"Earl Leofric of Mercia, as you see, keeps at a distance from Earl Godwin of Wessex. These noblemen are always opposed to each other; and I dread the consequences of such dissensions. Some earls rule only single shires. They ought more properly to be called aldermen ;—but our old English name is becoming unfashionable ; it has given way to the Danish appellation introduced under Canute, who, as I need scarcely tell you, Haco, really and truly conquered England.

"The earls thus constitute the second order of the witan. The third and lowest order in rank, yet by no means the least in importance, is composed of the thanes, who serve the king in time of war with the swords by which they are girt, and who are therefore called the king's ministers. The thanes are all landholders ; and no individual, however noble he may be, can sit amongst them, unless he is entitled to land. An East Anglian thane used to be required to possess a qualification of forty hydes, each containing from a hundred to a hundred and twenty acres. In Wessex, I believe, five hydes are sufficient ; but I am not sure, for our customs vary in almost every shire. We have no books in which they are set forth ; and the wisest clerk in Hampshire would be often puzzled, if you asked him what goes for law on the other side of the Avon.

"When the Witenagemot was last held at Oxford, I recollect conversing with some thanes who came from the Danish burghs, and here also may be others from the great cities of this kingdom. I understand that, in many of our ancient cities, the aldermen, law-men, and other magistrates, exercise their authority by virtue of the lands to which their offices are an-nexed. I dare say they are all in the house, but the place is so dark, that at this distance I really cannot distinguish their faces. As to that mixed multitude by whom the farther part of the hall is crowded, and who can be just seen behind the thanes, they consist, as far as I can judge, of the class of folks who come together in vast crowds at the meetings of our hun-dreds and our shires. It is usual, in these assemblies, that four good men and the reeve should appear from every upland or rural township ; their office being to give testimony, and to perform other acts relating to the administration of justice, and also to receive the commands of their superiors. In the Witenagemot, I believe, they are seldom or never called upon to act ; but they attend from ancient custom, deduced, per-haps, from the old time, when our kings were merely the aldermen of a single shire, and when the court in which they presided was merely the moot of their own little territory. And, whatever the rights or privileges of these churls might be in days of yore, I am tolerably sure of what they are not in these modern times. They have no weight or influence in the enactment of any law: voices, indeed, they may have, but only for the purpose of crying out—'Yea, yea!'—when the doom enacted by advice of the witan is proclaimed.

"Some of our old men have thought that this kind of assent is a recollection of the customs which prevailed amongst our forefathers, the old Saxons, before they quitted the forests of Germany, when, as it is said, the *leod*, or people at large, gave their consent to the laws which the ealdormen and priests had enacted in their solemn assembly. I am not learned enough to decide this point; it may be so; but nothing is said thereon by Alfric, or by Alfred, or by Bede; and now it is our principle, that he who is worth nothing in land, is nothing worth in public affairs, unless, as I have told you before, the place of land is supplied by learning. But Englishmen are sturdy, and not to be easily put down. I have heard strange things said about the charters granted by Athelstane to the townships of Malmsbury and Barnstaple; and if the churls in general should ever be led to imagine that they have a right to be members of the Witenagemot, I should not be surprised if they were, one day or another, to pluck up heart of grace, and cry out—'No, no!'—instead of affirming, as in duty bound, what their betters have thought best for them.

"Yet you must not suppose that these rustics are excluded by any perpetual bar. It was whilome the old English law, that if a merchant crossed the sea three times at his own risk, he obtained the rank of thane. Five hydes of land possessed by the churl for three generations, if held by him, his son, and his son's son, placed the family in the class of those who were gentle by birth and blood; 'Sithcundmen,' as such families were then called, before King Alfred's day; and though such laws are connected with usages and doctrines which have become obsolete, still we retain all the spirit of our ancient lessons of freedom; and, if qualified by station and property, there is no man between the channel and the water of Scotland, who may not acquire a share in the government of our empire.

"Haco, you well know how we call this assembly? A '*Micel getheaht,*' or great thought—a *Witena-gemot*, or 'Meeting of the Wise'—and at present it well deserves its name. Our *redes-men* or counsellors, the members of the legislature, ponder much before they come together, say little, and write less. All the dooms or statutes which have been

enacted since the days of King Ethelbert, would
not fill four-and-twenty leaves of that brass-bound
missal, which Thorold, the acolyte, has dropped
amongst the rushes on the floor.   Hence, our common
people know the laws and respect them; and, what
is of much greater importance, they respect the law-
makers—Long may they continue to deserve respect.
But I am not without apprehensions for the future.
We are strangely fond of novelty.   Since the days
of King Egbert, we have been accustomed to consider
the French as the very patterns of good government
and civilization.   And although we have seen king
after king expelled, there are numbers amongst us,
including some very estimable personages, who continue firm in this delusion.   I hear that, amongst the
French, they designate such legislative assemblies as
ours, by the name of a '*colloquium*,' or, as we should
say, a talk—which they render in their corrupted
Romance jargon, by the word *Parlement*; and, should
our Witenagemot, our Micel getheaht, ever cease to
be a meeting of the wise, or great thought, and
become a Parlement, or great-talk, it will be worse
for England than if a myriad of your northern
pirates were to ravage the land from sea to sea.

 "Haco, mark my words—if our witan ever enter
into long debates, consequences most ruinous to the
state must inevitably ensue—they will begin by con-

tradicting one another, and end by contradicting themselves. Constantly raising expectations which they never can fulfil; each party systematically decrying the acts of the other; the soc-men and churls, who compose the great body of the people, will at last fancy that the witan are no wiser than the rest of the community. They will suppose that the art of government requires neither skill nor practice; that it is accessible to the meanest capacity; that it requires nothing but Parlement, or great talk; and, leaving their ploughs and their harrows, armed with their flails and pitchforks, they will rush into the hall. They will demolish the throne, and, seizing the sceptre and the sword, they will involve the whole state in unutterable confusion and misery."

Allowing for a few anachronisms in the grouping of the individual characters, which do not alter the general truth of the picture, such was the aspect of the "Witenagemot," as far as it can be gathered from the documents which now exist; and, if you will take the trouble to consult the proofs appended to my larger work, you will find that I have mentioned no person by name who did not fill the station which I have assigned to him. Considered as a political congress, we may fairly say that the *micel gethealt* represented the whole realm. And whenever the assent of the witan was required by the monarch to

any measure of importance, the question was discussed in such an assembly. The extent of the
prerogative of the king is extremely undefined; but,
from the whole tenor of Anglo-Saxon history, we are
enabled to affirm, that every affair and matter which
concerned the empire, received the sanction of these
virtual representatives of the community.

As a legislative body, the authority of the Witenagemot appears to have been limited by the privileges
of the different states composing the Anglo-Saxon
empire; and which dominions, as I have often
remarked, had never amalgamated into one kingdom.
Kent, for instance, under the victorious Athelstane,
had lost all the appearance of an independent state.
But, when he had made a law, by the assent of the
witan of Wessex, he could not impose it upon the
men of Kent without their concurrence. He transmitted the enactment to them, and they then accepted
the proposition by an address which they returned to
their sovereign. I can quote the very words of such
a document :—

"Beloved lord, thy bishops of Kent, and all Kent-
shire, aldermen, thanes, and churls, return thanks to
thee for the directions which thou hast given unto us
concerning the conservancy of the peace, for great is
the benefit which results to all of us, both poor and
rich, thereby."

They then state the several articles or chapters of the statute, being ten in number, seriatim, and signify the manner in which they have received and modified the same. Grateful for the legislation thus bestowed upon them, the Kentishmen speak with thankfulness and humility ; yet the form of the proceeding implies that their assent, so asked, might have been refused. In proportion as the sovereign gained in prerogative, the powers of the Witenagemot of Wessex, the predominant kingdom, would gradually gain strength also. The minor states annexed to Wessex would tacitly submit to be bound by its legislation ; and, from the reign of Edgar, the lesser authorities seem, in most cases, to have been merged in the three leading states or territories of Wessex, Mercia, and Danelagh. Mercia clearly maintained its independence ; Northumbria equally so. East Anglia seems to have been sometimes considered as annexed to Mercia, sometimes as constituting a separate state, and sometimes as classing with Danish Northumbria. The laws which Edgar enacted at the request or with the assent of the witan of Wessex were to be implicitly observed by his own immediate subjects— including the Britons who inhabited the Anglo-Saxon shires. As to the others, they were to be adopted according the model enacted by the assembly. The laws were transmitted to the earls by writ ; it is most probable that they were usually received without hesitation : yet there was no absolute coercive power in the crown of Wessex ; and it was not until the reign of Canute that the Mercians received King Edgar's laws.

It is not to be supposed that the relations between the subordinate states and the paramount legislature were very accurately defined ; and we may suppose, that when defined, they were not always secure from violation. The American war took place, because the Parliament of Great Britain claimed an authority which the Assembly of New England refused. Both parties appealed to the same muniments of the same constitution ; and, whilst I am now writing, the colonial parliament of Lower Canada is at issue with the Government at home, upon many points of great weight and importance, considered as dubious, though arising out of a statute penned by a distinguished statesman now living ; who, if our legislation allowed of such a practice, might be called upon to explain the words upon which the contests arise. If such uncertainties prevail in the very midst of us, you will readily admit how hazardous it must be to theorize upon the exact rights which Northumbria possessed in the reign of the confessor. Nor will you be inclined to doubt the general accuracy of the theory which I have presented to you, though there may be doubts as to the minor details.

Recollect, also, that, in great measure, the same theory has always been familiar to us. Under one Crown, England, Scotland, and Ireland had their respective parliaments. The Isle of Man has a distinct legislature, called the "House of Keys;" and until the Duke of Athol sold the sovereignty of the island, he and the Stanleys, his ancestors, were, to all intents and purposes, kings of Man. The Norman islands of Guernsey and Jersey have their "estates," which are quite independent of the Parliament of the United Kingdom.

The theory of the rights of England and of the dependencies of the royal crown in 1683, admitted of no doubt; but the theory was not entirely respected by practical policy. When the English parliament changed the succession of the royal authority, by expelling the Stuarts, and bringing in the Prince of Orange, they did so, not only without the consent of the Irish, but entirely against their will. As for the Isle of Man, the King who then ruled was William Stanley, who sat in parliament as Earl of Derby. He possessed full rights of sovereignty within his narrow territory; yet, when the English Parliament declared that James had abdicated the throne, and the Scottish parliament voted that he forfeited his royal dignity, neither legislature thought it necessary to obtain any ratification of their proceedings from the Manx sovereign. And, lastly, if the Parliament of England thought fit to grant the supplies for a war against France, the minister did not think it necessary to wait for the concurrence of the bailiffs, jurats, and constables, who compose the supreme legislature of the Norman Isles.

This, then, was very nearly the state of the Anglo-Saxon dominions. And if, for England, Scotland, Ireland, Man, and the Norman Isles, you substitute Wessex, Northumbria, Mercia, East Anglia, and Kent, you will have a good idea of the general aspect of the mutual relations of the Anglo-Saxon states towards each other, and towards their common sovereign.

The Anglo-Saxon history, in every part and branch of it, is extremely obscure; and though I have done my best to discover the truth, still I am convinced that others, working with the same intent, may probably come to very different conclusions. No person ever can attempt any historical inquiry, who does not bring some favourite dogma of his own to the task— some principle which he wishes to support—some position which he is anxious to illustrate or defend —and it is quite useless to lament these tendencies to partiality, since they are the very incitements to the labour. And so strong is the effect of opinion, that, even in matters where there would seem to be the least possible reason for doubt, even our senses may be deluded by our passions and feelings.

The annals of justice furnish numerous instances of these hallucinations : but one of the most striking examples occurred a few years ago at Dublin :—

A pleasure-boat, belonging to a party of noted Brunswickers, having been moored on the River Liffy, near Carlisle-bridge, some of the bystanders on the adjoining quay were extremely incensed at the standard of defiance which the vessel displayed. The vane at the mast-head, like those of the ships of the conqueror, displayed an effigy—an orange-man trampling on a green shamrock. This affront, aimed at the feelings of the multitude, was not to be borne. The Milesians attacked the hostile Saxon bark by hurling a furious volley of paving-stones, and the unlucky crew, urged by danger or by apprehension, discharged their fire-arms, and wounded some of the surrounding assemblage. A great commotion was excited, the leaders of the belligerent parties were conducted to College-street Police-office ; amongst the witnesses who were called was the tin-man who had made the vane. And this worthy tradesman gave the most candid and unequivocal testimony, in full proof of the pacific intention of the pleasure-boat, though certainly somewhat to his discredit as an artist. The unlucky cause of so

much dissension and bloodshed, the supposed orange-
man trampling on the green shamrock, was in truth,
a flesh-coloured Mercury springing from a blue
cloud.

I will not stop to inquire whether the agitators
on both sides of the question might not derive some
useful instruction from this display of the effects
produced by opinion ; I will only ask you to apply
the lesson to history in general.

I have exerted myself to see the objects before me
clearly and distinctly. I have endeavoured to place
them in a proper light ; and I have approached them
as nearly as I could, in order to ensure the utmost
accuracy. However, when I took the pen in hand, I
had many an hypothesis of my own to elucidate ; nor
did I come to the task without having settled my
opinions on the most important points and doctrines
connected with history. And whilst I am most ready
to believe that my eyes may have often deceived me,
I hope that those who see differently, will admit, that
they also may, with equal unconsciousness on their
part, be labouring under a similar delusion.

Should I, therefore, be found on any occasion to
have erred, and to have mistaken green for blue, or
blue for green, I trust that those who know how
easily the tints may be confounded with each other,
will excuse the failing. Let me, however, lastly

observe, that I shall principally rest my claim for
lenient treatment upon this simple plea, that, deceived
or prejudiced as I may be—I have never thrown
stones ;—and with this appeal, I submit myself to
your judgment.

Yours ever faithfully,

FRANCIS PALGRAVE.

CONTENTS.

CHAPTER I.

CHAPTER VIII.

CHAPTER IX.

CHAPTER X.

CHAPTER XI.

CHAPTER XII.

CHAPTER XIII.

Arch-Druid in his Robes.   To face Chapter I.

HISTORY

OF THE

ANGLO-SAXONS.

Chapter I.

Ancient Population of Britain—Political State of the Provinces under the Romans—Formation of the States of Modern Europe, under the Tyrants of the Lower Empire—Tyrants of Britain—Invasions of the Saxons, Scots, and Picts—Britain finally separated from the Empire.

ACCORDING to a very ancient tradition, which, although not possessing scriptural authority, is grounded upon scripture, the "*Cymri,*" as they are still called in their own language, are decended from Gomer, the common ancestor of all the *Celtic* tribes; Britain having fallen to their lot, when the "islands of the Gentiles" were divided amongst the "children of Japhet, every one after his tongue, after their families in their nations."

Many nations have two or more designations; a name or names employed by foreigners, and a name which more properly belongs to them. Thus the people whom we know as *Bohemians,* call themselves *Czecki;* and the Hungarians call themselves *Magyar.* I mention these examples in order that you may understand how it happens that the "Cymri" are usually denominated *Britons* in our books, this latter name having been given to them

1

by the Romans from "*Prydain,*" or *Britain,* the country in which they were found.   In common English speech they are denominated *Welshmen,* a term formed from the old English or Saxon *Wilisc,* an adjective signifying any thing foreign or strange ; corresponding literally, both in etymology and application, with the Latin *Peregrinus.* * Hence *Italy* is the *Welschland* of the modern Germans, and their *Welschers* are the *Italians* :—foreigners to them, as the Britons were to the old English or Anglo-Saxon invaders.   Such double or concurrent appellations are very common ; and if their existence be kept in mind, you will be saved from much perplexity in your studies of history.

The people inhabiting the southern parts of the island, had, when the Romans first visited Britain, passed over more recently from *Belgic* Gaul, and differed from the Cymri in race, being of the *Teutonic* family of nations. But the lines of demarcation between the *Celts* and the *Teutons* were not then so well defined as in subsequent times.   The distinctions which now characterise the progeny of Adam have been continually increasing, since the children of men were first scattered abroad on the face of the earth.   And the more we ascend in history, the more apparent are the traces of that unity which subsisted, when we were all of one speech and one language, in the plain of Shinar.

Like all the other Gentiles, the Britons had abandoned the worship of the Almighty, and believed in false gods,

* The root *Wealh,* (A. S.) or *Wale* (Germ.) denotes a *foreigner* or *stranger;* and was so applied, as far back as any of the Teutonic dialects can be traced. In the very ancient gloss upon the Salic laws, the Romans dwelling amongst the Franks are called " *Wala Leodi,*" *homines Peregrini.—Wachter,* p. 1812.   The compass of this work does not admit of any lengthened disquisitions, and I shall therefore merely notice those etymologies which, upon consideration of the best authority, appear most plausible.

Ruins of Stonehenge.

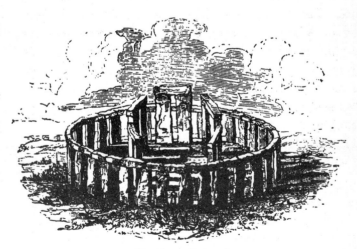

Stonehenge Restored.

British Coracles.

to whom they offered human sacrifices. They were so infatuated as to think that the favour of their idols could be obtained by slaying men and women. And this they did most cruelly; inclosing the victims in huge figures of wicker-work, and burning the wretched sufferers alive. The Druids were the priests of the Britons, and probably the lawgivers of the people. Amongst other rites, we are told that they used to cut the misletoe, with great ceremony, on the sixth day of the moon, employing for that purpose a sickle of pure gold. The oak is said to have been venerated amongst them; but, beyond a few particulars which have been preserved by Greek and Roman writers, we know little concerning their tenets. The doctrines of the Druids were not reduced into writing, but preserved by oral tradition; and when the Druidical priesthood was extinguished, their lore was lost, excepting the few vestiges which may be collected from the compositions of the British Bards, and the proverbial *triads* of the Cymri.*

The temples in which the Britons worshipped their deities, were composed of large, rough stones, disposed in circles; for they had not sufficient skill to execute any finished edifices. Some of these circles are yet existing; such is Stonehenge, near Salisbury: the huge masses of rock may still be seen there, grey with age; and the structure is yet sufficiently perfect to enable us to understand how the whole pile was anciently arranged. Stonehenge possesses a stern and savage magnificence. The masses of which it is composed are so large, that the structure seems to have been raised by more than human power. Hence, *Choir-gaur*† was fabled to have been

---

* Some of these memorials relate to law, others to history. As their name imports, each *triad* contains three facts, precepts, or definitions.

  † The " *Giant's Dance*"—the British name of Stonehenge.

4 HISTORY OF THE ANGLO-SAXONS. [Chap. I.

built by giants, or otherwise constructed by magic art. All around you in the plain, you will see mounds of earth or " tumuli," beneath which the Britons buried their dead. Antiquaries have sometimes opened these mounds, and there they have discovered vases, containing the ashes and the bones of the primeval Britons, together with their swords and hatchets, and arrowheads of flint or of bronze, and beads of glass and amber ; for the Britons probably believed, that the dead yet delighted in those things which had pleased them when they were alive, and that the disembodied spirit retained the inclinations and affections of mortality.

The Cymric Britons, though they lived in an island, had no boats or vessels except *coracles*, framed of slight ribs of wood covered with hides. These frail barks are still used by the Welsh fishermen on the Wye ; and it may be remarked that the Celtic tribes in general have never taken to the sea, whilst the Teutons seem always to have enjoyed the dangers of the ocean. But the valour of the Britons was displayed on land : they were brave and sturdy warriors ; and when they went forth to combat, they rode in chariots, with blades of scythes fixed to the axle-trees of the wheels. Engaged in battle, they urged their horses to their utmost speed, and the sharp edges of the scythes mowed down the enemy. But the prowess of the Britons was of little use or profit, for they were always quarrelling amongst themselves ; and it was in consequence of these dissensions that they were at last subdued by the Romans. If the Britons had made common cause, the Romans might not have prevailed against them : but the insular tribes or nations were divided and disunited ; envious of each other ; and when one tribe was conquered, the others

delighted in the misfortunes of their countrymen, and
then the same fate befel them in their turn.   The moral
deduced from the old fable of the bundle of sticks may be
applied with equal truth to families or nations.

Julius Cæsar was the first civilized stranger who attacked the island ;* but his incursions were confined to
the southern coast, and the Roman dominion did not
attain its full extent in Britain until Cnæus Julius
Agricola† took the command.

It does not appear that the Romans ever conquered
the more remote parts, beyond the Friths of Forth and
Clyde : the wall constructed by Lollius Urbicus, in the
reign of Antoninus Pius, and extending from Caer-riden
to Alcluid, or Dumbarton, was erected for the purpose
of protecting the Roman provinces against the inroads
of the unsubdued tribes,—who, under the names of
Caledonians and Picts,‡ inhabited the fastnesses beyond.
Other fortifications of the same description, between the
Solway Frith and the Tyne, constructed by Adrian and
Severus, constituted a second line of defence, stretching
from sea to sea.

Castles and towers,—"Burgi," as they were called by
the Romans,—ranged along these walls ; and these for-
tresses were constantly garrisoned by armed men.   The
stations were so near to each other, that if a beacon was
lighted on any one of the bulwarks, the warriors who
garrisoned the next station were able to see and to repeat the signal almost at the same instant ; and the next
onwards did the same ; by which token they announced
that some danger was impending.   So that, in a very
short time, all the soldiers who guarded the line of wall

* B.C. 52, 51.   † A.D. 78.
‡ The name of " Pict" does not appear till that of *Caledonians* began to go
out of use, but both probably denoted the same people.

could be assembled. The coast was protected with equal
care against any invading enemy ; and the ancient maritime stations, Garianonum and Portus Rhutupis, may
be instanced as fine specimens of Roman skill and industry. The Romans also fortified many strong cities
in different parts of the island, which they surrounded
by lofty ramparts. These "colonies," or "municipia,"
were peopled with Roman inhabitants, who came hither
from Italy, accompanied by their wives and children ;
and within the circuit of the fortifications, they built
temples, and palaces, and baths, and many other splendid
structures, living in great luxury and delight. Frequently it happens, that when workmen are employed
in digging the foundations of new erections in modern
towns, occupying the site of Roman cities, such as Gloucester, Cirencester, and Colchester, they find beautiful
tesselated pavements, composed of coloured stones, arranged in elegant patterns, the adornments of the Roman
palaces, though they now lie at a great depth below the
surface of the ground. And often you may see the
marks of the fire by which the dwellings themselves
were ruined, in the sieges which the cities sustained.

Many of our Roman cities have become entirely wasted
and desolate—Silchester is one of these. Corn-fields
and pastures cover the spot once adorned with public
and private buildings, all of which are now wholly destroyed. Like the busy crowds who inhabited them, the
edifices have sunk beneath the fresh and silent green-
sward; but the flinty wall which surrounded the city is
yet firm, and the direction of the streets may be discerned
by the difference of tint in the herbage ; and the plough-
share turns up the medals of the Cæsars, so long dead
and forgotten, who were once the masters of the world.

Garianonum (Burgh Castle, Suffolk).

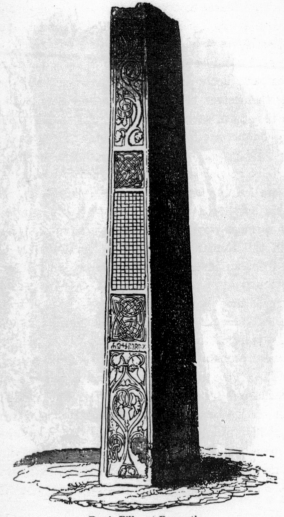

Runic Pillar at Bewcastle.

The Britons, or at least those tribes who inhabited the vicinity of the Roman colonies, soon adopted and emulated the customs of their masters, for evil as well as good. They learnt to speak the Latin language, adopted Latin names, clad themselves in rich raiment, and vied with the Romans in every luxury of corrupted Rome. In the earlier stages of the Roman conquests, the native Princes were, according to the usual custom of nations calling themselves civilized, when they deal with those whom they term savages, treated with merciless severity by the conquerors, for daring to struggle against their power. Boadicea, bleeding beneath the scourge, and Caractacus, or Caradoc, driven in fetters by the scoffing lictor, are familiar examples of this unrelenting tyranny. But this harshness was not always exerted; and other British princes were allowed to retain their dominions beneath the Roman supremacy. Cogidumnus, who appears, from an inscription discovered at Chichester, to have reigned in or near Sussex, the ancient territory of the Regni, may be quoted as one of these tributary governors. In such a country, the native population, having a ruler of their own race and blood placed over them, were probably less oppressed than in those parts where they were immediately beneath the rod of the Roman masters. But in other districts, and particularly towards the eastern side of the island, it should seem as if the British nobility and aristocracy had been entirely swept away, and the land allotted out to the Roman colonists, under whose power the British cultivators of the soil passed into a state of prædial slavery or villainage.

When we speak of the " Roman empire," we are apt to consider it as a consolidated power. We see only the

imperial standard, and contemplate only the majesty of
Rome. But the real state of things under the dominion
of the Eagle may in some measure be understood, by
considering the present condition of the provinces and
dominions subdued by the Russians, and added to the
dominion of the Czar. In some parts are flourishing
cities, Odessa for example, peopled by the conquering
race, speaking their language and governed by their
laws. In others (as in the Crimea generally) the Russians have become the owners of the soil, and the ancient
rulers, the Tartar Mirzas and Khans, have been expelled;
but the conquest has not displaced the ancient Tartar
peasantry, who retain their former customs, and, as yet,
are not greatly affected by the influence of the lords to
whom they belong. A third class will consist of such
provinces as Mingrelia, where the ancient rulers remain
in their seats, though entirely controlled by a governor
appointed by the Autocrat, beneath whose military sway
the kingdom is allowed to subsist. Furthermore, a
fourth class may be placed in provinces like Esthonia
and Livonia, which retain their former mixed government, though the ancient line of princes has become
extinct, and the sovereignty is vested in the Russian
Emperor. In Esthonia there is a " Land-tag," composed
of nobles and deputies of the towns. This assembly
exists in a state of respectable debility—not so strong
as to excite the jealousy of the emperor,—nor so weak
as to be entirely ineffective. By the Land-tag, laws may
be enacted concerning local regulations or affairs of the
province. Some taxes are apportioned by its power.
Yet, at the same time that the Autocrat of all the Russias
tolerates the existence of the Land-tag, his ukases, issued
from St. Petersburg, many overturn all the legislation

thus exercised; and he is, in theory, if not in practice, the uncontrolled master of the lives and fortunes of the Esthonian people, who, if he should think fit to act the despot, have no resource against his supreme authority. Lastly, in the so-called kingdom of Poland, there exists, by the grant and concession of the emperor, a "Diet," formed, in part, out of the original legislature possessed by the country when independent—but Russianized, remodelled, restricted, and re-formed—having a sufficient degree of consequence to prevent the Polish nation from being amalgamated into one mass with the Russians, and yet entirely incompetent to limit the Emperor's power, except so far as a discreet or benevolent Sovereign may think it just or expedient to give way to the opinion of his subjects, when respectfully expressed.

Now, if the Russian government were subverted, the cities to which I have alluded would still retain a portion of the organization which they have received. In the Provinces overspread by the Russians, the ancient races would regain their ascendancy, though they would probably retain (particularly in military discipline) many vestiges of the policy imparted by their late rulers. The third class of Provinces, or those whose dependent sovereigns are governed by the Court of St. Petersburg, would reappear in their primitive form, except so far as their Shahs or Sultans might think fit, as they probably would, to adopt such customs and principles as should tend either to enhance the splendour of their court, or to increase the authority which they would then enjoy, released from Russian supremacy. In the fourth class, in Esthonia and in Poland, the *Land-tag* and the *Diet* would gain in power, and acquire more consistency; and, under favourable circumstances,—assuming, for instance,

that these legislatures continued to exist quietly, until the
towns became opulent and the serfs free,—they might
become substantial checks upon the prerogatives of any
monarch by whom the country should be ruled.

All these suppositions are made upon the hypothesis of
a mere dissolution of the Russian empire ; but if that
dissolution were followed by an irruption of some much
less civilized nation, say the Mongul Tartars, the features
of the older dominion would be much more obscured ;
many of the laws and customs of the invaders would be
implanted by them : and the Russian laws and modes of
government would be kept down by the customs of a wild
nomadic people ; and yet the general relation of the parts
of the empire towards each other would remain the same,
unless it should happen that in any district all the ancient
inhabitants were violently expelled.

The parallel between the Russian empire and the Roman empire will not hold good in any of its minor details :
but in the general outline it is tolerably accurate ; and I
introduce it in this place, in order that the young reader
may understand how the Roman provinces were circumstanced, at the dawn of the history of modern Christendom.

The colonial policy of Rome sustained considerable
alterations in form, between the age of Agricola and the
fifth century ; but the main principles remain unchanged.
Taking the reign of Constantine as a middle point of
development, though not exactly of time, the whole
Roman Empire was then divided into four great "Prefectures, or governments, Britain being included in the
jurisdiction of the Prefect of the Gauls, who held his
court at Treves, and afterwards at Arles. The Prefectures were divided into " Dioceses."—Britain was a

Diocese—and the Dioceses into "Provinces," subjected to Presidents, or Consulars, and Vicars, or Vice-presidents, each in their degree invested with the various powers of judicial government and civil policy. The military command of the provinces was principally intrusted to the "*Comites*," each having his own district or territory. From the reign of Constantine, these functionaries held a conspicuous rank in the state. The *Comes*, or *Companion*, of Augustus was only his confidential friend; but the companions of the Cæsar were gradually erected into a dignified order, and the title became at length a designation both of military and civil dignity. Besides the military *Comites*, there were others in every department of the government. The title was particularly bestowed upon the attendants of the Imperial Court. There was a Count of the physicians, a Count of the wardrobe, a Count of the treasury, and a "*Comes stabuli*," or Count of the stable,* from whose station one of the proudest titles of the European monarchies was derived.

The Cities enjoyed considerable privileges, and possessed a distinct political existence. The ruling body, termed the *Curia*, was composed of *Senators* or *Decurions* : but, besides the main corporation, each city contained various "*colleges*," companies, or guilds, of traders and artificers; and if I were a freemason, which I am not, I should perhaps be able to ascertain whether the "Lodge

---

* As the *Comes stabuli*, or *Constable*, had the charge of the King's horses, he became, by an easy transition, the Marshal, or commander of the King's Cavalry, which in fact constituted the whole efficient body of the army. The hereditary Constables of Castile, of France, and of England, were all so powerful, that the sovereigns were glad to suppress a dignity which conferred an authority dangerous to the tranquillity of the monarchy. The office of Lord High Constable now exists only in Scotland, in the person of the Earl of Errol: on certain great occasions, some nobleman is made Lord High Constable of England *for the day*.

of Antiquity" at York is, as the members of the craft
pretend, a real scion from the Roman stock, subsisting
through so many changes.

The most absolute authority was vested in the Roman
emperor,—Louis the Fourteenth's saying, " *L'état; c'est
moi*," is only another version of the *Lex Regia*, an edict
by which, according to the theory of the civil law, all
the powers of the state had been concentrated in the
person of the " Imperial Majesty." As to the *Lex
Regia*, it is certain that no such edict was ever passed or
made by the Roman Senate, but the Emperors acted as
if it had; and a legal fiction, believed by government,
and which no subject can dare to dispute, has quite as
much validity as if it were the truth itself, and sustained
by the most lawful authority. The Prefects and other
Governors were, practically, and in their own depart-
ments, as despotic as the Emperor himself; yet a species
of controlling power existed in the provincial councils or
assemblies. The constitution of these senates cannot be
precisely defined. Some few particulars, however, may
be collected. Deputies, or Magistrates, from the cities
attended them. The great landed proprietors had also
seats; and perhaps the Bishops were admitted after the
establishment of Christianity. The Councils assembled
in course, and at stated times of the year, unless any
emergency arose, in which case they were summoned by
the rescript of the Emperor. If local regulations only
were required, the councils were authorised to enact
ordinances; but in matters of importance, and especially
if the Provincials needed the redress of any grievance,
they could only address their *petitions* to the Emperor.
The Prefect could not give his assent to such requests,
and the " Legates" to whom the bills were intrusted,

resorted for that purpose to the Presence-Chamber, or
according to the pompous phraseology of Byzantium,
" *the sacred consistory;*" and then the Sovereign, if he
thought fit, acceded to their request.

In point of form, this proceeding was very similar to
that adopted by the Cortes of Castile, the States-general
of France, and the Parliament of England. In all these
assemblies, the subjects pray to the King for redress,
and the answer to their petition constitutes the basis of
the *Fuero*,* Law, Ordinance, or Statute. But the members of the Roman provincial councils could not employ
any of those useful ways and means for obtaining the
attention of the sovereign, which render the decent and
humble language of supplication virtually equivalent to
a command. The Councils had no control over the
supplies. With the exception of the "*aurum coron-
arium,*" a *benevolence,* voluntary in name, but compulsory
by inveterate custom, taxation resulted from the arbitrary
decree of the Emperor; and to the edict by which the
Cæsar imposed a tribute upon the world, the assent of
the provincials was neither expected nor required. The
sovereign had nothing to hope from their gratitude; the
minister had nothing to fear from their displeasure. An
impeachment, under the entire management of the Prefect, was the only power of judicature which the Councils
possessed; and the laws which had been enacted upon
their request, might, at any time, be revoked or re-
scinded by the sovereign will and irresponsible declaration of the Emperor. In many parts of the empire, such
as Narbonensian Gaul, these councils appear to have
been engrafted upon the institutions subsisting among
the conquered nations before they were subdued.--Was

* The Castilian term for any law or enactment.

this the case in Britain?—The question is interesting, but difficult of discussion. It is sufficient to observe, that such local legislatures, however qualified their powers might be, contributed to keep alive a feeling of national or independent existence, and prevented those minor spheres of action, the provinces, from being merged in the vast orb of the empire. And, transmitted through the middle ages, they became one of the elements, at least, out of which the Parliaments, States-general, and other legislative assemblies of modern Europe were gradually formed.

The real power of the Roman state, however, was in the sword ; and we must now consider the station assigned to those by whom the sword was wielded. When the Roman republic subsisted in full vigour, the soldiers were rewarded by grants of land. An estate was allotted to the veteran, and he became entitled to the rents and profits as his retiring pay, instead of receiving a stipend from the treasury. Such policy was wise and considerate. It was right that the public should enable those whose strength had been worn out in the service of their country, to enjoy the quiet and comfort of repose in their old age : the boon was the discharge of a just debt, and at the same time this act of justice added greatly to the security of the commonwealth. The grey-headed warrior, who had served the republic with honour, was bound to his allegiance by gratitude. He taught obedience and loyalty to his son, and encouraged the youth to walk in the same path, and to hope for the same reward ; so that, when his time of toil and danger should be fulfilled, he also might become the peaceful citizen of the state which he had defended.

But another character was soon imparted to these

donations.   Civil wars arose amongst the Romans; and the generals who obtained the victory, treated the allies and subjects of Rome with the same severity which they had used towards their enemies.   Sylla, and afterwards Augustus, confiscated or seized the lands of several of the Italian cities, and divided these possessions amongst the soldiers who had fought in their service against other Romans.   It was a sad day when the poor people of Mantua were compelled to quit the farms which they cultivated, and to give up their fields and their vineyards to the insulting stranger.   I have mentioned Mantua, because we have the clearest description of the afflictions of this city in the ninth eclogue of Virgil.   For thus was that great poet deprived of his little patrimony and reduced to the greatest distress, and compelled to seek his sustenance in the great city of Rome, where the talents which had been given to him became the means of raising him to imperishable fame.

The grants made to the soldiers who hàd served the Triumvirate, were not, like the donations which had in the elder time been bestowed upon the veterans, the well-earned reward of honourable valour. Gifts received in recompense for services performed in civil war, were, in truth, a recompense for evil-doing ; and instead of encouraging the people to defend their country, the military were excited to hatred and dissension.   All departure from justice is as foolish as it is wrong, and the Romans afforded full proof of this maxim.   It became an easy step to bestow land upon the " Barbarians," in the expectation that they would become useful allies to the emperors.   This was one of the principal causes of the decline of the empire, because the provinces were filled with inhabitants adverse to the well-being of the state; who served the sovereign merely for profit, and who opened the path to their kinsmen, the implacable enemies of the Roman name. The Romans acted like a man who, being afraid of robbers, hires the brother of the depredators to stand as sentinel before his door.

First, these donations were made at the expense of other barbarians; but before the reign of Diocletian, the "*Liuti*," or "People,"* as thay are emphatically called, both by themselves and the Romans—the latter merely changing the term into *Læti*—were domiciled throughout the empire upon the "*Lætic*" lands, of which they received possession by the writ or rescript of the emperor. Two German tribes, the Quadi and the Marcomanni, were thus rewarded by the possession of lands in Britain. The progeny of the Tungrians, who, brought over as allies by Agricola, warred against the Caledonians, became the owners as well as the defenders of the wilds which they subdued.† The word *Liuti*, or *Læti*, is purely German, but it was extended from the Teutonic auxiliaries to all others of the same class. This is the usual progress of language, and we exemplify it in many cases; for instance, by giving the name of *Hussars*, which originally signified *Hungarians*, to all light cavalry, mounted and armed like the original Hungarian troops of that description. The *Læti* were also called *Gentiles* (a translation of their former name). And upwards of forty of those barbarian legions, some of Teutonic origin, and others Moors, Dalmatians, and

* In the Anglo-Saxon, *Leod;* in other dialects *Liuti* and *Leute*, Folks, nation, or people; probably from the same root as λαος. Hesychius calls the public lands λαιτα.

† The existence of the Tungrian cohort appears from an inscription found near *Castle Cary*. For the general proofs of the statements here given, relating to the civil and military government of Roman Britain, I must refer the reader to the Rise and Progress of the English Commonwealth, chapters x. and xi.

Thracians, whose forefathers had been transplanted from the remotest parts of the empire, obtained their domicile in various parts of our island, though principally upon the northern and eastern coasts, and in the neighbourhood of the Roman walls.

The donations of these Lætic lands had branched abusively out of the general system of defence; which, with few exceptions, was founded upon the principle of paying the soldier by giving him land.   Thus the *March* or border countries were granted almost exclusively to the " Limitanean" soldiery, upon conditions which have been well described as containing the germ of the " feudal tenures."   The valleys and passes of the mountains, and the banks of the great frontier rivers, were tilled by the martial husbandmen, who could only secure their harvests by warding off the incursions of the enemy.   Such land could not be alienated to a non-military owner.   The property descended from the father to the son, and the son at the age of eighteen years was compelled to gird himself with the baldrick, and to join the legion to which his parent belonged.

The " Limitanean" soldiers, as their name imports, continued settled on the borders; but in the same manner, or nearly so, were all the other Roman legions rooted and fixed in the interior of Britain.   After the establishment of the Imperial government, they were not, like our regiments in the colonies, changed and removed from time to time, but permanently established on and in the island.   The son of the veteran was compelled to follow the profession of his father.   Military service was an imperative obligation upon all of military race.   The soldiery constituted not only an " Estate" distinct from the rest of the people, but also

a ruling Caste, from whose will the sovereign power
was derived.

Perhaps there was never any community in the world,
civilized or semi-civilized, in which the succession to the
supreme authority was so utterly without law or rule as
the Roman empire.   Good fortune was the only standard
of legitimacy.—Aurelian, a sturdy Dacian, is hailed as
emperor by the legions on the shore of the Danube.
Quintilian is recognized by the voice and suffrage of the
legions of Rome, and the approbation of all Italy; but
Aurelian prevails, and he is considered as the lawful
possessor of the Roman world.

The General who could only retain a Province or a
Diocese, is called a Tyrant; that is to say, an illegal
Pretender.   But let an example be selected, and the
justice of such a title will entirely disappear.—Gaul and
Spain and Britain, or the Prefecture of the Gauls, were
erected into a flourishing empire by Posthumus, the
" Tyrant," who denied obedience to Gallienus, the
" Emperor " of Rome.   Posthumus had been called to
the government by the voice and affection of the people,
and accepted by the legions.   And if the palsied Senate,
assembled on the Capitol, branded this change of government as a rebellion, the " Court of Treves " might very
reasonably question the rights devolving upon Gallienus,
a son who enjoyed his dignity merely because he allowed
his father Valerian to languish, during nine years, in
hopeless captivity; or, ascending a degree higher in the
pedigree, they might impugn the title of Valerian, and
inquire by what means the legions of Rhetia had acquired the authority of imposing him upon the dioceses
of the east or the prefectures of the west.

From the history of Avitus, who, after being saluted

as emperor by the legions at Toulouse, was invested with
the imperial purple by the " Honorati " of Arles, we
may estimate the share which the provincial legislatures
possessed in the nomination of the provincial " Tyrants."
The soldiers elected the Emperor, the Council ratified
the election; and in the eye of reason, it may appear
that these sovereigns, who are stigmatized as usurpers,
had, perhaps, a better title than the rulers who are
considered as legitimate merely because they were
recognized at Rome.—What was the Roman Senate ?—
Certainly it bore an honoured and venerable name ; but
the Patricians who trembled in the chairs of Cato and
Cicero were the mere creatures and nominees of the
Emperor ; whilst the provincial assemblies participated
in all the feelings and opinions of their countrymen, and
virtually represented the wealth and respectability of the
land.   Unconscious of the ends which they were destined
to accomplish, the Provincial Emperors may be considered as the precursors of the barbarian dynasties.
The revolutions sustained by the provinces under their
government gave an impulse, which ultimately caused
the kingdoms of modern Christendom to spring out of
the fourth great monarchy of the Gentiles.

The political ancestry of the ancient monarchs of
Anglo-Saxon Britain, must therefore be sought amongst
the sovereigns who are expunged from the regular series
of the Cæsars, and put at the bottom of the page by the
chronologists of the empire.   Britain was said to be
singularly fertile in " Tyrants ;" or, in other words, the
opulent province made strong efforts to detach itself from
Rome, and to acquire independence.   But the history of
these times is extremely imperfect.   The jejune and
feeble writers of the Augustan history afford our chief

materials (A.D. 280); and though we know that the first
of these British Tyrants was slain by his competitor
Probus, we are not able to tell his name.

Carausius obtained a more durable ascendency. He was
a Menapian by birth. The nation whence he originated had
been divided by its migrations into several colonies (A.D.
287-294): one was settled in Hibernia, another was found
in the islands of the Rhine; and the Menapia, or Menevia,
of Britain, now St. David's, seems also to have belonged
to these tribes. Carausius was born in Britain, according to an authority which we are at present compelled to
receive with some hesitation, and opposed to the Roman
writers, who call him the "foster son of Batavia." Yet,
for the credit of Richard of Cirencester, the writer to
whom I allude, it may be remarked that the same
uncertainty prevails with respect to many of the
Emperors, and most of the "Tyrants." The contradictory statements of contemporary writers were evidently occasioned, not so much from incorrect information, as from the difficulty of finding accurate language.
In one narrative, perhaps, the individual is described
according to his *race*; in another according to his *local
birthplace*; in a third, according to his *political domicile*;
just as Napoleon might be described as an *Italian*, a
Corsican, or a *Frenchman*. Carausius, perhaps himself a
pirate, had been accustomed to the sea from his earliest
youth; and he was raised, by his valour and talent, to
the command of the navy destined to repress the incursions of the Franks and Saxons, and other barbarians,
who ravaged the shores of Britain and of Gaul. In
this station, dark suspicions arose respecting his collu-
sion with the enemy; and it being anticipated that he
would throw off his allegiance to Diocletian and Maxi-

mian, the Emperors who then ruled, orders were sent from Rome to put Carausius to death. But he evaded the fatal messenger; and the wealth which he had earned by his exploits, as well as the reputation which he gained in his victories, persuaded the British legions and auxiliaries to hail him as Augustus, and to bestow upon him the imperial diadem.

Maximian, who made some fruitless attempts to rid himself of this rival, was repelled with disgrace. The Emperor of Britain—whose dominions included Boulogne, and the adjoining coast of Gaul—used every exertion to maintain his sovereignty; he built vessels of war, and raised great forces, inviting to his service the barbarians against whom he had fought, and to whose native courage and maritime skill was now added the regular discipline of the Roman soldier. The numerous medals struck by Carausius are no inadequate tokens of the wealth and splendour which graced his reign; and the inscriptions and devices with which they are impressed, display the pomp and state which he assumed in his island empire. Ruling in Britain, " Marcus Aurelius Valerius Carausius," for he had borrowed these impressive names, was ranked as the " brother" of Diocletian and Maximian. The fleets of Carausius sailed triumphant; and from the columns of Hercules to the mouths of the Rhine, his standard ruled the seas. When Constantius was associated to the purple, he prepared to dispossess Carausius of his dominions; and by a bold and fortunate enterprise, the British fleet stationed at Boulogne was compelled to surrender. Constantius then prepared for the invasion of Britain; but in the meanwhile, domestic conspiracies had arisen (A.D. 294-297), and Carausius was slain at York by the dagger of

Allectus, his friend and minister, who succeeded to the imperial dignity.

The details of the succession of the provincial emperors, so improperly called "Tyrants," who either ruled in Britain alone, or in Britain as a part of the prefecture of the Gauls, must be omitted until we arrive at the reign of Maximus, an able and fortunate general. By some historians he is described as a Briton, and yet as allied to the imperial family. He disputed the empire with Gratian (A.D. 382-388) ; and the Bretons of Armorica, or the " *Lesser Britain*," in Gaul, believed that their nation sprang from the flower and youth of this island, who accompanied him in this enterprise. The exploits of Maximus belong rather to the general history of the Roman empire, than to the particular history of Britain. It is sufficient to observe that, after his death at Aquileia, Theodorus reannexed the province of Britain to his dominions, which he transmitted to his son Honorius, his successor in the empire of the west. But the authority acquired by the "Robber of Richborough," as Maximus is termed by Ausonius, was not entirely lost to his posterity. And if we consult the genealogies of the Cymri, we shall find there were princes reigning in Britain long after the extinction of the Roman power, who traced their descent from "Maxen-Wledig," "Maximus the Emperor," and who were proud to consider him as their ancestor.*

When the Empire began to decline, the Romans, as well as the Romanized Britons, were incessantly exposed to the hostility of the *Picts*. These were originally Britons, who, living beyond the Roman frontier, had continued in the enjoyment of their independence, and

* *Gwledig* does not literally signify *Emperor*, but it denotes supreme and paramount authority.

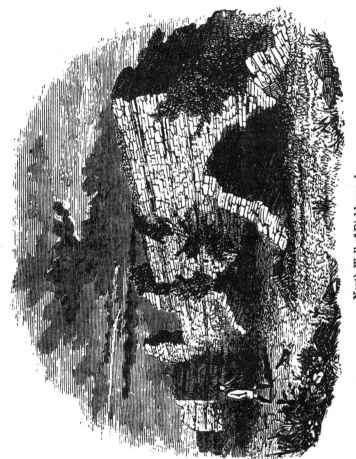

North Wall of Richborough.

Ornaments and Patten of Ancient Britons.

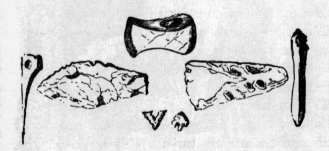

Ancient British Weapons.

Coin of Carausius.

whose primitive rudeness was unaffected by the civilization which the Roman conquests had imparted to their
brethren.   Tamed animals are always persecuted by the
wild creatures of their own species, and the Picts bore
the greatest antipathy to their ancient kinsmen.   The
first inroads of the Picts (A.D. 306) were easily repelled.
But when the *Scots* arrived from the opposite coast of
Erin, the union of the forces of these barbarians enabled
them to pursue their operations with great success.   The
united hordes of the Picts and the Scots rushed from the
North like a torrent; attacked and plundered London;
and though this invasion was repelled by Theodosius
(A.D. 367-368), still the northern districts were never
afterwards reduced to order and tranquillity.

The *Scots* were the relatives of the Cymri, being another branch of the great Celtic nation, and who, at a
period far beyond all authentic history, had established
themselves in *Hibernia, Erin,* or *Ireland.*   Hence, that
island, from its predominant population, was generally
called *Scotia,* or *Insula Scotorum,* by the writers of the
sixth and seventh centuries.   This is a circumstance
which has often been forgotten, but it is of great importance to recollect it, for the name of Scotia, or Scotland,
as applied to the northern portion of Britain, is comparatively of modern origin.   These Irish Scots appear to
have begun by spreading themselves in straggling settlements on the coast of Argyle and the neighbouring
shores, forming little clans, or even families, not owing
obedience to any common chieftain, and without any
regular government.   The land was sterile, the Pictish
population thin and scanty, and therefore the original
inhabitants do not appear to have opposed the Scottish
settlements.   Reuda, who arrived with rather a large

train of followers, seems to have been the first who
acquired any permanent authority amongst the British
Scots; and from him they are said to have been called
Dalreudini or *Dalriads*. But the princes afterwards
governing these nations (A.D. 986), claimed to be descended from Fergus, the son of Erc, who, with his
brother Lourn, reigned towards the close of the fifth
century. There was probably a flux and reflux of
population; and the history of these tribes is much
clouded by fable. But the main facts are satisfactorily
established; and there is no reason to doubt but that
the Scots had emigrated from Ireland, and obtained a
small tract of country, as before described. Another
colony was settled, though at what period is uncertain,
in the country called Galloway: here they appear also
to have been blended with the Picts, perhaps some of the
tribes who had assisted in the war.

We must now advert to another nation, destined to
effect an entire alteration in the fortunes of Britain.
Carausius had been brought to notice, and afterwards
raised to power, by his warfare against the Franks and
Saxons, Teutonic tribes, who much infested the coasts
of Britain and of Gaul. They were repelled, but his
successes had only a transient effect upon the power of
the enemy; and the name of the " Saxon shore " given
to the coast of Britain from Branodunum or Brancaster,
in Norfolk, to the portus Adurni (perhaps Pevensey) in
Sussex, is a proof of the ascendency which the associates
of the Franks had obtained. This district, in the last
ages of the Roman empire, was placed under the
command of a military Count, called " *Comes litoris
Saxonici.*" It has been supposed that this shore was so
called merely because it was open to the incursions of the

Saxons; but it is most probable that they, like the Scots, succeeded in fixing themselves in some portion of the district; for it appears a strange anomaly, that a country should be named, not from its inhabitants, but from its assailants; and in the "Littus Saxonicum" of Gaul, afterwards included in Normandy, they had obtained a permanent domicile not far from Baieux.

Either flocking from these settlements, or passing from beyond the sea, the Saxons joined the Picts and the Scots in their great invasion. The victory of Theodosius (A.D. 368) produced a temporary calm; but he was compelled to follow the host of the pirates to the extremity of the British islands, and the distant Orcades were drenched with Saxon gore.

Whilst these events were taking place in Britain, hordes of barbarians continued pouring into Gaul and Italy. The Roman emperors, Arcadius and Honorius, were compelled to abandon Britain to its fate (A.D. 406-418). Marcus and Gratian, successively hailed as Emperors by the British legions, passed away like shadows. Constantine, who was raised from the ranks by his well-omened name, and promoted to the Imperial dignity in Britain, obtained more considerable, though transient power. At length the connexion between Britain and Rome was entirely severed. Britain broke, as it were, into various independent and rival communities—and the sovereigns contended amongst themselves for the empire, whilst the hosts of the enemy were thickening around them.

As far as we can judge, two great parties prevailed in the southern tracts of our island. A Roman party, headed by Aurelius Ambrosius, a chieftain of imperial descent, who claimed or acquired the Imperial dignity;

and another, supporting the cause of the too famous
Vortigern.   During these contentions, the Scots and
the Picts continued their predatory warfare, and reduced
the country to the greatest misery (A.D. 430).   Any
degree of union amongst the Britons might have enabled
them to repel their enemies.   The walls of the cities
fortified by the Romans were yet strong and firm.   The
tactics of the legions were not forgotten.   Bright armour
was piled in the storehouses, and the serried line of
spears might have been presented to the half naked
Scots and Picts, who could never have prevailed against
their opponents.   But the Britons had no inclination to
lift the sword, except against each other.   Humbly and
pitifully imploring the Romans for help, they lost all
courage, except for faction, when the Romans could not
comply, but left them to their own resources.   The most
ancient historian of this disturbed and lamentable period,
is Gildas, himself the son of a British king, and he bears
a most forcible testimony against his countrymen.   The
British kings were stained with every vice—ruling, not
for the protection, but for the spoil of their subjects,—
and their misconduct soon involved both kings and
people in one common ruin.

Conflict between the Romans and the Saxons.

1

6°   4°   2°   0   2°

58   58

Scandinavians

BRITAIN
under Ella the first
BRETWALDA
of Saxon Race
A.D. 491.

North Picts

South Picts

56   56

Scots of Dalriada

Gododin

Alcluid   B R Y N E I C H

R E G N U

Picts & Scots   R   e   d

Caer Luel   B R E N S E A

D E I R

54   54

Caer Ebrahc

Caer Loidcot

Caer Legion

Caer Lirion

Caer Gorangon

52   52

Caer Leon ar Wisk

Caer Glou

Caer ceol

Caer Ceri

Caer Lundene

Caer Baddon   Caer Segent   Cantwaraland Brobi Jutes

L O E G R   Caer Gwent

Caer Dori   Saxons

uster

4°   2°   Meridian of 0 Greenwich

London. William Tegg.   J.& C. Walker. Sculpt.

Chapter II.

*Hengist and Horsa: their supposed Transactions with Vorti-
gern—Progress of the Invaders—Conquest of Britain by the
Jutes, Angles, and Saxons—Kingdoms founded by them—
Kent, Sussex, Wessex, East Anglia, Essex, Deira, Bernicia,
Mercia—Subjugation of the Britons.*

THE "three tribes of Germany"—the *Jutes*, the *Angles*,
and the *Saxons*, by whom Britain was subdued, seem
originally to have constituted but one nation, speaking
the same language, and ruled by monarchs who all
claimed their descent from the deified monarch of the
Teutons, *Woden* or *Odin*. They frequently changed
their position on the firm land of Europe, as the stream
of population rolled forward, impelled by the secondary
causes, prepared and destined to act in fulfilment of the
decree by which the enlargement of Japhet had been
foretold.

The Jutes, together with their neighbours the Angles,
dwelt in the peninsula of Jutland, or the "Cimbric
Chersonesus," and in the adjoining Holstein, where there
is still a district called *Anglen*. That, in fact, is the
real *Old England;* and, properly speaking, our "Old
England" is *New England*, though now we give that
name to a province in America. The Saxons were more
widely dispersed. Ptolemy places them in the Cimbric
Chersonesus, near the Jutes and Angles; but they afterwards occupied a much larger extent, from the Delta of
the Rhine to the Weser. After the migration of the
Saxons to Britain, the name of *Old Saxons* was given
to the parent stock. One very large body of Saxon

population occupied the present Westphalia; but the
tribes by whom Britain was invaded, appear principally
to have proceeded from the country now called Fries-
land; for of all the continental dialects, the ancient
Frisick is the one which approaches most nearly to the
Anglo-Saxon of our ancestors.

It is necessary, however, to remark, that the name
" *Saxon* " appears rather to have been intended to denote
a confederacy of tribes, than to have originally belonged
to any one nation.—Learned men have sought for the
etymology of the term in the " *Seax* " or short sword, a
weapon with which they were armed.   These and other
suppositions, upon which I have not room to enlarge, are,
however, after all, only ingenious sports and fancies.
We possess but a very small number of authentic facts
concerning the early history of the barbarian nations of
the West; and, though the general outline of their position upon the ethnographical map can be understood
with tolerable precision, yet we must be always uncertain
concerning the details.

Whilst Vortigern was contending with Aurelius Ambrosius (A.D. 446), two Jutish *Ealdormen*, or Chieftains,
Hengist and Horsa, arrived in the Isle of Thanet with
three *keels* or vessels, and a small train of chosen followers. According to some of the Chroniclers, Vortigern
invited Hengist and Horsa as his allies.   Others represent them as exiles from their native land.   All seem to
agree that the Jutes warred successfully against the Picts
and Scots; and that, in order to reward their services,
the Isle of Thanet was bestowed upon them, in the
manner which, as I have before described, was practised
by the Romans in favour of their Lætic or Gentile auxiliaries.   The land was given to the Jutes as their pay.

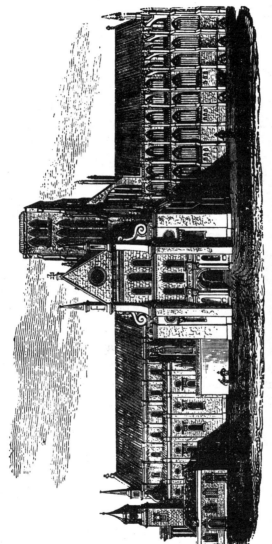

Old St. Paul's Cathedral, South View.

Elevated and Richly-ornamented Saxon Seat.

It is said by some writers, that Vortigern married Rowena, the daughter of Hengist. She was very beautiful; and when introduced by her father at the royal banquet of the British King, she advanced gracefully and modestly towards him, bearing in her hand a golden goblet filled with wine. Young people, even of the highest rank, were accustomed to wait upon their elders, or those unto whom they wished to show respect, and therefore the appearance of Rowena as the cupbearer of the feast was neither unbecoming nor unseemly. And when Rowena came near unto Vortigern, she said, in her own Saxon language,—" *Wœs heal, hlaford Conung;*"—which means " Health to thee, my Lord King." Vortigern did not understand the salutation of Rowena, but the words were explained to him by an interpreter. " *Drinc heal,*"—" Drink thou health,"—was the accustomed answer, and the memory of the event was preserved in merry old England by the *wassail-cup* —a cup full of spiced wine or good ale, which was handed round from guest to guest, at the banquet and the festival. Well, therefore, might Rowena be recollected on high tides and holidays, for the introduction of this concomitant of good cheer.

The expectations of the Jutes increased with their power. Further demands were made upon the Britons —an increase of reward—a larger territory. Refusal provoked hostility; the Jutes joined with the Scots and Picts, and ravaged Britain from East to West. An interval of ill fortune ensued, during which the Jutes were compelled to leave the island, but they speedily returned with greater force. They craved peace from the Britons, and a banquet was held to celebrate the pacification. The treacherous Hengist instructed his companions to conceal their short swords beneath their garments. At the signal, which he gave by exclaiming, "*Nimed eure saxes,*"* they drew their weapons. The British Nobles were slain; Vortigern was taken prisoner, and the Jutes gained possession of Kent, and extended their dominion over a considerable portion of the adjoining country.

These details have been told so often, that they acquire a kind of prescriptive right to credit; but I believe that they bear no nearer relation to the real history of Anglo-Saxon England, than the story of Æneas, as related by Virgil, does to the real history of the foundation of Rome. Nothing can be more unlikely than that Vortigern should have invited over these implacable enemies of Britain, "the Dragons of Germany," as they are called by the bards, for the purpose of warring against the Scots and Picts, with whom they or their kinsmen had been so recently allied. We may seek for the groundwork of the narrative, in the historical ballads of the Anglo-Saxons, in which their early enterprises were commemorated. And even the names of *Hengist* and *Horsa*† seem only to be epithets derived from their standard, the snow-white steed, which still appears as the ensign of Kent in England, as it anciently did in the shield of the "Old Saxons" in Germany.‡

Connecting the history of the Jutes with antecedent events, it appears most agreeable to probability, that their landing was the result of such a piratical expedition as had so often harassed Britain in the Roman ages.

* Take your *seaxes.*

† *Hengst*, or *Hengist* signifies a stallion. *Horsa* or *Hross* does not require any explanation. It may be remarked, however, that in Danish *Hors* signifies not a *Horse*, but a *Mare.*

‡ Hence the White Horse is borne on the shield of Brunswick-Hanover.

Their acquisition of the Isle of Thanet from the British King may perhaps be credited. As I have observed, it was a grant in the nature of those which the Romans made to the *Liuti*, yet not so much as the price of aid to be obtained from the threatening colony, as for the purpose of warding off further hostility.

Thanet is now divided from the rest of Kent by a narrow rill, crossed by an arch of the smallest span. The rill was then a channel, nearly a mile in width; and in this isle, the Jutes, possessing the command of the sea, could well maintain themselves against their disunited enemies. Several years, however, of constant warfare elapsed before "*Cantwara Land*," or Kent, became their dominion (A.D. 457, 473, 488); and Eric, the son of Hengist, appears to have been the first real king of the country; for he, and not his father Hengist, was honoured as founder of the Kentish dynasty. From the spear which he wielded, or the vessel which bore him over the waves, he was surnamed "*Æsc*," or *Ash-tree*; and *Æscingas*, or *Sons of the Ash-tree*, did the kings of Kent, his descendants, call themselves so long as their dynasty endured. When Æsc was fairly settled in his rich and fertile kingdom, he laid down the sword: his son and his son's son lived equally in peaceful obscurity. Ethelbert, fourth in descent from Æsc, gave great splendour to the state (A.D. 568-616); but Kent soon sunk into the condition of a dependent principality, beneath the sway of its more powerful rivals and neighbours. No portion of our island has continued more truly Anglo-Saxon than "Cantwara Land." The fair-haired Kentish yeoman bears in his countenance the stamp of his remote ancestry; and the existence of the *gavel kind* tenure in Kent, or the custom whereby the land becomes divisible among all the children, instead of descending to the eldest, is a singular proof of the steadiness or good fortune which enabled the Kentish men to assert their franchises, when all England yielded to the Norman sway.

Whilst the Jutes were conquering Kent, their kindred took part in the war. Ship after ship sailed from the North Sea, filled with eager warriors. The Saxons now arrived—Ella and his three sons landed in the ancient territory of the Regni (A.D. 477-491). The Britons were defeated with great slaughter, and driven into the forest of *Andreade*, whose extent is faintly indicated by the wastes and commons of the Weald.

A general confederacy of the Kings and "Tyrants" of the Britons was formed against the invaders, but fresh reinforcements arrived from Germany; the city of *Andreades-Ceastre* was taken by storm, all its inhabitants were slain, and the buildings razed to the ground, so that its site is now entirely unknown. From this period, the kingdom of the *South Saxons* was established in the person of Ella; and though ruling only over the narrow boundary of modern *Sussex*, he was accepted as the first of the Saxon Bretwaldas,* or Emperors of the Isle of Britain.

Encouraged, perhaps, by the good tidings received from Ella, another band of Saxons, commanded by Cerdic and his son Cynric, landed on the neighbouring shore, in the modern Hampshire (A.D. 494). At first they made but little progress. They were opposed by the Britons; but Geraint, whom the Saxon Chroniclers celebrate for his nobility, and the British Bards extol for his beauty and valour, was slain (A.D. 501). The death of the Prince of the

---

* *Bretwalda* is literally the Dominator of Britain ; but as a title, it was equivalent to Emperor.

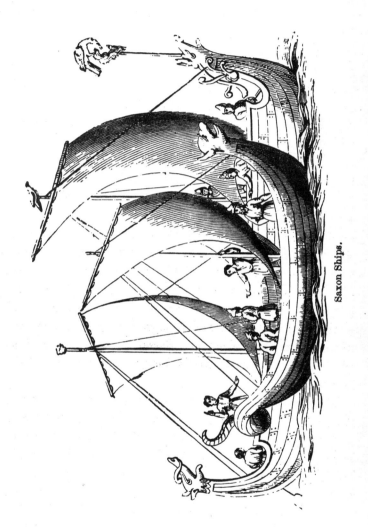

Saxon Ships.

Capital of a Column in the Crypt of Canterbury Cathedral.

"Woodlands of Dyfnaint," or Damnonia, may have been avenged, but the power of the Saxons overwhelmed all opposition; and Cerdic, associating his son Cynric in the dignity, became the King of the territory which he gained. Under Cynric and his son Ceaulin, the Saxons slowly, yet steadily, gained ground. The utmost extent of their dominions towards the North cannot be ascertained; but they had conquered the town of Bedford: and it was probably in consequence of their geographical position (A.D. 571) with respect to the countries of the *Middle* and *East Saxons*, that the name of the *West Saxons* was given to this colony. The tract north of the Thames was soon lost; but on the south of that river and of the Severn, the successors of Cerdic, Kings of *Wessex*, continued to extend their dominions. The Hampshire *Avon*, which retains its old Celtic name, signifying *the Water*, seems at first to have been their boundary. Beyond this river, the British Princes of Damnonia retained their power; and it was long before the country as far as the Exe became a Saxon March-land, or border.

About the time that the Saxons under Cerdic and Cynric were successfully warring against the Britons, another colony was seen to establish itself in the territory or kingdom which, from its geographical position, obtained the name of *East Saxony*; but whereof the district of the *Middle Saxons*, now *Middlesex*, formed a part. London, as you well know, is locally included in *Middle Saxony*; and the Kings of *Essex*, and the other sovereigns who afterwards acquired the country, certainly possessed many extensive rights of sovereignty in the city. Yet, I doubt much whether London was ever incorporated in any Anglo-Saxon kingdom; and I think we must view it as a weak, tributary, vassal state, not

very well able to resist the usurpations of the supreme
Lord or Suzerain, Æscwin, or Ercenwine, who was the first
King of the East Saxons (A.D. 527). His son Sleda was
married to Ricola, daughter to Ethelbert of Kent, who
afterwards appears as the superior, or sovereign of the
country; and though Sleda was King, yet Ethelbert
joined in all important acts of government. This was
the fate of Essex—it is styled a kingdom, but it never
enjoyed any political independence, being always subjected to the adjoining kings.

Thus did the Jutes and the Saxons resort to Britain;
and now came the Angles—and in such numbers, that
Old England was almost emptied of its inhabitants; and
the district continued very thinly peopled, even in the
days of Venerable Bede. The tribes dwelling in the
adjoining tracts did not occupy the country, although
they continued pouring forth their colonies into many
other parts of the world; nor was it replenished by the
progeny of the Angles who had been left behind. And
this circumstance is worthy of note, because it shows
how little the movements or multiplication of mankind
are regulated by those uniform theories of population
which, on paper, exhibit so much plausibility and ingenuity. Some of these Angles, first conducted by unknown chieftains, and apparently divided into two great
tribes, the *North-Folk* and the *South-Folk*, acquired the
eastern part of the island (about A.D. 597), afterwards
denominated *East Anglia*, of which the modern counties
of *Norfolk* and *Suffolk* constitute the greatest part. Here
they were almost separated from the rest of Britain; for
a wide expanse of marshes bounded their territory towards the west; and these watery wastes being connected
with each other by numerous shallow streams, in many

places expanding into *meres* and *broads*, the country had nearly the appearance of a peninsula. At the isthmus where these natural defences ended, the East Anglians cast up a very strong fortification, consisting of a deep moat and a lofty rampart. In the middle ages it was often called the "*Rech dyke*,"* or *Giant's dyke :* the common people attributed it to the Fiend. The heath through which the rampart extends, not having been subjected to cultivation, the *Devil's Dyke* is yet very entire, and is one of the most remarkable monuments of its kind. But the marshes have been drained, and Croyland and Thorney no longer rise like islands in the midst of a marshy lake ; though still the nature of the fen countries is not entirely altered; and the traveller can easily picture to himself the ancient state of the district before it was recovered from the floods. Uffa was the first of the East Anglian chieftains who acquired the title of a King, within the boundaries which I have thus described. And as the kings of Kent were known as *Æscingas*, so were the sovereigns of East Anglia distinguished by the patronymic of *Uffingas*, or sons of *Uffa*. But their annals have been almost wholly lost; and the history of East Anglia is nearly a blank in the Chronicles of England.

The British kingdoms of Deyfyr and Bryneich (latinised into Deira and Bernicia), extending from the Humber

---

* Not, as Camden supposes, from the village of *Retch* (Cambridgeshire), but from *Recke* or *Riege*, (Germ. and Isl.) a Giant, a Hero, a being possessed of preternatural power. The term may be found in all the Gothic dialects. Like the cognate *Rex* and *Rajah*, it is primarily to be deduced from *Rich* or *Reich*, dominion or power. *Wealth* is power, and hence *Rice*, or *rich*, assumed the secondary sense which it now bears. In the Anglo-Saxon, however, it more usually (though not invariably) retains its primary sense—*e.g.* "He awearps the *rican* of setle. Deposuit *potentes* de sede." He hath put pown the mighty from their seat. In the phrase " *Ricos* hombres," the Castilian has retained the Gothic appellation of his ancestors. King*rick*, for kingdom, remained in use, till recent times, in Scotland.

to the Frith of Forth, were divided from each other by a
forest, occupying the tract between the Tyne and Tees;
and which, unreclaimed by man, was abandoned to the
wild-deer.   Properly speaking, this border-land does
not seem originally to have belonged to either kingdom;
but, in subsequent times, the boundary between Deira
and Bernicia was usually fixed at the Tyne.   The trans-
humbrane countries were exposed at an early period to
the attacks of the Jutes and Saxons.   Some chroniclers
say, that Octa and Ebusa, sons of Hengist, conquered a
portion of the country.   At the onset, the invaders made
little progress.   The Britons of the neighbouring Reged
and Strathclyde,   governed by valiant Princes, the
descendants of the Roman Maximus, appear to have
possessed more unity than their brethren in the South;
and their efforts supported the population of Deira and
Bernicia in resisting their enemies.   The scale was
evenly poised until the English Ida landed at the pro-
montory called Flamborough Head, with forty vessels,
all manned with chosen warriors (before A.D. 547).
Urien, the hero of the Bards, opposed a strenuous
resistance, but the Angles had strengthened themselves
on the coast.   Fresh reinforcements poured in; and Ida,
the "Bearer of Flame," as he was termed by the Britons,
became the master and sovereign of the land which he
had assailed.   Ida erected a tower or fortress, which was
at once his castle and his palace; and so deeply were
the Britons humiliated by this token of his power, that
they gave the name of the *Shame of Bernicia* to the structure which he had raised.   Ida afterwards bestowed this
building upon his queen, Bebba, from whom it was, or
rather is, denominated *Bebban-Burgh*, the Burgh or fortress of Bebba, commonly abbreviated into *Bamborough*.

The massy keep yet stands; and the voyager, following the course of the Abbess of St. Hilda, may yet see

> " King Ida's castle huge and square
> From its tall rock look grimly down,
> And on the swelling ocean frown."

Ida's dominions were intersected by tracts still belonging to the Britons, who ultimately yielded to the invaders. In Deira, the progress of the Angles or English was slow : York, it is true, had been plundered by the Saxons (A.D. 504), and Archbishop Sampson compelled to take refuge in Armorica or Brittany; but until the accession of Ella (A.D. 559-560), Deira is not known to have been subjected to an English king. Ella was not of the same family as Ida. Both were children of Woden; but Ida was descended from the fifth son of the fabled monarch, whilst Ella traced his ancestry to Baldeg, the sixth son, from whom the kings of Wessex were also descended. Ida had twelve sons. Six of these are said to have reigned in succession after him, one after another. This statement seems to be improbable; and I should rather think that they took distinct principalities, or portions of the kingdom. Ella, king of Deira, appears to have compelled the sons of Ida to become tributary to him (A.D. 559-560). And the two houses of Bernicia and Deira continued, during several years, in a state of rivalry and hostility. Deira ultimately prevailed in the person of Edwin. The two states were now usually known by the collective name of *Northumbria* (A.D. 617). Though not united into one community, they were generally governed by one monarch; and the kingdom became, for a time, the most powerful in Anglo-Saxon Britain.

The country adjoining the English settlements of East Anglia and Deira, and which bordered on the lands of the British tribes, obtained the name of the *March*, or

boundary. The English chieftains who settled in it,
seem originally to have considered themselves as freed
from any control; but Creoda, their first king (A.D. 585-
593), who appears to have been the Ruler of the Middle
Angles, must have been a vassal under the supremacy of
Northumbria. Penda, a fierce and valiant warrior, cast
off this allegiance: the *March* or *Mercia* was now established as an independent state (A.D. 626-655); and though
more than once reduced to subjection, either by Northumbria or by Wessex, its sovereigns continued to extend
their dominions at the expense of the Britons, until at
length, having acquired all the midland parts of Loegria,*
the Britons of Cambria were exposed to their constant
hostility. That a portion of the dominions of Wessex
passed into Mercia, has been already noticed. London
was afterwards wrested by the Mercians from the West
Saxons, and the geographical extent of the state perhaps
exceeded any other of the Anglo-Saxon kingdoms. But
Mercia never became compact. The population was
greatly mixed; the Britons approached nearly to the
number of the English, and the chieftains, or Ealdormen,
who ruled the minor states of which it was composed,
possessed great power; so that the kingdom contained
within it the seeds of disunion and decay.

In this manner were formed the states of the so-called
Heptarchy, an erroneous term, but one which has become
so familiar by usage, that there is some difficulty in
discarding it from history. It must, however, be rejected,
because an idea is conveyed thereby, which is substantially wrong. At no one period of our history were there

---

* The Britons divided the island into three great territories. *Cambria*,
bounded by the Severn and the Wye ; *Loegria*, south of the Humber, *Albania*
to the north.—*Map* I. The boundaries of Albania were afterwards contracted to
the country north of the friths.

ever *seven* kingdoms independent of each other. And if we include those kingdoms which were subservient to larger states, the number must be increased. The nephew of Cerdic ruled the Isle of Wight with regal title. In Mercia, the chieftain of " *Hwiccas*"* had as much authority in his good city of Worcester, as the king of Essex had in London. But, however divided, the nations whom we term Anglo-Saxons were thus possessed of the best parts of Britain, whilst the Cymri were driven to the western side of the island, and principally those districts where the natural fortifications of moors and mountains, and lakes, and woods, enabled them to withstand their invaders.

Part of the Britons retained possession of Strathclyde and Cumbria, extending from Alcluyd, now called Dunbreton, or Dunbarton—the *Dun* or fortress of the *Britons,* —to the southern borders of Lancashire; whilst the ridge of mountains, not unaptly termed the British Apennines, separated them from Northumbria.†

Another great mass of British population continued in possession of *Damnonia* or Devonshire, with its dependancy, *Cernaw* or Cornwall, which countries the Saxons called *West Wales* (about A.D. 638). Here the Britons, although their enemies were daily gaining ground upon them, still dreamt that they retained the monarchy of Britain, until Cadwallader, surnamed " Bhendyged," or the Blessed, resigned his crown, and went to Rome, where he died, a penitent and a pilgrim. Many of the Britons fled beyond sea to Armorica: those who remained behind seem to have consisted chiefly of the peasantry. The Britons then took their stand beyond

* Gloucester, Worcester, and part of Warwickshire. See *Map* II.
† See *Maps* II. and IV.

the Exe, and afterwards beyond the Tamar, until at
length they submitted to the English ascendency, and
lost every trace of national power.

Lastly, the noblest of the Britons maintained themselves in Cambria, or Wales. The Anglo-Saxons, and
particularly the Mercians, more than once overran their
country; but the Cymri defended themselves amidst
their fastnesses. They detested the Saxons, and would
neither conform to the Saxon customs nor the Saxon
laws. The Romanized Britons of Loegria appear to have
united more readily to their invaders. I apprehend that
they possessed less nationality; and sometimes even
national prejudices are the safeguards of independence.
In the kingdoms or principalities of the Western Cymri,
of which, according to a nomenclature of perhaps later
origin, the states of Gwynedd, Deheubarth, Powys, and
Gwent,* were the most important, the old lines or
dynasties of Princes continued unbroken: many subsist
in the nobility and gentry of Wales at the present day;
and the whole body of the people continued in possession
of their native soil, and unmingled with the stranger.
Yet, though unconquered, they were overshadowed by
the supremacy of the Anglo-Saxon sceptre: they bent
before the Anglo-Saxon throne, and rendered tribute to
the Anglo-Saxon kings.

Thus did the dominion of the Britons pass away: thus
were the British people either banished from their own
country, or reduced into vassalage. And the island,
from the "Pictish sea"† to the shore of the Channel,
became the inheritance of the Anglo-Saxons, who caused
their own language, and their own customs and laws, to
become paramount in Britain.

* See *Map* II.   † The Frith of Forth.

Chapter III.

*Heathenism of the Anglo-Saxons—Deities worshipped by them—
Origin of the Papal Authority—Pope Gregory undertakes
the Conversion of Anglo-Saxon Britain—Missions of Augus-
tine and Paulinus—Temporal Effects of the Introduction of
Christianity—Ethelbert of Kent and Edwin of Northumbria
—Conversion of those Kings—Foundation of the Sees of
Canterbury and London.*

AMONGST the heathen, we may discern several shades or
gradations of delusion.   Some nations, like the Mexicans,
have so entirely renounced the Divine assistance, as to
be allowed to fall into absolute devil-worship ; knowingly
and wittingly worshipping the sources of evil, and
attempting to propitiate the demons whom they adore,
by actions which they must confess to be crimes.   Others
have erred, not so much by denying the Almighty, as by
bestowing his attributes upon his creatures, to whom
they have rendered the worship due to the Creator.
The sun going forth in his course, the moon walking in
brightness, and the starry host of heaven, have all
received the honour appertaining only to the power by
whom they were framed.   Nor has this idolatry been
confined to inanimate objects ; for the lawgivers, the
rulers, and the warriors of the people, have been deified
by the ignorance or fraud of their subjects or disciples.
This sin against the Divine Majesty may exist in fact,
although not acknowledged in form.   Whenever any
veneration is rendered to human virtue, any respect paid
to human wisdom, or any confidence placed in human
power, in such a manner as to render us unmindful that

our talents are the free gifts of Providence, we err, even as if we offered the hecatomb to Apollo, or burnt the incense before Baal.

The religion of the Anglo-Saxons, in general,—it is not in our power to distinguish between particular tribes,—was evidently a compound of the worship of the celestial bodies, or *Sabœism*, as it is termed, and of hero-worship; and the Anglo-Saxon names of the days of the week enable us to give a compendium of their creed.

Sunnandœg and *Monandœg*, or Sunday and Monday, scarcely need a version. It must be remarked, however, that, contrary to the mythology of the Greeks and Romans, the Sun was considered by all the Teutons as a female, and the Moon as a male deity. They had an odd notion that if they addressed that power as a goddess, their wives would be their masters.

The third day of the week, following the two great festivals of Sun-day and Moon-day, was known amongst many of the German nations by the name of "*Dings-tag*," or the Court-day, the popular tribunals being then held. But the Anglo-Saxons called it "*Tiues-dœg*," or Tuesday. Some learned men suppose that "*Tiue*" is the "*Tuisco*" noticed by Tacitus as a deity, whom the Teutons praised in their hymns, and from whom the Teutonic nations were named. Others identify him with *Tyr*, one of the twelve companions of Odin, much venerated in the north.

Wodnesdœg, or Wednesday, was consecrated to the great *Woden*, or *Odin*. The worship of this hero was common to all the Teutons. He was their king, from whom their science and lore had been derived—the song of the bard and the incantation of the sorcerer had been taught by Odin—and all the princes and rulers of the

Anglo-Saxons claimed, as I have before observed, to be considered as his progeny. In the Scandinavian "*Sagas*," or romances, Odin appears as the leader by whom the " Asi," or Northmen, were conducted to the shores of the Baltic from their original clime, perhaps the neighbourhood of the Black Sea; and the learned historians of Sweden and Denmark, by the ingenious device of supposing that there were *three* Wodens or Odins at different periods, have contrived to reduce the adventures ascribed to him to a kind of consistent chronology. Woden must, however, be considered merely as a mythological creation; and though it is very probable that there is some authentic foundation for the historical character of the " Furious One,"*—such being the meaning of his name, —yet it is quite impossible to analyse the elements of which it is composed.

Thor, the patron deity of *Thorsdæg*, or Thursday, follows in the rank immediately after Odin. Thor, like the Roman Jove, to whom the same day was assigned, was worshipped as the Thunderer; his thunderbolt was a hammer, which he wielded with irresistible force; and many tales and fables are told of his achievements and battles against giants and demons.

Freya was the wife of Odin, and gave her name to *Freya-dæg*, or Friday. She was the Venus of the North.

Lastly came *Sæter*, from whom Saturday was named. He was represented as standing upon a fish, and he held a bucket in his hand, so that he appears to have been a water deity.

Besides the before-mentioned deities, many others received their share of honour. *Saxnote*, the son of Odin,

* *Wood* still means *mad* in the actual dialect of Scotland.

was venerated by the old Saxons of Germany, and probably by their kinsmen in Britain, almost as highly as Odin himself; and from him the Kings of Essex were descended. On the Continent, the Slavonians, who spread themselves into Europe out of Asia, at a later period than the Teutons, had possessed themselves of the shores of the Baltic, where the old Saxons dwelled. The Russians are Slavonians; but this great nation consisted of many tribes, and the wild people who advanced as far as the Elbe were also called *Slavo-Winidi*, *Vendi*, or Vandals. Their mythology had some affinity to the system which now prevails amongst the Hindoos. Their idols were often many-headed, and covered with symbols. The Slavonians or Vandals adopted some of the Teuton gods from their Saxon neighbours: the latter equally borrowed from the Slavonians; and Sæter appears to have been one of these foreign deities.

In Britain, especially in Deira, the Angles appear to have united their own idolatry to the ministration of a druidical hierarchy. This flexibility of opinion was not the result of unsteadiness. Ignorantly worshipping, and knowing not how to seek the truth, they felt the insufficiency of their belief, and yearned for a better creed. Rocks, and running streams, and green trees, were considered as objects requiring libations and sacrifices. Not that the Anglo-Saxons believed that stocks and stones, or the water, could listen to them; but they offered their prayers beneath the shadows of the forest, or on the banks of the rushing torrent, as being the places more particularly haunted by the *Elves*, or subordinate deities who filled this sublunary globe, though unseen to mortal eye. Yet, notwithstanding these and many other similar delusions, the Teutonic nations retained some faint reminiscences of the truths revealed or shadowed to the Patriarchs.   Possibly the week of seven days, as used by them, may be considered as one of these vestiges.   They had a very firm conviction that the soul did not perish with the body.   Of their conception of the essence of the Divine Being, the Anglo-Saxon language affords a singular testimony, for the name of *God* signifies *Good*. He was goodness itself, and the author of all goodness. Yet the idea of denoting the Deity by a term equivalent to abstract and absolute perfection, striking as it may appear, is perhaps less remarkable than the fact, that the word *Man*, which they used, as we do, to designate a human being, also signified *Wickedness ;* showing how well they were aware that our fallen nature had become identified with sin and corruption.   They held the doctrine, that this visible world was to be judged and destroyed, preparatory to a new and happier state of being.   Though wild, and ferocious towards their enemies, they were less corrupted than the more polished Greeks and Romans.   They were faithful, chaste, and honest— turning towards the light, and seeking amendment. The ground was good; and when the sower cast the seed, it brought forth an abundant harvest.

Whilst the Jutes, the Angles, and the Saxons were establishing their temporal dominion in Britain, the means of imparting to them the saving truths of the Gospel were preparing by the intervention of Gregory, who then held the station of Bishop or Patriarch, or, as his office is now more usually termed, of *Pope* of Rome.

The possession of the Roman Bishopric gave great rank and pre-eminence to the Prelate by whom this dignity was enjoyed.   After the Romans, and the

nations constituting the Roman empire, had been converted to Christianity, it appeared expedient, that,
when the Bishops of the different cities and provinces
were assembled for the purpose of deliberating on the
rule and government of the church, certain Prelates
amongst them should be appointed to preside and keep
order in these councils of the Clergy. And this duty
was assigned to the Bishops, sometimes called Patriarchs,
whose chairs or "*Cathedræ*" were placed in the mother,
or principal churches of the most important dioceses;
for this latter term, which is now exclusively applied to
ecclesiastical divisions, was used according to the imperial nomenclature—as I have before observed—to
denote one of the classes of the temporal governments
into which the empire was divided. The first, or
Primate, of the Cathedral Bishops, was the Patriarch of
Rome, who was complimented with an honorary pre-
cedence over other Bishops, because Rome was anciently
the capital of the whole empire. Constantinople, or New
Rome, had a Patriarch, who also possessed the rank of
a President; because that city, when the empire was
divided, became the capital of the Empire of the East.
Jerusalem was the seat of a Patriarch, out of respect to
the Holy City; Antioch and Alexandria, as the chief
cities of Asia Minor and of Africa, also possessed Prelates, invested with the patriarchal dignity; and many
other cities enjoyed the same honour.

Bishops derive their order and spiritual functions from
the Apostles. But the arrangements relating to the
places where they are fixed, and to the endowments of
their sees, form a part of the civil government of the
church; and as they are not essentially connected with
her doctrines, they may be altered by competent authority.

The Church of Rome perverted many human institutions into articles of faith ; and the pre-eminence assigned to the " Chair of St. Peter," unconnected as it was with any thing except the temporal government of the empire, became the origin and source of the vast dominion which the Popes afterwards assumed over the other churches of the Christian world.

Pope Gregory had become much interested in the welfare of the Anglo-Saxons, in consequence of an incident which happened to him at an earlier period of his life. It chanced that he passed through the market at Rome (about A.D. 588), where certain dealers had just arrived from foreign parts with various kinds of merchandise. Amongst other articles, there were slaves for sale, like cattle. This wicked traffic had existed from time immemorial ; and though Christianity had alleviated the lot of the slave, it had not succeeded in breaking his bonds. Gregory, therefore, could only pity the captives ; and he was particularly interested by the appearance of some poor little lads, who stood trembling in the expectation of being consigned to a new master. They were beautiful children, with ruddy cheeks and blue eyes, and their fine yellow tresses flowing in long curls upon their shoulders. Long hair, in those days, was a token of dignified birth. Only kings and nobles were accustomed to allow of its growth : persons of an inferior or servile class were closely shorn. Gregory must, therefore, have felt an additional motive for compassion, since he perceived that these children had sustained some great reverse of fortune—and their sufferings must be comparatively much more poignant than if they had been accustomed to privation and labour. The father of the boys had probably been killed in war ; and the children,

brought up in ease and comfort, were now exposed to
hopeless captivity, passing from the tender care of their
parents to the power of a merciless task-master in a
strange land.

"To what nation do these poor boys belong?" was
the question which Gregory asked of the dealer. "They
are Angles, Father." "Well may they be so called for
they are as comely as angels; and would that, like
angels, they might become cherubim in Heaven! But
from which of the many provinces of Britain do they
come?" "From *Deira*, Father." "Indeed," continued
Gregory, speaking in Latin, "*De irâ Dei liberandi sunt*"
—From the wrath of God they are to be delivered.
And when, on asking the name of their king, he was
told it was Ella, or Alla, he added, that *Allelujah*—praise
ye the Lord—ought to be sung in his dominions.

This conversation may appear trifling; but it was
destined to produce the most important effects. The
state of Britain having been introduced to the notice of
Gregory, he brooded over the thought, and determined
to proceed hither in the character of a missionary.
Impediments arose, which prevented him from carrying
this design into effect, but the impression continued firm
in his mind; and when he became Pope of Rome he
despatched Augustine to fulfil the task, the accomplishment of which he had so earnestly desired (A.D. 596-601).

At this period, Kent was governed by Ethelbert, a
monarch of great power and ability, who had compelled
the other sovereigns of the island, whether Britons or
Anglo-Saxons, to acknowledge him as their superior
(A.D. 597-598). He had married a princess named Bertha,
the sister of Charibert, King of Paris. This lady was a
Christian; and, by permission of her husband, she had

caused a deserted church, built by the Romans in the neighbourhood of Canterbury, to be repaired and fitted up for divine service.   Ethelbert, therefore, was not altogether unacquainted with the character and functions of Augustine and his forty companions, who, when they had landed in the Isle of Thanet, sent a messenger to him, soliciting an interview.   Still he had a strange opinion that they might be magicians ; and, by a still stranger idea, he fancied they were less likely to be able to hurt him by their enchantments, if he received them in the open air.

Augustine and his companions proceeded to the appointed place, and advanced towards the king, chanting the Litany, and praying earnestly for the Divine blessing and protection.*   Ethelbert did not at first yield much attention to the Missionaries.   He excused himself from attending to their exhortations ; but he received the Priests with kindness, and allowed them free liberty to preach to the people.   Ethelbert himself soon became a listener and a convert ; and within a short period, all the inhabitants of Kent were convinced of their folly in worshipping Thor and Woden, the idols of their ancestors.

So earnestly indeed did the men of Kent listen to

---

* " For ever hallowed be this morning fair,
    Blest be the unconscious shore on which ye tread,
    And blest the Silver Cross, which ye, instead
Of martial banner, in procession bear ;
    The Cross preceding Him who floats in air,
    The pictured Saviour !—By Augustine led,
    They come—and onward travel without dread,
Chanting in barbarous ears a tuneful prayer,
    Sung for themselves, and those whom they would free !
    Rich conquest waits them :—The tempestuous sea
Of ignorance, that ran so rough and high,
    And heeded not the voice of clashing swords,
    These good men humble by a few bare words,
And calm with fear of God's divinity."—WORDSWORTH.

Augustine, that upwards of ten thousand of them were baptized on one Christmas-day. And we have yet a friendly and confidential letter, addressed by Pope Gregory to Eulogius, his brother Patriarch of Alexandria, containing an account of the joyful success attending the missionaries who had laboured amongst the English, "in the most remote parts of the world." He speaks nearly in the same tone which we should now adopt, if relating the fruits of a mission in Polynesia.

Ethelbert was extremely anxious to afford to Augustine and his companions the means of performing divine worship with decency and solemnity; and he surrendered to them his own palace, that they might live therein, and erect a church adjoining : at the same time, he bestowed many ample possessions for the maintenance of the priests who were to become its ministers. This church is now the Cathedral of Canterbury. The present structure, though ancient, is of date long subsequent to the age of Augustine. After a great fire, which consumed the cathedral in the eleventh century, it was rebuilt by Lanfranc, and other portions are of yet later periods. Still the Cathedral retains its original consecration; and venerable as the fabric appears to the eye, it acquires a greater title to our respect, when we recollect how long the spot has been hallowed by the worship of the Lord.

Sebert, the King of the East Saxons, was the nephew of Ethelbert, being the son of his sister Ricola, and the Christian missionaries therefore obtained an easy access into his dominions. London was still noted for its opulence; its fame was diffused far and wide; and the city was the resort of merchants from all parts of the world. I say, *still*, because it had been equally pre-

eminent in the Roman times.   And the great confusion
consequent upon the Saxon conquest had scarcely in-
jured the prosperity of London, which has continued
increasing from the time of the Romans till the present
day.

London was quite unlike the great metropolis which
we now inhabit.   Its extent was confined to what is now
termed " the city," then surrounded by a wall, built, as
it is supposed, about the age of Constantine, and of
which a few fragments are existing.   All around was
open country.   Towards the north-east a deep marsh,—
the name is yet preserved in Moorfields,—extended to
the foot of the Roman ramparts.   On the western side
of the city, and at the distance of nearly two miles, the
branches of a small river which fell into the Thames
formed an island, so overgrown with thickets and brush-
wood, that the Saxons called it " *Thorney*," or the " Isle
of Thorns."   The river surrounding Thorney crept
sullenly along the plashy soil; and the spot was so wild
and desolate, that it is described as a fearful and terrible
place, which no one could approach after night-fall without great danger.   In this island there had been an
ancient Roman temple, consecrated to Apollo.   And
Sebert, perhaps on account of the seclusion which Thorney afforded, resolved to build a church on the site, and
he dedicated the fabric to St. Peter the Apostle.   This
Church is now Westminster Abbey; the busy city of
Westminster is old Thorney Island, that seat of desolation; and the bones of Sebert yet rest in the structure
which he founded.   Another great church was built by
Sebert, in the city of London, upon the ruins of the
heathen temple of Diana (A.D. 604).   This church is now
St. Paul's Cathedral; and Mellitus being appointed the

first Bishop by Ethelbert and Sebert, the succession has continued to the present day.

During the lifetime of Augustine, the Anglo-Saxons to the north of the Humber continued strangers to Christianity. Their conversion took place under the reign of Edwin, who, after many vicissitudes of fortune, attained the supreme dignity, and became the Bretwalda or Emperor amongst the Kings of the island of Britain.

Edwin had married Ethelburgha, the daughter of Ethelbert; and at the request of Eadbert, her brother—who succeeded to the kingdom of Kent, upon the death of Ethelbert—he had permitted Paulinus, a missionary despatched by Justus, Archbishop of Canterbury, to enter his dominions. Paulinus was received with courtesy, and his conduct continued to command the respect which, at first, had been yielded to his station. Instead of injudiciously urging the object of his mission, he waited until the way should open before him. About this time, Cwichelm, the King of Wessex, unable to withstand the power of Edwin, treacherously attempted to destroy him by assassination (A.D. 625-626). Eomer, the agent chosen for this nefarious purpose, approached the throne of Edwin in the character of an ambassador; and when the King stretched forth his hand to welcome the stranger, the latter drew his sword, and attempted to transfix the King. But Edwin's faithful Thane, Lilla, whose keen eye had caught the gesture of the murderer, threw himself between his master and the point of the weapon. Yet so fierce and fell was the thrust, that it passed through the body of the Thane; and though Edwin's life was saved, he received a dangerous wound. Amidst this alarm, Ethelburgha was seized by the pangs of child-birth, and the mother, as well as the infant, ap-

peared in the greatest danger. The prayers of Paulinus
were offered for the queen and her babe : they both
recovered ; and twelve of the royal household, as well
as the infant, were baptized by Edwin's permission and
request.

Edwin himself still hesitated : he was about to engage
in war with Cwichelm, for the purpose of punishing his
treachery. He asked Paulinus for a sign, and declared,
that, should he succeed against his enemies, he would
adopt the Christian faith.

As soon as Edwin recovered from his wounds, he
collected his forces, marched against the men of Wessex,
and inflicted a signal punishment upon all who had
conspired against him. On his return, he performed his
vow in part : he abjured idolatry ; no longer did he
sacrifice to the false gods whom he had adored ; and he
anxiously laboured to put himself in the right way.
Much of his time he passed in discussion with Paulinus,
and also with his counsellors and nobles, but more in
communing with his own heart, in solitude, in reflection,
and in prayer.

Edwin was one day alone in his chamber (A.D. 627),
being in that state of imperfect conviction, when the
feelings of religion, alloyed by human doubts, impart
more distress than comfort to the soul,—Paulinus
suddenly entered, placed his hand upon Edwin's head,
and announced a great deliverance from his enemies.
The appearance of Paulinus, his attitude, and the
intelligence which he thus communicated, corresponded
with a foreboding or presentiment which Edwin had
received, probably by a dream, when in exile at the
court of Redwald, King of the East Angles ; and
Paulinus, availing himself of the impression thus created,

earnestly exhorted Edwin to acknowledge that Power by whom he had been protected and rescued from temporal danger. Edwin now began to yield the assent which he had so long delayed ; and he declared unto Paulinus, that he would receive the sacrament of baptism, provided the wise law-givers of his kingdom would sanction his conversion, and also adopt Christianity.

Edwin had even yet only a wavering faith : humanly speaking, however, his conduct was palliated by the circumstances in which he was placed. The Kings of the Anglo-Saxons did not possess a despotic authority. They were forced to act by the advice of their nobles, many of whom were Sovereigns in their territories, though the vassals of the King ; and if the Northumbrian chieftains had continued contumaciously averse to Christianity, Edwin would not only have been unable to protect the Missionaries, but he might himself have been in danger of losing his crown, and perhaps his life. And that the course so adopted was prudent, may be understood by the ready assent given by Paulinus, to the proposition which Edwin had thus made.

Edwin, therefore, convened his nobles and counsellors —and craved their advice upon the important question which he propounded : each was to give his opinion separately from the rest, and each was asked by the King to declare his mind concerning Christianity.

The first who spake was the High Priest of the heathen gods, Coifi by name, who acknowledged the utter vanity of those idols which he had served. He had found that these imaginary deities could not reward the good ; we must suppose that he equally acknowledged their want of power to punish the evil doer; and he concluded by declaring, that if any better doctrine could be taught to him, he would adopt it without hesitation or delay.

Then spake another of the nobles, who, addressing himself to Edwin, compared the present life of man to the flight of a swallow : whence it comes we know not, nor whither it proceeds : our human existence is a gleam in the midst of darkness. "We know nothing of our origin," said he, "nothing of our end; and if this new doctrine can teach us anything certain of our destiny, well is it worth that we should follow its law."*

All the other nobles and counsellors delivered opinions to the same effect : not a dissentient voice was heard; and Coifi, the High Priest, proposed that the heathen places of worship should be destroyed, or burnt with fire. But who is to execute this task ? The High Priest answers, that he himself will set the example of destroying the pristine objects of idolatry.

From the tone in which the question was put and answered, it is probable that some danger was apprehended from the anger of the people, and Coifi began his work in such a manner, as to show the most complete abandonment of the heathen law. According to the

* I cannot deny to myself and my readers the pleasure of inserting the lines by which Wordsworth has rendered the text of Bede :—

"Man's life is like a sparrow, mighty King,
That, stealing in, while by the fire you sit
Housed with rejoicing friends, is seen to flit
Safe from the storm, in comfort tarrying.
Here did it enter—there, on hasty wing
Flies out, and passes on from cold to cold ;
But whence it came we know not, nor behold
Whither it goes. E'en such that transient thing
The human soul ; not utterly unknown
While in the body lodged, her warm abode—
But from what world she came, what woe or weal
On her departure waits, no tongue hath shewn :
This mystery if the stranger can reveal,
His be a welcome cordially bestowed !"

ritual of Deira, a priest could not bear a weapon, or ride on a horse. Coifi girt himself with a sword, and grasped a lance in his hand, and mounting one of the royal steeds, he galloped to the temple of " Godmundingham."

This place of worship appears to have been encircled by several concentric enclosures, like the morais of Polynesia, and as soon as Coifi came within reach of the fane, he hurled his spear against its walls. When the people first saw him sally forth, they thought some sudden insanity had seized him. How much more must they have been astonished at this act! Yet no opposition was offered; within a very short space of time, the fabric was levelled to the ground; and after the lapse of so many centuries, its name, but slightly altered,* continues to attest the truth of the history.

Baptism was then performed by immersion, and so general and so fervent was the zeal of the Northumbrians, that Paulinus was employed during thirty-six successive days, from morning to night, in baptizing the eager multitude (A.D. 628).

Before a century had elapsed, Christianity was firmly and sincerely believed throughout Anglo-Saxon Britain; and, in the state of society which then prevailed, the establishment of the true religion became the means of conferring the greatest temporal advantages upon the community. A large proportion of the population consisted either of slaves, or of churls or villains, who were compelled to till the ground for the benefit of their masters. These classes immediately gained the comfort of rest, one day in seven; and they whose labour had hitherto been unremitted, without any pause, except when fainting nature sunk under incessant toil, could

* Now " Goodmanham," Harthill Wapentake, in the East Riding of York.

now expect the Sabbath of the Lord, as a day of holiness and of repose. So strictly did the temporal laws protect the observance of the seventh day, the right and privilege of the poor, that the master who compelled his slave to work on the Sunday, was deprived of the means of abusing his power,—the slave obtained his freedom.

A tenth part of the produce of the land was set apart for the maintenance of the clergy, and the support of the destitute. Charity, when resulting from the unaided impulses of humanity, has no permanence. Bestowed merely to relieve ourselves from the painful sight of misery, the virtue blesses neither the giver nor the receiver. But, proceeding from the love of God, it is steady and uniform in its operation, not wayward, not lukewarm, not affected by starts and fancies, and ministering to more than the bodily wants of those who are in need.

Paupers, such as we now see, then rarely existed. Bad as it was, the system of slavery had given a house and a home to the great mass of the lowest orders. And the laws, which placed the middling classes under the protection, and at the same time under the control of the more powerful, prevented all such as really belonged to society, from experiencing any severe privations in those years when the people were not visited by any particular misfortunes. But mankind were then subjected to many calamities, which have been moderated in our times. If crops failed, and the earth did not bring forth her fruit, vessels arrived not from distant parts, laden with corn. Hunger wasted the land. Sickness and pestilence followed, and thinned the remnant who had been left. Families were broken up, and the survivors became helpless outcasts; for the people of each country raised only as much grain as was sufficient for their own use, and could not supply their neighbours. War often produced still greater miseries. In all these distresses, the spirit of Christianity constantly urged those who were influenced by this enduring spring of action, to exert themselves in affording relief;—to clothe the naked and feed the hungry,—to visit the sick —and bury the corpses of the departed.

The higher or ruling orders saw, in the plain letter of the Bible, the means of amending the rude and savage laws which had governed their forefathers; and religion also afforded the means of improving the whole fabric of the state. In addition to their piety, the clergy were the depositaries of all the learning of the age. All the knowledge which distinguishes civilization from savage life was entrusted to them. Admitted into the supreme councils of the realm, they became an Order, possessing acknowledged rights which could not be lawfully assailed. And though they may occasionally have attempted to extend their privileges beyond their proper bounds, yet, in a monarchy, the existence of any one rank or order invested with franchises which the king must not assail, is in itself a strong and direct protection to the privileges of all other ranks of the community. Powerful as the nobles may have been, it is doubtful whether they could have maintained their ground, had they been deprived of the support which they derived from the bishops and abbots, who stood foremost in the ranks, amongst the peers of the monarchy. Many a blow which would have cleft the helmet turned off without harm from the mitre; and the crozier kept many an enemy at bay, who would have rushed without apprehension upon the spear.

To the successors of the Anglo-Saxon prelates, we mainly owe the preservation of the forms and spirit of a free government, defended, not by force, but by law; and the altar may be considered as the corner-stone of the ancient constitution of the realm.

Chapter IV.

Royal dignity not existing amongst the Saxons and Jutes before their arrival in Britain—Kings—Royal authority amongst the Barbarians, how deduced from the Roman authority— Clovis—Bretwaldas or Emperors of Britain—Ella—Ceawlin —Ethelbert—Redwald—Edwin—Oswald—Oswio—Subjugation of the smaller States—Rise of the Kingdom of Mercia— Ethelbald—Offa—His Conquests of the Britons—Decline of Mercia, and Rise of Wessex—Egbert—His early adventures —Obtains the dignity of Bretwalda.

IF by the royal dignity we are to understand a permanent authority, enabling the Sovereign to give laws to his subjects in time of peace, to command them to follow him in time of war, and to impose taxes or tributes upon the nation at all times, such an authority was wholly unknown to the Jutes, Angles, and Saxons, before they settled in Britain. Their chieftains were called *Ealdormen* or *Aldermen*, in plain English, *Eldermen*, a title originally employed to denote only the very highest of the chieftains,—Cerdic and Cynric, or Hengist and Horsa,—but which was afterwards given by courtesy to almost every person in command. It was common to all the Teutonic nations; but those who adopted the Latin language translated the title into *Senior*, the origin of the *Seigneur*, *Senor*, and *Signor* of the French, Spaniards, and Italians.

To return to our Anglo-Saxon and Jutish Aldermen— they constituted a kind of ruling Caste or Tribe, all sons of Woden, perhaps anciently invested with sacerdotal functions—the priests, as well as the lawgivers and leaders of the nation. Collectively as a caste, and individually over their own immediate followers and retainers, they possessed great dominion and influence; but there was no political power of any wide extent, vested in any one individual, excepting during hostilities. A chieftain was then elected to lead the nation, but his rule expired with the urgency which had given it birth, and all the Aldermen were alike again. Such was the government of the "*old Saxons;*" but amongst others of the Teutonic nations, the authority of the chieftains had greatly extended. The Romans not unfrequently bestowed the title of " Rex " upon the leaders who had submitted to them, and who were by no means unwilling to purchase an increased authority over their subjects, by compromising their own political independence. Instances of this practice are found as early as the time of Julius Cæsar, and they afford a curious exemplification of the course pursued by the Romans in the days of their strength. When the empire decayed, grants of similar titles were the result of the weakness of the imperial power. Clovis may be our example. He was the conqueror of the Gauls; he had come in by right of the sword; and yet he was happy to receive the consular diploma and the purple robe from Anastasius, the Emperor of the East; and, invested with the imperial insignia, he rode in state, scattering gold and silver as he paced on his steed, whilst he was hailed as Augustus by the surrounding multitude. Here was policy on both sides;—Anastasius, by conferring such dignities upon Clovis, kept himself in the position of a superior; and Clovis, by accepting his dignity from Anastasius, not only obtained a firm hold upon his conquered subjects, the Romanized inhabitants of Gaul, but laid the foundation for a dominion over his own Frankish warriors, of a far different nature from that possessed by his fur-clad ancestors in the forests of Germany.

The Anglo-Saxon Aldermen, who, on the other side of the North Sea, were balanced by the authority of very many others, all as good as themselves, felt themselves in great measure relieved from that check, when they settled in Britain. Their power had ample verge and room to expand. The chieftains accompanying the captains of the expeditions, were principally younger branches belonging to the family, who were contented to accept a share of the conquest with a subordinate authority. Cerdic thus bestowed the Isle of Wight upon his nephews, who held it as a subordinate kingdom, which subsisted until the reign of Alfred under monarchs of its own. All the powers of the British kings were assumed by the Saxon victors. The conqueror entered into the palace, encircled his shaggy locks with the diadem, threw the Dalmatica over his shoulder, and became entitled to the riches and ample domains of the British sovereigns. The very word " Cynge," or King, as exclusively appropriated to the sovereign, seems to have been derived from a Celtic term, Cen, or Cean, signifying Head or Chief. I am compelled to differ from my friends and contemporaries, who had been employed upon the history of England,* and to declare my opinion,

* Mr. Allen, in his most learned inquiry into the rise and growth of the royal prerogative, adopts the etymology of Lye, that " Cyning" is derived from Cyn,—this means kindred, family, tribe, or nation ; but the termination " ing " being a patronymic, he supposes that Cyning was considered as the son or child of the nation. Sir James Mackintosh follows Adelung, who derives the word from Konnen. to be able, which corresponds to our verb can. But Ihre admits that the term was strange in the north, and substituted for the term Drottnar. In the Mæso-Gothic it never occurs, the corresponding term being Thiudans. Amongst the Burgundians, the Sovereign was called Hendinus, and I cannot get out of the maze in any better manner, than by adopting the supposition in my text.

that the Teutonic dialects do not offer any satisfactory etymology. This, however, is of little consequence; it is sufficient to know that the word "King" gradually became restricted to denote a sovereign power; whilst the chieftains, now subordinate, because their compeers had been raised above them, and who held the smaller districts, retained the old title of "*Aldermen*," which continued applied to them until the Danish conquests. There were certainly exceptions either way. At one period we read of five *kings* of Wessex being killed in battle, who could only have been minor chieftains; yet these irregularities in the state nomenclature were not so numerous as to derogate from the general rule.

But there was a prouder honour than that of King; for the title of "*Bretwalda*," Ruler or Emperor of Britain, placed the possessor as much above the kings, as each king was above his aldermen.

That Ella, who first assumed the title of Bretwalda, must have obtained this dignity in consequence of his dominion over the Britons, is easily proved by inspection of the map ;* for the South Saxons and the Jutes had then alone established themselves; and it would have been preposterous in Ella to have founded so wide a claim merely on his supremacy over this narrow angle of the island. The title was evidently assumed in imitation of the Roman imperial authority, whether as exercised by the legitimate Emperors or the British Tyrants; and the idea of such a supremacy is wholly foreign to any species of government existing amongst the Saxons before they came to Britain. It was exercised with as much show of Roman style and splendour as could be attained. The coin of the Bretwalda, rudely

* No. 1.

copied from the medal of Carausius, exhibits the wolf and twins, the ensigns of old Rome; and the Roman ensign, borne before him, demonstrated the rank which he had claimed, and which he endeavoured, with more or less success, to extend, not only over the Britons, but over all the other nations of the island.

Ella,—Ceawlin of Wessex,—and Ethelbert of Kent, successively held this dignity. Redwald of East Anglia obtained it; but whether in the lifetime of Ethelbert (A.D. 477 to 616), or after his decease is somewhat uncertain. I incline to the latter supposition. From Redwald, the empire passed to Edwin of Northumbria. His authority extended over every part of Britain which was inhabited either by the Cymri, or by the English and Saxon natives (A.D. 617-633). The Menavian islands, or Man and Anglesea, were equally subjected to his power; and the name by which we denote the latter, meaning the "island of the English," is thought to have been derived from the colonies transplanted there by Edwin: but the Britons must have returned again, for the English colonies disappeared amidst the races by whom "Mona, the mother of the Cymri,"* was possessed.

Penda, the Mercian, resisted or rebelled against the authority of Edwin; and allying himself with Cadwallader, the King of the Western Britons, they marched their forces against the King of Northumbria. Edwin was overpowered by their numbers, and slain in the battle of Heathfield; and Northumbria became, for a time, the prey of the victors.

Oswald, the nephew of Edwin, who united in his own person the claims of the families both of Deira and Bernicia, regained all that his uncle had lost (A.D. 634-635).

* "Mon Mam Cymri."

Britain acknowledged him as "Emperor;" and the title was given to him in such a manner as to shew that it was equivalent to that of Bretwalda. He ruled supreme over all the nations and provinces of the island, divided, according to the expression of Bede, into four nations: the Angles, the Picts, the Cymri, and the Scots. Oswald's virtues, perhaps, assisted in enabling him to acquire this dominion. Humble and lowly-minded, full of piety and active charity, the qualities which caused him to be canonized after his death, obtained the love and veneration of his subjects when living; and the epithet of "Bounteous-hand," bestowed upon him by the Britons, is a singular testimony of respect shewn to a "Sassenagh" sovereign.

Oswald, like Edwin, fell in battle with the Mercians (A.D. 642); and the miracles supposed to be worked in the field of "Maserfelth,"* were accepted as testimonies of the sanctity ascribed to the Northumbrian king. Oswio, the brother of Oswald, after some interval—for his authority over the Northumbrian kingdoms was disturbed and contested even by his own son—obtained the dignity of Bretwalda, like his predecessor; and the Picts and Scots, as well as the other natives of Britain, acknowledged his supremacy.

I have said that the Bretwaldas are to be considered as the successors of the Roman Emperors, or *Tyrants*. But the remark must be extended; and we may affirm, that when and so soon as the royal authority became developed amongst any of the barbarians who settled on Roman ground, all their kings took upon themselves, as far as they could, to govern according to the spirit of the Roman policy, and agreeably to the maxims prevail-

* Perhaps Oswestry.

ing in the decline of the empire, and declared in the
imperial law. At the same time, this copy of the Roman
majesty was very rude and inartificial. The edifice was
the handiwork of unskilful artists working by eye,
and in coarse materials. The " *Witan* " (sages), and
" *Rædgifa* " (givers of counsel), of the Anglo-Saxon
and other of the barbaric kingdoms, used the codes and
codicils and rescripts of the Emperors, even as their
church architects attempted to imitate the models
afforded by the sacred structures of imperial Rome.
Yet, though the column be disproportioned, and the
capital rude, and the moulding misshapen, we must
acknowledge that the cathedral of Charlemagne would
never have assumed its characteristic form, if the archi-
tect had not sought a prototype in the Basilica of
Constantine.

This assumption of power was not unchecked or
uncontrolled. Whilst the kings of the barbaric nations
were striving to clothe themselves with an imperial
authority, the people, or, to speak more correctly, the
communities or bodies of people which they governed,
strove equally to maintain their old Germanic freedom;
and the nobles, in particular, were fully able to resist all
coercion from the royal power. Some of the rights
claimed by the monarch were, perhaps, mere pretensions :
others were contested ; and, at the same time, whatever
prerogatives the king possessed as an ancient Germanic
chieftain, were still enforced by him, to the utmost of
his might.

The infusion of Roman or Romanized doctrines into
the administration of the monarch, did not derogate
from the full exercise of all the laws and legal customs
of the barbarians, which the Teutonic warriors considered

as their birthright and best privilege. Taking all these
things together, we must consider the practical government of the State as resulting from two opposite
principles, often discordant, and sometimes entirely
hostile to each other—a Roman law which the king
endeavoured to introduce into the administration of the
state—and a Germanic law, upon which that Roman
law was imposed; and by adverting to these circumstances, many of the problems of history may be solved.
Thus, in the kingdom of the Franks, the "Comites"
and "Duces," (such being the titles by which the
subordinate chieftains were distinguished), appear sometimes as hereditary, and sometimes as deriving their
authority from the sovereign. Now, if it be assumed
that the sovereign, in continuation of the Roman policy,
delegated his power to local governors—but that these
local governors were usually the old heads or rulers of
the subordinate nations or tribes, this contradiction will
disappear. By accepting the royal diploma or com-
mission, the *Senior* accumulated the royal jurisdiction
upon his own, and they became inseparably blended
when, in process of time, the distinction between his
rights as a Teutonic chieftain, and his duties as the
king's officer were neglected or forgotten. This may be
illustrated by a familiar comparison :—supposing the
Lord-lieutenancy of Merionethshire had been invariably
granted, since the reign of Henry VIII., to the Wynns
—from father to son ; and that when the male line
ceased, the office was equally continued in the female
line : that we had no regular record or register relating
to such appointments ; and that the country was in
great turbulence and warfare :—under these circumstances, the Wynns and the people of Merionethshire

might very naturally be induced to suppose, that all the
powers of the lieutenancy were inherent in the descendant of Owen Gwynedd, and that they belonged to him
by inheritance, like his estates, independently of the will
of the King of England.

No monarch of Northumbria, after Oswio, possessed
the title of Bretwalda; and, in the course of his reign,
he sustained a great loss of dominion. He slew Penda
and subdued Mercia (A.D. 655); and, without doubt,
declared in his manifestoes that it was a just war, which
he had undertaken for the purpose of reducing the
ancient dependency of his Northumbrian crown. But the
conquest profited not to Oswio. The Mercian nobles or
Ealdormen submitted with an ill will (A.D. 656): they
concealed Wulfere, Penda's son; and in less than a
year, Wulfere was king of the Mercians and Middle
Angles—for the two nations continued distinct. Wulfere extended his conquests into Wessex; and the title
of king of all the "Australian Regions," shews that he
possessed the authority of a Bretwalda in all the island
south of the Humber.

Northumbria was on the wane; and "Ethelbald the
Proud" greatly increased the power and fame of the
Mercian kingdom (A.D. 716). The Mercians continued
pressing against the Britons who inhabited Powys and
Gwynnedd, and Ethelbald waged an obstinate warfare
against them. Over his own race Ethelbald claimed
the rights of a Bretwalda, and at one period all the
kings of the English were subject to the supremacy of
the "King of Britain." Ethelbald was not wise in his
power. His authority over the West Saxons was accompanied by so many acts of vexation and oppression, that
Cuthred, and his people, resolved to make a desperate

effort for the purpose of relieving themselves from a yoke which had become intolerable. At Burford, the two sovereigns met in battle. Ethelbald's army consisted of his own people, the Mercians, the men of Kent, the East Saxons, and the East Angles (A.D. 752). Cuthred's troops were led on by Ethelhun,—" the presumptuous Alderman," as he is called in the Chronicles—bearing the Golden Dragon, the ensign of Wessex. Ethelhun had recently been at war with his lord, Cuthred; but Cuthred defeated him, and they were good friends again ; and Ethelhun was strenuous in his sovereign's cause. The conflict was extremely obstinate and bloody, but at length Ethelhun and Ethelbald engaged in single combat. Hitherto, Ethelbald had found no equal in prowess; but now his strength failed him, and he betook himself to shameful flight : not long afterwards he was slain by treachery, and his dominion passed to Beorred the Tyrant, who usurped his throne (A.D. 757).

Beorred fully deserved the epithet of Tyrant, taken in its worst sense. He appears to have been one of the many Aldermen whose dominions were united beneath the Mercian crown. He governed the people according to his will, and not according to law. And when his intrusive government had become so oppressive, that the Mercians could bear it no longer, the whole people, gentle and simple, rose as one man ; and, expelling Beorred, they elected or recognized Offa as their king. Offa was a " Patrician" of the " right royal line" of Mercia, being descended from Wibba, the son of Creoda ; but he had been compelled to take refuge with the King of Hwiccas, who probably was his kinsman. The historical romances of the Anglo-Saxons celebrated two monarchs of the name of Offa. The first was the son of

Wahrmund or *True-mouth*, being the name which the
Franks spell as "*Pharamond*." *Wahrmund* and *Offa*
really do appear in the genealogies of the kings of
Mercia. And the tales of the Northmen repeat the same
fables concerning *Varmund Vitri*, or the *Wise*, and *Olaf*,
or *Uffa Litilate*, or the *Meek*, which had become consecrated by the lays of the Scandinavian Scallds. Offa
the Second is fabled to have been miraculously restored
from deformity and debility, to symmetry and vigour;
and his marriage with the fair but profligate Druda is
accompanied by all the machinery of romance. These
fictitious Offas must not be confounded with the true
one; and it is difficult to discover any slender vestiges
of truth which may exist amongst these fables.

Offa's right to the crown of Mercia was joyfully
acknowledged. Clergy and laity crowned him as king,
and he speedily extended his power, far beyond the
boundaries which Mercia had possessed under his predecessors. Against the Britons, "Offa the terrible" was
particularly successful. These people had been slowly
reduced. Occasionally they rallied in great strength;
but the English were steady in their plans of conquest,
and the kingdom, or principality of "Ferreggs," now
called Herefordshire, but to which the Anglo-Saxons
gave the name of *Hecana*, had been gained by the Mercians before the reign of Wulfhere. Offa continued to
advance in the same direction. Fair and fertile Powys-
land was almost wholly subjugated by him (A.D. 777).
Flying from Pengwern, now called Shrewsbury, the
princes of this country were compelled to fix their residence in the Halls of Mathraval, whilst the best and
most valuable part of their dominions was planted with
Saxon colonies. To secure these acquisitions, Offa cast

up a vast entrenchment, reaching from the neighbour-
hood of Chester to the Wye. " Clawdh Offa," or Offa's
Dyke, it is called by the Welshmen to the present day. The
Britons, however, did not submit tamely to the invader
(A.D. 792). Issuing from their mountain fastnesses, they
continually, though unavailingly, attacked the English
Mercians, who, on their part, retaliated by ravaging the
British territory. During one of these incursions, a
memorable battle took place at Rhuddlan. Caradoc,
King of Gwinnedd, or North Wales, was slain, together
with the flower of the British youth and nobility. The
British bards mourned this defeat by composing a
lament, entitled, " Morva Rhuddlan :" the strain is often
played upon the harp in Wales : and we may yet listen
to the rich and plaintive melody, which, to us Saxons,
commemorates the victory of the Mercian Offa.

Upon the conquests of Offa and his predecessor it is
necessary to make one important observation, namely,
that the political subjugation of Powys and the adjoining
countries did not necessarily lead to the total expulsion
of the British tribes. English colonists were partially
introduced ; but the British peasantry continued to
dwell upon the soil, though the domain was transferred
to other lords; and so numerous were they, that the
country continued British in appearance even until the
reign of King John, when, in common language, Hereford was still considered to be in Wales. In fact, the
whole of this border was held and peopled nearly as we
see Monmouthshire at the present day. The mass of the
people are *Cymri*, speak their ancient British language,
and continue to give the ancient denomination of *Gwent*
to the lands on which they dwell. But the higher orders,
the gentry and the clergy and the magistrates, are almost

wholly of English race; and the county is an integral
part of the realm of England. Very many of the territories ruled by the Anglo-Saxons had thus a double
aspect; Anglo-Saxon, if you considered them as a state;
British, if you viewed the populacy by which they were
filled: and by recollecting this circumstance, we may
reconcile and explain many seeming anomalies and con-
tradictions in our history.

The results of these conflicts seem to have confirmed
the authority of Offa over the Britons of Cambria, who
became the vassals of his crown. Offa lived to accomplish the subjugation of all the Anglo-Saxon states south
of the Humber. Kent was conquered in open battle
(A.D. 775-776). The West Saxons, after losing part of
their territories, submitted by compromise. The East
Saxons were subdued; and the great and opulent city
of London, with the " Pagus" of Middlesex, had been
annexed to Mercia, perhaps by the voluntary submission
of the inhabitants.

East Anglia was acquired by deliberate treachery.
Ethelbyrht, the king of this country, was desirous of
marrying one of Offa's daughters (A.D. 792); and he
proceeded with much pomp to the court of the Mercian
King, who usually resided at Tamworth, for the purpose
of obtaining her hand. It was most usual in those days
for kings and princes to woo by deputy; and the old
romances, whose fictions often afford the best represen-
tations and memorials of the manners and customs of
real life, describe the scenes which ensued. If one king
sought the daughter of another, he would send ambassadors—grave men, old soldiers, or learned clerks;—
when they arrived, they inspected the young princesses,
who stood up all in a row, and made a report of the

Shrine of Ethelbert, King of the East Saxons.

Inscription on the Shrine.

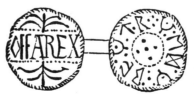

Coin of the Bretwalda Ethelbert.

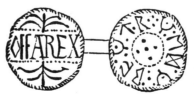

Silver Penny of Offa, King of Mercia.

Danish Warriors.

appearance and character of the damsels to their master. The eldest, they might say, was distinguished by her beauty, the second by her wit, but the youngest by her modesty and discretion. Ethelbyrht thought it best to judge with his own eyes, though caution ought to have suggested, that some harm might ensue to him. The once-powerful kingdom of East Anglia had rapidly declined : its history is merely a blank in our annals. Even the names of the greater number of its monarchs are lost; and we can only surmise, that from the death of Redwald, it had usually submitted to the reigning Bretwalda. Offa asserted his supremacy, and many dissensions had arisen between him and Ethelbyrht. But the latter relied upon the honour of a king; and he proceeded without doubt or hesitation to the palace of his intended father-in-law.

Cwendritha, the queen of Offa, was cruel and crafty. "You have your old enemy in your power," quoth she to Offa; "him whose kingdom you have so long coveted." The Mercian, easily yielding to advice which agreed with his wishes, caused the young and valiant Ethelbyrht to be beheaded, and then despatching a powerful army against the East Angles, he took possession of the country. Neither the " Giant's dyke," not the rivers and waters of their frontier, could enable them to withstand their enemy.

An Anglo-Saxon king was not always certain that his son would succeed him in his dominions. The royal authority was vested in the royal families; but no individual of such family had any determinate or absolute right. The new king was generally designated by the assent of the nation ; and if the son of the late king was not able to exercise the functions of royalty, the brother of the deceased monarch, or even some more remote relation, was called to the throne. Such a mode of succession was not unwisely adapted to the exigencies of the age. An Anglo-Saxon king, in the earlier times, was the chief-justice or magistrate of his people in time of peace. He was also their commander-in-chief, both by land and sea, in time of war; and ill would the affairs of the nation have been sped, had they been entrusted to an infant mind or an infant hand. In cases, however, where the heir was approaching to mature age, the deviation from lineal succession, though often practised, was less expedient; nor could it be pleasing to a father to anticipate the exclusion of his son, from the dignity which he himself had possessed.

Offa, therefore, adopted a scheme, not hitherto employed in England, though many examples had been found in foreign nations (A.D. 785). He summoned a great council; and, with the assent and concurrence of the prelates and nobles of Mercia, Ecgfrith, his son, was associated to him in the royal dignity. So long as Offa lived, Ecgfrith was styled King of Mercia; he sat by the side of his father, and he succeeded to the throne without opposition after Offa's demise.

Whilst Charlemagne claimed for himself the title of the most powerful of the kings of *Eastern* Christendom, he addressed Offa in the same manner, as the most powerful of the kings of the *West*. He uses the titles interchangeably, and as if he wished to imply that Offa was to be considered as his compeer in authority; and in this and many other notices preserved concerning Offa, we can ascertain that he attained great celebrity and fame. His regal palace at " Tamworth Town " has been long since levelled to the ground, and the entrench-

ments, faintly raised above the grass, just enable us to
trace the site of the royal residence.   But the medals
coined by Offa, and which in beauty and workmanship
excel those of any other Saxon monarch, afford a proof
of the cultivation of those arts whose progress is
favoured by opulence and tranquillity.   The prosperity
of Mercia was, however, of very short duration.   The
welfare of the country was not founded upon right
government and justice.   It was a tower built upon the
sand; and after the death of Offa (A.D. 795), upon
whose personal character the vigour of the government,
during his long reign of forty years, had prinicpally
depended, the splendour of Mercia declined, and the
fortunes of its rival, Wessex, prevailed.

Where lineal succession, that is to say, the rule that
the son of a king takes the dignity which had been held
by his father, is fully established, it has the good effect
of preventing most of those disputes which give rise to
civil wars.   It is very easy to tell who is the eldest son of
the late king : no doubt can arise about that fact; but it
is not so easy to determine who is the bravest or the
wisest candidate or competitor, because the electors, in
such a case, will ascribe all the requisite qualifications to
that prince from whom they expect the greatest favours.
Hence all persons are now agreed that, if you have a
king, it is best that the dignity should be inheritable
according to primogeniture; that the eldest son should
take the crown in preference to the younger brothers,
and also in preference to his uncles.   For, by this means,
all the disputes are avoided, and if the heir be deficient
in wisdom, he may perhaps be provided with good
ministers, by whose advice he can be guided.

As I have before observed, this rule of lineal succession did not anciently prevail amongst the Anglo-Saxons : and therefore cases of contested successions occasionally arose between the members of royal family.   Properly speaking, the *Witenagemot*, " the assembly of sages," or great council, had the right of election or nomination ; but if a dispute arose, the knot was usually cut by the sword.   When Beortric, king of the West Saxons, was raised to the throne (A.D. 786), his succession was opposed by Egbert, the son of Alchmund, who claimed a better title to the dignity.   But Egbert had few partisans ; and in order to save his life, he took refuge in the dominions of Offa.   Such a pretender, stationed in the adjoining kingdom, might well alarm Beortric ; and he despatched ambassadors to Offa, with two earnest requests, that he, Offa, would be pleased to bestow upon Beortric the hand of his daughter Eadburgha, in marriage (A.D. 787) ;— and that Offa would also kindly surrender up the rebel Egbert to the just vengeance of his rightful sovereign. Offa assented without any hesitation to the first request ; he well knew that he would gain by ridding himself of his daughter.   The second request was denied ; yet Offa's protection was withdrawn from the pretender. Egbert was compelled to fly from Britain, and he took up his residence in France, where he continued during the whole of Beortric's reign.   These years of exile, how-ever, were not years of misfortune.   France, governed by Charlemagne, then excelled all the other states of Western Christendom in good order and civilization. And our ancient historians have remarked, that it was well that Egbert should have been thus disciplined by adversity before he exercised the wide dominion which he afterwards attained.

Eadburgha, the Queen of Beortric, had inherited all

the cruelty and ambition of her father, Offa. Constantly did she labour to excite jealousy between the king and his subjects (A.D. 799-800). She became hateful to all, and she returned that hatred; and when she could not wreak her vengeance in any other manner, she had recourse to poison. Having prepared a mortal potion, which she intended for the bane of one of the noblemen who attended the court, it chanced that Beortric drank of the cup, and died. The crime could not be concealed; Eadburgha was degraded from her station, and banished; and the men of Wessex, not contented with the punishment inflicted upon the criminal, determined to abolish the rank which she had possessed; they decreed, that thenceforward the consort of the king should neither be called queen, nor sit on the throne, nor be in any wise associated to the royal dignity. Eadburgha fled to France, disgraced, but wealthy, for she had carried off great store of gold. In that country she sank into the most abandoned profligacy: miserable poverty followed. From France she wandered to Italy. During the last years of her life, she was a common beggar in the streets of Pavia. Thus ended the line of Offa.

Beortric having perished by the wickedness of his queen, as I have before described, the vacant throne was filled by Egbert, who returned from France, and succeeded without any domestic opposition (A.D. 800); and having concluded a peace with the Mercians who had taken up arms against him, he had full leisure to establish himself in his kingdom. The first nine years of his reign are nearly a void in all the authentic chronicles; but in those narratives which are less trustworthy, the vacant space is partly filled up by the account of a parliament held at Winchester, in which Egbert decreed,

that South Britain should take the name of " England."
It is tolerably clear, that, in consequence of the greater
preponderance of Angles, the nations whom we usually
term Anglo-Saxons were often called English; but our
country was not denominated England till a much later
period, and the parliament of Egbert is a pure fable.

According to the usual course of policy amongst the
Anglo-Saxons, Egbert pursued the Britons with fierce
hostility; yet I believe that it was not for the purpose
of expelling them from the country, but rather to reduce
them into a state of tributary subjection. The Britons
of the West opposed a strenuous, but unavailing resistance (A.D. 809 to 814). Great was the slaughter on
both sides; but Egbert prevailed; he was equally successful against those who dwelt on the northern shore
of the estuary of the Severn; and lastly, all, or the
greater part of, modern Wales submitted to his authority
(A.D. 783). We must now direct our attention to Kent,
of which Alchmund, the father of Egbert, had been king;
and, as it should seem, after the line of the *Æscingas*
had failed. If you ask me how, and when, and in what
manner, Alchmund was placed upon the throne, I cannot answer these questions, otherwise than by telling
you that the Anglo-Saxon sovereigns in general, but
more particularly those of Wessex, were accustomed to
provide for their sons by settling them in what the
French term "apanages;" that is to say, by granting
them some smaller kingdom or state, which they held in
due subjection to the elder royal branch; just as, in
private life, a nobleman, when his son comes of age,
surrenders to him a decent property on which he can
marry and settle, and bring up his children, until he
succeeds to the principal estates of the family.

Alchmund. then, was one of those kinglets, or *Roitelêts* as the French term them; and, as I suppose (but recollect, that this is only my hypothesis), he had been appointed king in Kent by the power of Wessex. But before and during his time, there were many other kings of Kent, some of whose dominions were, perhaps, not more extensive than the "Lathes" into which the country is divided.* This petty state was in great confusion; and after the reign of Alchmund, one Eadbert, surnamed Pren or Prynne, obtained the kingdom. The ancestry of Eadbert is not known (A.D. 796-797); some people think that he was a priest or monk, who, having quitted his church or monastery, exchanged the clerical tonsure for a crown. The Mercians, as you have heard, had already been the conquerors of Kent; and Cynewulf, the king of the Mercians, who had succeeded to Ecgfrith, the son of Offa, resolved to gain possession of the country, which he attacked with a powerful army. Eadbert Pren could not make any defence: the "Men of the Marsh" or Merscwara, supposed to be the inhabitants of the neighbourhood of Romney, betrayed him into the power of his enemies. Eadbert is accused of great tyranny; but he was treated with a degree of cruelty which no tyranny could justify. The Merscwara put out his eyes, and struck off his hands; and, thus blinded and maimed, the agonized captive was loaded with chains and fetters, and conducted into Mercia.

Cynewulf had erected a church or monastery at Winchecombe, and on the day when the fabric was consecrated, his heart inclined to mercy. Cynewulf manumitted the captive Eadbert before the altar, in the

---

* Kent contained Five Lathes, which were analogous to the Tithings in Yorkshire.

presence of the applauding multitude; but there his clemency terminated. He took the crown of Kent and placed it on his own head; and then he grasped the sceptre in his hand, and proclaimed himself to be king of the country, which was now subjected to the dominion of Mercia. Kent continued thus subjugated during several years, though the Mercians frequently appointed "under kings" or dependent sovereigns, who governed the land as vassals of the Mercian crown; the first sovereign of this description after the Mercian conquest, being Cuthred, the brother of Cynewulf, who received the country as an apanage.

Under the earlier Bretwaldas, the greater Anglo-Saxon powers had been pretty nearly balanced; but Northumbria, as I shall shortly have occasion to explain to you, was now in the last stage of weakness and disunion; and the kings of this country were entirely out of the field. A fierce rivalry prevailed between Wessex and Mercia; they divided all Britain south of the Humber. I say "all Britain," because all the British princes were subjected to one or other of them. It was clear that either would brook no rival; and, under Egbert, the fate of Mercia was speedily decided (A.D. 823). Having defeated Beornwulf, King of Mercia, in a great battle at "Ellandune," now called Wilton, he marched a very large body of troops into Kent, under the directions of his son, Ethelwulf, or "Noble Wolf," and other experienced warriors, the Alderman Wulfhard, and Alstane, bishop of Sherborn, who thus joined in commanding an army; a strange, but not unusual employment for a churchman in those turbulent times. As soon as the army of Wessex had occupied Kent, Baldred, the Mercian "Subregulus," or "under king," fled beyond the

Thames, and the inhabitants of the country unanimously
declared in favour of Egbert.   Surrey, Sussex, and
Essex followed the example of Kent.   They all considered that Egbert was their rightful king by descent
and blood, and that they had been wrongfully separated
from the dominion of his ancestors ; and I present this
fact to you prominently, because it is one of those which
show how zealously the old English or Anglo-Saxons
were attached to the families of their sovereigns.
Egbert, upon acquiring possession of Kent and the
adjoining countries, acted according to the policy which
I have before noticed.   He granted these dominions to
his son Ethelwulf as an apanage ; the latter held them
until his accession to his father's throne ; and, thereupon,
the apanage passed to Ethelwulf's son, Athelstane.   The
mode of descent, therefore, if the Danish invasions, of
which I shall shortly speak, had not unsettled the
kingdom, would have been nearly like that of the
principality of Wales, which is held by the heir-apparent
for the time being of the English crown.

These prosperous events were followed by another
acquisition of power.   The East Anglians, who after the
murder of Ethelbyrht had become the subjects of Mercia,
threw off this hateful supremacy ; but Beornwulf, who
had usurped the throne of Mercia, asserted his intention
of regaining the authority, however unjust, which his
predecessors had acquired (A.D. 821).   Thus harassed,
the king of the East Angles and his people placed themselves under the protection of Egbert, requesting his aid
and protection against the Mercian power ; in other
words, they became his vassals (A.D. 823) ; and it is
worthy of notice, that the chronicle expresses their submission in the terms employed in the official acts, by

which the subjects of the Carlovingian empire recognised the authority of their sovereign. Egbert most willingly accepted their homage, and promised to afford them that protection which their submission had earned, for in all such cases the obligation was reciprocal.

Beornwulf was a stout warrior. His name means " Bear-wolf," and I almost suspect that, as amongst the North American Indians, the appellations of the Anglo-Saxon chieftains were sometimes given to them in mature age, from the qualities which they possessed, or of which they wished to be thought the possessors. Beornwulf showed great pugnacity; and, collecting a powerful army, he invaded East Anglia (A.D. 825), denouncing vengeance against king and people; but they encountered him with equal obstinacy, and Beornwulf fell in the conflict. Ludica, who can be traced as an Alderman in Mercia, was raised to the throne; but he also was slain by the East Anglians. Upon the death of Ludica, the choice of the Mercian chieftains fell upon Wiglaf, Alderman of the Hwiccians, a collateral kinsman of Offa; but before he could collect his forces, Egbert advanced into Mercia, and expelled him from the kingdom. Wiglaf was now a fugitive: he wandered from place to place and concealed himself in the wastes of Croyland, where he sought to escape the vengeance of the victor. But about two or three years afterwards (A.D. 828), Egbert, moved by pity, restored the kingdom to him, to be held in tributary subjection.

By the conquest of Mercia, Egbert had become lord of all the states south of the Humber; and he now marched his forces against the Angles of Deira and Bernicia. Unable to resist the invader, the Northumbrians, and their king Eanred, proffered their homage to Egbert, and became his tributaries (A.D. 828-830). About the same time, Swithred, King of the East Saxons, was expelled by the conqueror. The Britons north of the Severn, in other words, occupying the territory of the modern Welsh, were utterly subdued; and Egbert became fully established in the state and honour of the eighth Bretwalda, or supreme Emperor of the Island of Britain.

Chapter V.

*The Danish Invasions—Facilitated by the Dissensions of the
Anglo-Saxon States — Regnor Lodbrok and his Sons —
Martyrdom of Edmund, King of the East Angles—Ethelwulf—His Marriage with Judith—West Saxons Rebel against
him—Cedes the best part of his Kingdom to his Son Ethelbald—Death of Ethelwulf—His four Sons become successively
Kings of Wessex—Ethelbald—Ethelbert—Ethered—Alfred.*

THE victories of Egbert were facilitated by causes which
ultimately brought disgrace and ruin upon the Anglo-
Saxon name. Although the Anglo-Saxons were quite
sensible, in theory, of the advantages resulting from
good order and regular policy, the first element of
government was wanting. Peace could never have been
ensured in a country where the different subordinate
chieftains retained the full right of declaring war against
one another; and, on the very day of Egbert's accession
(A.D. 800), a bloody battle was fought between the men
of Wilts and the men of Hwiccas, under the command
of their respective chieftains. Ethelmund, whom the
Chronicles call the *Alderman*, was the ruler of the latter
people; he also assumed the title of "Subregulus,"
whilst in the metrical account of the Abbey of Wilton,
he figures as "King of the March," though he was only
a vassal of the Mercian crown.

Our Milton, who, great as he was as a poet, had no
peculiar talent for historical enquiries, expresses his
opinion that such conflicts are as unworthy of notice
"as the fights between the kites and the crows." Burke,

the celebrated orator, who, like Milton, failed as an historian, has repeated the same comparison; and it has been borrowed by many other writers of great eminence. With submission, however, they are in the wrong. A simile which may eke out a verse, or embellish and relieve a speech, may, nevertheless, be a very invalid argument; these distinguished writers were entirely deluded by the picture presented to their fancy. And the popularity which the comparison has attained—for it is in every body's mouth—has tended, in no small degree, to encourage an erroneous mode of investigating the truths of history.

Whether the kites or the crows gain the battle, may certainly be of little consequence to us, as an abstract question; but if we are employed in investigating the natural history of these birds, then it becomes very important to know how, and when, and for what reasons, they carry on their hostilities. Their pugnacity is a fact which elucidates their habits, and which must not be neglected by the enquirer. For, assuming that kites and crows do wage war amongst each other, according to Milton's supposition, the inference to be drawn is, that the nature of the genera to which kites and crows belong, differs most essentially from the genus of rooks, who are quietly directed in their course, without ever engaging against an enemy.

He who wishes to understand history, must learn to estimate the importance of facts and details, especially those relating to remote or obscure periods, not by their apparent value, but in proportion to the insight which they afford into the general character of society. The skirmish to which I have alluded, was probably an ordinary occurrence, exciting no attention at the time;

but such petty warfare could not have taken place, if the Anglo-Saxon monarchs had possessed that degree of supremacy over their people, which we now consider as an essential attribute of royal power. This loose and imperfect government accustomed the people to strife and dissension ; and the Anglo-Saxon states were miserably divided by internal feuds.

The misfortunes sustained by the men of Kent had been greatly occasioned by their quarrels, during which the line of the Æscingas had become extinct. But the chief scene of strife was laid in Northumbria. As one faction or another prevailed, the kings, who were, in truth, only the puppets of these factions, were expelled or restored : hailed as monarchs, or slain as traitors and usurpers ; and the greater part were of dubious lineage. Amongst a rude people, who, whether justly or not, considered the royal authority as appertaining to a peculiar caste, this defect of ancestry alone was enough to prevent any efficient authority, by depriving the kings of that foundation of opinion, upon which all peaceable dominion is grounded.

Against such misrule and anarchy it was not difficult for Egbert to prevail ; but his authority was gained at the expense of the Anglo-Saxon people ; and much as his imperial dominion may have contributed to his personal aggrandizement, it added nothing to their strength and security. It has been said that Egbert consolidated the Anglo-Saxon power ; but this assertion is most incorrect. Each state and people continued as distinct as before : there was no common legislature, and no means of concentrating in the supreme government the strength and resources of the community. Rivalry is always as injurious to those who indulge in this misleading passion, as it is wrong in its origin.   All the Anglo-Saxon states professed one faith, spoke one language, and the depression of any one kingdom ought, in truth, to have been considered as the misfortune of the whole community.

The Romans and Anglo-Saxons had successively prevailed over the Britons, principally by reason of their dissensions, which had prevented them from withstanding their common enemies.   Alcuin, the friend of Charlemagne, in the epistles which he addressed to his English countrymen, exhorted them to bear in mind the example afforded them by the ancient annals of the island.   From his cloister, he bade them turn to the pages of Gildas, and employ the history of the past in its best use, as a lesson for the present time.   But no warning could prevail; and the conquerors, in their turn, were now about to become the victims of the same short-sighted passion and folly : they continued turning their spears against each other, unmindful of the foemen who were preparing to reduce them to the utmost misery.

The Scandinavian nations and their kindred tribes, who about this period were usually called Danes or Northmen, were never at peace.   Like the piratical states of Barbary, they depended wholly upon war and plunder; but after the settlement of Northumbria by the Angles, all communication between Britain and " old England" seems to have ceased.   During this period, it is probable that the Scandinavians and Jutes were much engaged in warfare with the Finns and other inhabitants of the north.   Such civilization as they had once possessed was greatly impaired, and a more stern and savage character was imparted to their idolatry.

In the same year when Offa acquired the supremacy of

Wessex (A.D. 787), three strange vessels made the shore of Dorsetshire, and landed their crews near one of the "king's towns." Badohard, the Reeve, or Mayor of the town, quite unsuspicious of any danger, rode to meet the strangers, probably thinking that they were traders, and with the intent of claiming the customs due upon their merchandize. If such was his object, he received payment from the Danish battle-axe : his attendants shared the same fate, and fell before the invaders.

From this era, the Danes became the incessant and inveterate foes of Britain and its inhabitants, visiting every part of the island with fire and sword. They are always before us ; we always see the horizon reddened with flame, we always hear the tramp of war. It is certain that they must have recollected their kindred with the Anglo-Saxons ; but this circumstance rather heightened than mitigated their ferocity. They considered the English, for this familiar name now began to be in use, as apostates and recreants from the warlike virtues of their ancestors. They viewed them as cowards who, contemning the banquet of Valhalla, had yielded up its joys for the song of the priest and the mummery of the quire.

Another cause of hostility is obscurely indicated : some of the Danish chieftains imagined that they possessed a right to the government of the Anglian states of Britain. The Danish kings were sons of Woden, like our Anglo-Saxon monarchs. *Wahrmund* and *Offa*, who appear in the genealogies of Mercia, as before-mentioned, were the ancestors of the Norwegian " sea kings." And the allusions in the Sagas to the conquests effected by the Danish heroes in Britain, at very early periods, can only be explained by supposing that they relate to the chieftains by whom our island was colonised. This opinion is corroborated by the very strong traditional belief which has prevailed concerning the pertinacity of the Danes in keeping up the remembrance of their rights. In the thirteenth century, the French imagined that part of the dowry of the unfortunate princess Inge-burgha (who was married to Philip Augustus, and was most shamefully treated by him) consisted of the pre-tensions which Denmark possessed to the dominion of England. The peasantry of Ireland firmly believe, that when a Danish nobleman bestows his daughter in marri-age, he always makes an ample Irish settlement upon her ; giving her, in part of her fortune, or sometimes as the whole of it, a fine estate in the county Clare, or county Wexford, to which his family have been legally entitled ever since they were dispossessed, in the tenth century. And, but a very few years ago, a party of surveyors employed in measuring Lord Reay's country, in the shire of Sutherland, were mistaken by the highlanders for a detachment of the Host of Lochlin, about to reclaim their old inheritance. These traditional opinions are not to be engrafted into history as facts ; but yet they are usually the recollections of facts, and not without their value in elucidating the transactions of remote periods, and in connecting and explaining the fragments of information which we possess.

During the last years of Egbert's reign, the Northmen or Danes had been continually gaining strength. Their attacks were principally directed towards the western districts, thickly peopled with discontented Britons. Gladly did the Britons or *Wilisc-men* of Devon join the invader (A.D. 832-833-835), by whose aid they hoped to be delivered from the empire of the sons of Cerdic, and

released from the thraldom of their Saxon lords.   Egbert
defeated the allies, both *Welsh* and Northmen; and soon
afterwards he died (A.D. 836); and the throne devolved
upon Ethelwulf, his son, King of Kent; who, upon
becoming King of Wessex, resigned this apanage to his
son, Athelstane.*

During a period of about fifteen years, Ethelwulf was
just able to keep the Danes in check, but without gaining any permanent advantage.   The heathens became
bolder and bolder: they sailed repeatedly up the Thames
(A.D. 837 to 851).   London was stormed and pillaged:
Rochester and Canterbury shared the same fate; and the
southern districts were attacked and ravaged.   The
Mercians were assailed with equal hostility; and the
need of co-operation against the common persecutors
became so manifest, that they and the West Saxons
agreed to unite for the purpose of repelling the enemy.
A great congress was held at Kingsbury, in Oxfordshire,
composed of the prelates and nobles of the two nations;
and as Ethelwulf could not attend in person, he
despatched his ambassador in his stead.   Oslac, the
nobleman thus honoured, was Ethelwulf's father-in-law,
and a man of great fame; and in this assembly the
Witan deliberated on the best mode of resisting the
enemy.   Soon afterwards, we find that Burhed, King of
Mercia, marched against the Danes, perhaps in conformity
to the resolutions of the council of Kingsbury, but with
ill success; for he was defeated by the enemy.   Ethelwulf was more fortunate.   The King of Wessex, and his
son Ethelbald, gave battle to the Northmen and entirely
routed them (A.D. 851).   Vast numbers of the heathen-
folk were slain; and other advantages were gained at

* This Athelstane must not be confounded with the celebrated King of Wessex.

Sandwich. Athelstane, King of Kent, and Elchere, the Alderman, defeated the Danes and took many of their vessels, and the state of affairs seemed to promise a temporary security.

Ethelwulf, about this time, had four surviving sons, his children by his wife Osburgha, the daughter of the noble Oslac. Ethelbald, now the eldest, and who had assisted his father in defeating the Danes,—Ethelbert—Ethered—and Alfred. The latter was the best-beloved child of Ethelwulf; and for the purpose of securing the succession to him, he was sent to Rome, where Pope Leo anointed him with holy oil, and consecrated him as a king (A.D. 853-855). Ethelwulf also proceeded to Rome; and whilst he was on the continent he espoused Judith, the daughter of Charles the Bald, King of the Franks. The royal diadem was placed upon her head by Hincmar, Bishop of Rheims; and she was inaugurated and crowned as queen, with great solemnity.

Ethelwulf's journey was ill-timed. It is said that he was dull and stupid, and wanting in ability to govern and defend his people: and that, if he ever shewed wisdom, it was when acting under the advice of Alstane, Bishop of Sherborne, who had assisted him in making the conquest of Kent, and of Swithin, Bishop of Winchester, a great statesman in those days, but who is now only recollected as the patron of rainy weather. During Ethelwulf's absence, the discontent which prevailed against him assumed the shape of an organized revolt. The conspirators, headed by Ethelbald, the eldest son of Ethelwulf, who was already king of some apanage or dependant state, assembled in the forest of Selwood, and resolved to prevent Ethelwulf from ever returning to the government of Wessex. Bishop Alstane, Ealhere, Duke of Somerset, and other powerful noblemen, had joined in the plot. Many, however, of the nobles of Wessex sided with the old king; and a most unnatural civil war between the father and son appeared to be impending.

Ethelwulf had alarmed the jealousy of Ethelbald by the coronation of Alfred, who was thus obviously designated as his father's successor. Equally, or perhaps more offensive to the West Saxons, was the recognition of Judith as Queen. You will recollect, that, in consequence of the crimes of the wicked Eadburgha, the dignity of Queen had been altogether abolished; and the coronation of Judith, with great pomp and solemnity, was regarded as a violation of the constitution. It must also be observed, that Ethelwulf, in order to make way for Judith, had put away Osburgha, the mother of his children. This fact is not mentioned in express terms in our ancient historians; but Osburgha is noticed in a manner which cannot be explained by any other hypothesis; and such conduct must have greatly added to the discontent which prevailed.

Upon the arrival of Ethelwulf in England, his party gained much strength, and he might, perhaps, have expelled Ethelbald. But the general characteristic of the Anglo-Saxon kings was mildness towards their own people. Ethelwulf shrank from the responsibility of occasioning internal dissensions. He was gentle towards his disobedient child; he also appears to have been much attached to his Frankish queen; and a compromise was effected. Ethelwulf took to himself the government of the eastern states appertaining to Wessex; namely, the ancient kingdom of Kent, together with Sussex, Surrey, and perhaps Essex: whilst the kingdom of Wessex-proper, which of right belonged to the head of the family, became

Winchester.

the portion of Ethelbald, though with a nominal subjection to his father.

Ethelwulf survived these events about four years. Upon his death, Ethelbald immediately married his own step-mother, Judith (A.D. 857-860). This incestuous marriage caused great scandal; but nothing further is recorded concerning him.

He was succeeded by his brother, Ethelbert, who had already been in possession of the kingdom of Kent, with its dependencies (A.D. 860). Immediately upon his accession, the invasions of the Danes were renewed. They had been busily employed in Gaul. Paris was burnt, together with many of the principal cities of that country; and so extensive were their operations, that whilst some of their squadrons ascended the Scheld, others passed through the Straits of Gibraltar; and sailing up the Mediterranean, had visited the southern shores with their fury. And now their unsatiated thirst of rapine was again directed against unhappy Britain. Winchester, the ancient capital of Wessex, shared the fate of Paris. The city was burnt to the ground (A.D. 860). As the Danes were returning to their vessels, laden with spoil, they were attacked by the men of Hampshire and Berkshire, under the command of their respective Aldermen, Athelwulf and Osric, and some of the invading detachments were dispersed. The Saxons called this a victory; but such victories produced no more permanent effect than the fanning of your hand through a cloud of mosquitoes; they give way, and instantly they come together again, as numerous and as teasing as before.

Though the Danes had not yet acquired any dominion in Britain, they had occupied Thanet, where they fixed

their winter-quarters (A.D. 864-865); and this isle became
a rallying point for their forces.   The same spot on
which the Jutes first established themselves against the
Britons, was fated to become equally detrimental to their
descendants.   The men of Kent concluded, or, to speak
more accurately, bought a treaty of peace.   They paid a
large sum to the pagans as the price of their forbearance.
The Danes took the gold, but they calculated that they
could earn more by war than by peace.   They secretly
and treacherously quitted their position, and fearfully
ravaged the country, whose inhabitants relied upon the
compact which they had concluded.

The death of Ethelbert and the accession of Ethered,
at this calamitous period (A.D. 866), are events which
appear scarcely discernible amidst the distress and tur-
moil of the war.

Halfdane, Hingwar, and Hubba, the sons of Regner
Lodbrok, now descended on the coast of East Anglia,
having proceeded, as the chroniclers believed, from the
Danube ; that is to say, from their own northern country,
which the ignorance of the monks confounded with the
ancient Scythia.

According to the romantic history of the Scandinavians, this invasion was the result of filial piety.   Ella,
King of Northumbria, had caused Regner Lodbrok to be
cast into a pit full of vipers, by which he was " stung to
death;" and it is said that this expedition was undertaken by the sons of Regner, to avenge the fate of their
father.   No warrior of the north is more celebrated than
this Regner Lodbrok, the son of Sigurd.   Volumes have
been filled with his adventures, and with disquisitions
thereupon.   I, however, have not space to enlarge upon
them, nor indeed am I entirely persuaded of their

authenticity. His surname, "*Lodbrok*," was derived
from the ingenious device which he employed for his
protection when encountering a dragon, by whose death
he was to win the hand of the beauteous Thora. It is
hardly necessary to observe,—the fact being familiarly
known to the merest tyro in romance—that all dragons
spit fire and poison; and, in order to resist the venom
of the beast, Regner, with as much ingenuity as "More
of More Hall," clad himself in garments of shaggy
leather, of which that portion, which, if he had been a
highlander, he would *not* have worn, was so remarkable
in its appearance, that the name of *Lodbrok** adhered to
him during the remainder of his life. It would have
been well if the raiment itself had covered him in the
cave of vipers; but it did not; and whilst the reptiles
were "stinging" him, he composed his celebrated death-
song, called "*Krakamal*," the foundation of his history;
and this ode he sung whilst he was expiring.

Of such materials is the life of Regner composed; and
the Danish historians, in order to reduce his adventures
into due chronology, are obliged to have recourse to
their usual theory of multiplication. *Torfœus* divides
Regner Lodbrok into *two*. This will not suffice for
Suhm: he supposes there were *three* successive Regners,
and *two* successive Ellas, by whom the three Lodbroks
were killed. Some of our chronicles attribute the expedition to the revenge of a Northumbrian noble, one
Bruern Brocard, irritated to madness, like another Count
Julian, by the affront which he had received from the
lust of Osbert, the King of Northumbria. And, according to a third narrative, Regner Lodbrok having been
cast ashore in East Anglia, was slain by Beorn, the

* *Villosa femoralia*, as expounded by Saxo. Grammaticus.

huntsman of the king. But I must dismiss these tales, which I have quoted merely as specimens of the fables intermixed with our authentic history.

As soon as the Danes landed, the pirates were converted into an army of cavalry. They "horsed" themselves forthwith; and their wonderful activity and bodily energy rendered them as formidable by land as by sea. Upon the ample folds of the standard which floated at the head of their host, was depicted the Raven, the bird of Odin. The magic banner had been woven and worked by the daughters of Regner Lodbrok, in one noontide; and the Danes believed that their national ensign was endued with prophetic powers. If victory was to follow, the raven stood erect and soaring before the warriors; but if a defeat was impending, the raven hung his head and drooped his wings.

Had the Northumbrians and the Mercians cordially concurred, at this crisis, with the West Saxons, their united forces would have sufficed to repel the invaders. But even the imminent danger to which they were exposed, failed to produce any degree of union.

The Northumbrians were most unhappily employed in contending amongst themselves; the kingdom being divided between Osbert, who is called the legitimate king, and Ella, the usurper. Osbert and Ella now plainly saw that their situation was desperate; they suspended their rivalry, and marched against the heathen, who had occupied the city of York; and the Northumbrians became the assailants of their enemies. The conflict was stubborn; but the Danes gained the victory (A.D. 867). Osbert and Ella were slain, and the Northmen became the masters of the country which they occupied.

Thus were the Northumbrians punished. Mercia now felt the scourge. The heathens crossed the frontier, and took the town of Nottingham. King Burhred and the Mercians implored the aid of Ethered and Alfred, who readily advanced to their assistance, but with little effect, for the Danes retained possession of the town. Henceforth, Nottingham was reckoned among those which were especially denominated the " Danish Burghs." The others were " *Northweorthig*," Leicester, Lincoln, Stamford, York, and Chester, forming a connected chain of strong positions, which equally commanded the English population of Mercia and of Northumbria. In these burghs there appears to have settled a large and effective population composed of the higher classes of the Danish warriors ; and the name of " *Northweorthig* " was altered by them to the appellation of *Deorby*, or Derby, which the town or borough now bears.

Other similar changes of name took place. Streoneshalch, the monastery of St. Hilda, acquired the name of Whitby : and it is probable that the greater part of the names of places in Yorkshire, Lincoln, Nottingham, and other shires of the *Danelagh*, which now terminate in the syllable " *By*," were fixed on them by the Danes, in whose language *By* signifies a place of abode. At a subsequent period, the Danish burghs were recovered by the Anglo-Saxons, but the Danish Thanes were not displaced : and as late as the reign of Ethelred, we can trace their existence as a privileged community, distinct from the kingdom in which they were included. Lincolnshire, or Lindesey, as it was then called, was attacked by the enemy, who advanced simultaneously from Mercia and Northumbria (A.D. 868-870). Here, as the traditions of the country inform us, they were resisted with more

conduct and valour than in other parts of England. Three
Danish kings were slain in one battle ; and the place
where they were buried by their followers, acquired the
name of *Trekingham*, or Thrikingham,* which it still
retains. But fresh reinforcements of the invaders more
than supplied the loss. Five kings, Godrun, Bacseg,
Halfdane, Oskettel, and Hamond, and five *Jarls,* or earls,
Frena, Hingvar, and Hubba, and the two Sidrocs, the
father and the son, poured their barbarian hordes into
the country ; and a victory, which they gained as much
by artifice as by numbers, placed the land wholly in their
power. Great numbers of the inhabitants were slain ;
and all the monasteries, Croyland, Medhamstede (afterwards Peterborough), Thorney, Ramsey, and Ely, were
levelled with the ground.

The Danes had acquired considerable skill in the art of
war ; and if you trace their operations on the map, you
will find, that, however desultory their attacks may have
been, they had evidently formed a settled plan of operations. They sought to post their forces across the island,
and also to occupy the best stations on the sea-coast ;
and hence they now directed their hostility against East
Anglia.

At this period, the East Angles were governed by
Edmund, a king of singular virtue and piety, and who
defended his people against their enemies with great
valour. During their invasion of this kingdom (A.D.
870), the Danes displayed even more than usual ferocity.
Edmund was defeated and made captive. It is said,
that this event took place at Hoxne, in Suffolk. Being
hotly pursued by his foes, he fled to this town, and
attempted to conceal himself by crouching beneath a

* In Aveland Hundred, Kesteven Division.

bridge, now called *Goldbridge*. The glittering of his *golden* spurs discovered him to a newly-married couple, who were returning home by moonlight, and they betrayed him to the Danes. Edmund, as he was dragged from his hiding-place, pronounced a malediction upon all who should afterwards pass this bridge on their way to be married ; and so much regard is paid to this tradition by the good folks of Hoxne, that now (or at least till within the last twenty years) no bride and bridegroom would venture along the forbidden path. It is not because I wish you to place any great reliance upon the minute details of such traditions, that I mention them ; but they enable you to connect the general outline of history with the geography of England, and hence they may be always recollected with utility.

A particular account of Edmund's death was given by his sword-bearer, who, having attained a very advanced age, was wont to repeat the sad story at the court of Athelstane. Edmund was fettered and manacled, and treated with every species of cruelty and indignity. The heathen Danes bound their captive to a tree, beat and scourged him, and shot their arrows at him as a mark— taunting him, and urging him to deny his faith ; but he continued steadfast amidst his sufferings, until Hingvar, wearied by his constancy, commanded that he should be beheaded. His corpse, privately buried by his followers, was, in process of time, removed to a town originally called Badrichesworth, but now St. Edmund's Bury—a monastery having been founded there to his honour by King Canute. Of this building, once the most sumptuous in England, only a few fragments remain ; but the name of " Edmund," transmitted from generation to generation in the families of Norfolk and Suffolk, attests the respect anciently rendered in East Anglia to the martyred sovereign.

We must now return to the Danes. Elated by the victories which I have briefly narrated, they attacked the kingdom of Wessex (A.D. 871), fighting their way as they advanced, and sustaining many changes of fortune. A bloody battle was fought at Ashdown:* King Bacseg was slain, together with many other Danish leaders—Sidroc, and Osbern, and Frena, and Harold,—whose names had become the terror of the English nation. A single thorn-bush, which grew in the midst of the field, marked the spot where the fight had raged most furiously; and it was surrounded by heaps of corpses when the English became the masters of the "field of slaughter." No permanent advantage, however, was gained by this dear-bought victory. Less fortunate conflicts ensued, and the scale was turned against the English, by the continued reinforcements which filled the ranks of the pagan armies. In one of these battles, Ethered received a wound, which, though not immediately fatal, was the cause of his death; the effects of the injury being probably aggravated by the disquiet and mental uneasiness which he sustained.

* Perhaps *Aston*, near Reading. According to Dr. Kennet, *Ashenden* in Bucks.

Chapter VI.

Accession of Alfred—Great Successes of the Danes—Their Conquest of Mercia and Northumbria—Rollo the " Ganger" and the Danes, or Northmen, settle in Neustria or Normandy—Danes conquer the greater part of Wessex—Alfred compelled to secrete himself in Athelney—Alfred rallies his Forces—Recovers his Kingdom—Treaty between Alfred and Guthred—Danish Kingdoms of East Anglia and Northumbria—Hasting invades England—is defeated—Death of Alfred.

ALFRED, during the life of his brothers, was possessed of a subordinate royal authority. Some writers think that he was acknowledged as king by the Britons of Wales; but this point is not clear. According to the expression employed by Asser, his contemporary biographer, he was invested with a "secondary" power, but no further contemporary exposition is obtained.

Alfred was already so much distinguished, both by his good sense and valour, that he might, had he chosen to do so, have obtained the title of King of Wessex, to the prejudice of Ethered; but he did not covet the dignity; and when, upon the decease of his brother, the voice of the nobles and people designated him as Ethered's successor, he unwillingly accepted the laborious honour.

In those days, royalty, never an easy or enviable station, was accompanied by great danger and toil. A king was compelled to sleep on the hard ground, to encounter every privation and difficulty, and to expose his life for the defence of his crown and people; and, had Alfred been a sluggard, it might have been supposed

that love of ease rendered him unwilling to undertake
an office of so much peril.   But his conduct, both before
and after his accession, disproves this supposition ; and
we may, therefore, fully believe that he was actuated by
the motive assigned for his reluctance, and transmitted
to us by Asser, his biographer and friend.   He knew
that he could not be furthered in his attempts to govern
well, except by the continual aid of providence ; and he
feared that such help might not be granted unto him.
With this full sense and conviction of his own utter
weakness and inability to help himself, did Alfred begin
his reign, during which he was enabled to acquire a
better reputation than any other monarch of Western
Christendom.

England sustained extreme misery and devastation at
the period of Alfred's accession to the throne (A.D. 871-
872).   Nine pitched battles were fought between the
English and the Danes in the course of one year.   The
minor conflicts and skirmishes were innumerable.   These
wars were conducted by the most savage ferocity ;
neither old nor young were spared by the Danes.   They
were enemies who tore the screaming babes from the
mother's arms, and tossed them on the point of the spear.
If they took any prisoners, they never spared the lives
of their captives, excepting for the purpose of extorting
money from their relatives by way of ransom ; and they
often put their victims to death with the most cruel
tortures.   Against such foes did Alfred contend.   The
Mercians had utterly lost all courage, and made what
was called a peace (A.D. 873-874).   This was observed
by the Danes just as long as it was convenient to them.
They established their head-quarters in Lincolnshire,
until they had a good opportunity of attacking King

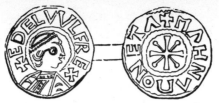

Silver Penny of Ethelwulf.

Anglo-Saxon Cup found at Halton (Lancashire).

Silver Coin of Egbert.

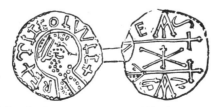

Silver Penny of Ceolvolf, King of Mercia.

St. Cuthbert. (From Durham Cathedral.)

Burhred, whom they defeated without difficulty. He escaped beyond the sea to Rome, where he ended his weary days, and was buried in the "school" or college of the English nation.

Mercia was now entirely in the power of the Danes; but, according to their cunning policy, they did not immediately assume the government of the country. There was one Ceolwulf, a Thane, or "minister" of King Burhred, whom they found to be a convenient tool: and they installed him as king; but upon condition that he should be ready to give up his kingdom whenever he should be required by his masters. Coelwulf, invested with this precarious dominion, acted like a Turkish Pasha: he only endeavoured to make the most of his government. Mercia had been completely ravaged; the greater part of the nobility had fled, or had fallen in battle; few but the peasantry or churls were left. These were plundered most pitilessly by Ceolwulf, who continued to commit every act of oppression, until his Danish masters needed him no longer. As soon as it was convenient for them to do so, they deprived him of his disgraceful authority (A.D. 877).

Northumbria, as you will recollect, had been already overrun; but the Danes had not yet entirely reduced the country. After the death of Osbert and Ella (A.D. 867), they appointed one Egbert, a Northumbrian, to govern, or rather to oppress, Bernicia, as a vassal king, under their supremacy. In one of the revolutions which desolated that country, he was expelled (A.D. 875-876), and Ricsig, a Dane, was appointed in his stead; but the inroads of the enemy were renewed. The pagans, under Halfdane, destroyed all the churches and monasteries. The ruin of the cathedral of Lindisfairne, in particular, was lamented as the greatest misfortune of the age. Cuthbert, one of the prelates of this see, canonized by the grateful veneration of the English, was considered as the patron saint of the north; and the island of Lindisfairne was viewed as holy land. A considerable tract between the Tyne and Wear, part of the ancient marchland between the two Northumbrian kingdoms,* had been granted to the bishops, and brought into cultivation by their tenants. This territory was desolated by the Danes, who extended their devastations over every part of Northumbria: nor did they spare the adjoining districts: Picts, Scots, and Cumbrians—all were equally ravaged by them. Halfdane completed his conquest by dividing great part of the Northumbrian territory amongst his followers, who, settling amongst the Angles, were at last so mixed with them, as to form almost one people.

During these transactions, a continual predatory warfare was carried on in every part of Britain by the Danish or northern chieftains. They infested the coast of France with equal pertinacity. Sometimes they were defeated; but after every reverse they seemed more powerful than ever. " If thirty thousand are slain in one day "—said

---

* As before noticed, Carlisle, with a territory of twelve miles round about it, had been granted to the bishopric by Egfrith of Northumbria (A.D. 685). The body of St. Cuthbert was saved when the church of Lindisfairne was destroyed, and after many migrations it was deposited in the cathedral of Durham, to which city the see of Lindisfairne was transferred (A.D. 990); the present Bishops of Durham being the successors of the Bishops of Lindisfairne. The corpse of St. Cuthbert was deposited in a magnificent shrine, which was destroyed at the time of the Reformation. According to the traditions of the catholics of the north, the relics were saved, and secretly interred in the cathedral; and, as they assert, from that time to the present day, there have always been three Benedictine monks residing at Durham, to whom the trust is confided. When one dies, the two survivors elect a successor, so as to ensure a transmission of the secret, until the time when the Catholic worship shall be restored. In 1827, a skeleton, supposed to be that of St. Cuthbert, was disinterred by the Rev. James Raine. The body had been deposited with some most curious relics of the Anglo-Saxon age.

the English—"there will be double that number in the
field on the morrow."

The Danes were remarkable for the celerity of their
movements, both by sea and land. As soon as they
disembarked from their ships, the pirates become a force
of cavalry, and dashed through England. This activity
magnified their apparent numbers ; yet they were really
very numerous, and commanded by the most valiant and
experienced of the sons of Odin.

Amongst these chieftains was one Hrolf, or Rollo,
whom his own countrymen called the " *Gange*," or the
"Walker" (before A.D. 786). It is supposed that he was
marvellously tall and bulky, and some Danish historians
assert that he was always compelled to walk or go on
foot, as no horse could bear his weight; and that he
hence derived his name. "No,"—say other grave
Danish historians ;—"·Rollo did ride, but when he was
on horseback, his long legs almost touched the ground,
and thus he seemed to be walking." Since this diversity
of opinion exists among the learned, I may have an
hypothesis of my own : and I will conjecture that he
acquired the name of the " *Ganger*," from his incessant
movements against his enemies. Rollo, after an expedition against the Hebrides, landed in England. Defeated,
or at least checked, in an obstinate conflict, he drew off
to France, where a brighter fortune awaited him. After
a long series of events, Rollo succeeded in gaining
possession of the province of Neustria (A.D. 912), which
the King of the French, Charles the Simple, was compelled to yield to the Danish pirate. This cession, however, was made upon condition that he should consider
himself as the vassal of Charles, and that the King of the
French should be accepted as the superior of the Duke of

the Northmen. Rollo had little reluctance to enter into this stipulation ; and the scene which took place, when he was invested with the territory, will show what kind of subjects the Northmen were likely to prove. It was the custom in Gaul, that the vassal who received a donation should kiss the king's foot; which, after all, being the accustomed form, was no more humiliating than the act of kissing the king's hand. Rollo refused—he said he would bow to no one; but at last he consented to perform the ceremony by deputy, and he beckoned to one of his soldiers to come forward accordingly. The gruff and surly Dane obeyed; but seizing hold of the king's foot, he raised it to his lips with so much rudeness and violence, that Charles the Simple was thrown upon his back, amidst the shouts and laughter of the surrounding multitude. Rollo, the " Ganger," who took the name of *Robert*, thus became the first Duke of Normandy. Berengarius and Alan, the chiefs of the Britons of Armorica, submitted, as his vassals, to his power; and the English, in after times, had reason enough to rue the day on which Rollo abandoned Britain for the opposite shore.

Whilst one great body of the Danes found employment in reducing the kingdom of Mercia, others continued their operations against Alfred and the West Saxons (A.D. 877). An army of these barbarians marched against Exeter; whilst their navy, stationed at the mouth of the Thames, sailed westward, for the purpose of joining the land forces. Exeter seems at that time to have been a free city, almost independent of the Kings of Wessex : and the Britons, as you may recollect, were rebelling against the English government; so that the Danes wisely attempted to assail Alfred in the most vulnerable portion of his dominions. Alfred, who was fully sensible of the importance attached to naval warfare, had ordered "long ships," or vessels calculated for warfare, to be built in all the ports, wherewith he intended to intercept the pirates; but he was unexpectedly assisted by the elements : a great storm arose, and many of the Danish ships were lost. Alfred's army was sufficiently numerous to allow him to invest the Danes in Exeter, but he could not take the city ; and a peace, or truce, was negotiated between the besieged and the besiegers.

The Danes took oaths, and gave hostages, for the due observance of the peace. In the preceding year they had broken a similar engagement contracted in the most solemn manner—by swearing on the "holy ring or bracelet," consecrated to Odin. But they were not believers, even in their own misbelief : they had violated their promise ; and the truce into which they had now entered, was infringed by them with equal readiness. The faithlessness of these barbarians was only to be equalled by their ferocity ; and such as they were, would the Anglo-Saxons have become, had it not been for the introduction of Christianity.

In the depth of the winter, a season in which military operations can seldom be pursued, the Danes made a sudden irruption into Wilts, and the adjoining shires (A.D. 878). So fearful was their incursion, that a great portion of the inhabitants fled to the Isle of Wight : others submitted. Alfred, almost wholly deprived of his authority, was driven with a small but trusty band of followers,—and his old mother, Osburgha, also accompanied him,—into "Athelney," a secluded spot, at the confluence of the Thone and the Parrett, sur-

rounded by marshes and moors, which served at once
for his concealment and his defence; and great were the
hardships and privations which Alfred here sustained.
He now lived like an outlaw. His daily sustenance
depended upon chance and accident. Sometimes the
waters furnished him with food : sometimes he hunted
the wild-deer; and sometimes he was compelled to
forage in the country occupied by the Danes, and to seize
by force the stores of the enemy. Yet these misfortunes
neither damped his courage, nor subdued his energy.

Amongst other adventures, it chanced that he was
sheltered in the cabin of a neatherd. Here an adventure
happened to him which has been often told. Crouching
before the fire, he was busily employed in fitting his bow
and arrows : round the hearth were the loaves which the
wife of the neatherd had prepared. Alfred had been
commanded by her to take care of the batch; and intent
as he was upon his other task, he did not perceive that
the bread was caught by the fire. The good-wife, who
had quicker eyes, ran to the hearth and turned the
loaves; and she rated Alfred soundly for his careless-
ness. "Why, man,"—she cried out at the top of her
shrill voice—" with such idleness and neglect, how can
ye come to good in the world, be ye who you may?"—
And she continued her vituperations, telling him that
he, who was ready enow to devour the loaves when
baked, was surely bound to be more attentive during
the baking. To these reproofs, Alfred listened with
great patience, turning the loaves as he was bid by the
shrew, and never replying to her upbraidings. Our
historians must have considered this obedience as a great
trial, for it holds a prominent station in all their
histories. We know that Alfred was wont, when

happier times arrived, to recount his adventures to his listening friends; and this anecdote may have been among those which originally rested upon his own testimony.

One very curious fact remains to be added. The king wore an ornament, probably fastened to a necklace, made of gold and enamel, which being lost by him at Athelney, was found there, entire and undefaced, in the seventeenth century. It is now preserved at Oxford;* and the inscription which surrounds it, "*Alfred het meh gewircan*,"—"*Alfred caused me to be (worked) made*,"— affords the most authentic testimony of its origin.

Whilst Alfred was thus concealed, the men of Wessex gained a signal victory (A.D. 878). Biorn-Ironside and Hubba, who attempted to land in Devonshire, were killed, together with many of their followers. Hubba was buried under a cairn,† which, in after ages, retained his name. The Danes lamented their chieftain with loud outcries; but it was not their custom to grieve long over their dead; and ten times the number of the slain would scarcely have occasioned any perceptible diminution of their forces. Their magical banner, the Raven, had, however, become the prize of the enemy; and this loss, added to the death of their leaders, served to dispirit them, and to impress them with feelings of inferiority, hitherto unknown. The news of the battle reached Alfred in his seclusion in Athelney, and he determined upon bolder operations. Disguising himself as a minstrel or *Glee-man*, he stole into the camp of the Danes, and was gladly received by the rude chieftains,

---

* In the Ashmolean Museum. It is very accurately engraved in Mr. Gorham's entertaining History of St. Neot's.

† *Hubbelow,* or *Hubblestanes.*

as one who increased their mirth and jollity. So skil-
fully did Alfred act his part, that whilst he entirely
escaped suspicion or detection, there was no object
which he did not observe, both with eyes and ears. He
thus abode amongst the Danes for several days, till he
had satisfied his mind upon every matter which he
wished to investigate, and he then returned to his
hiding-place.

About Easter, Alfred and his followers had completed
a "work" or entrenchment, at Athelney, which he destined, and successfully, as the key of his position against
the enemy. Seven weeks afterwards, having been joined
by the men of Somerset, he sallied forth and took his
position at "Egbert's stone," on the verge of the forest
of Selwood; which by the *Welsh*, or British inhabitants
of Somerset, who perhaps constituted the majority of the
population, was called by the name of "*the great forest*,"
or "*Coit-mawr*." Here he unfurled his standard. All
the inhabitants of the adjoining districts of Somerset,
Dorset, and Hampshire, mustered beneath the banner of
Alfred with the utmost zeal. They rejoiced to see him
again amidst them; and whatever causes of discontent
had existed, these were now wholly forgotten.

With the forces thus raised, and at the head of an
army of warriors who, for the first time, could venture
to hope that their country might be delivered from the
enemy, Alfred prepared for the struggle. Two days
were employed in making ready for battle. On the
third, the king assembled his army; and, taking advantage of a commanding height, he encamped there. The
following morning, he advanced to a spot called Ethan-
dune,* in front of the enemy. Alfred then addressed

* Perhaps Eddindon, near Westbury (Wilts).

his troops : his speech was short and energetic, exhorting them to avail themselves of this, perhaps the last, opportunity of rescuing themselves from shameful slavery. The battle began by a flight of arrows. The English and British lances were next hurled against the Northmen ; and when the missiles were expended, the combatants engaged hand to hand. After a murderous conflict, the English were left masters of the field ; whilst the scattered remnants of the Danish army, under Guthrun, were compelled to take refuge in their entrenchments. Here they were blockaded by Alfred during fourteen days. No succour could be afforded to them by their countrymen ; and at last, being well nigh hunger-starved, they were compelled to accept the terms which Alfred imposed.

Alfred, though victorious, could not expel the Danes from the island of Britain : he was compelled to cede an extensive territory to these invaders, and to Guthrun their king—namely, from the mouth of the Lea to its source, thence to Bedford, and thence along the Ouse to Watling Street, or the ancient Roman road ;—and this territory, together with Northumbria, became from henceforth known by the name of the *Danelagh*, or " Dane-law."*

In East Anglia, and in the portions of Essex and Mercia thus ceded, the Danes settled and established themselves : not as enemies, but as vassals to Alfred's crown. Guthrun became a convert to Christianity— Alfred was his godfather ;—and the Danes followed the example of their king. They appear to have been wearied out by their own barbarism. A compact, or treaty, was concluded between Guthrun and Alfred (A.D.

* See Map III.

878-880), for the confirmation of peace and friendship between the two nations ; and such laws were established, by mutual consent, as were best calculated to ensure a reasonable conformity to the Anglo-Saxon policy, though many of their old customs were still retained by the Danes.

It may be thought that Alfred would have acted more wisely by insisting that the Danes should entirely quit Britain.   But, had he done so, how would he have prevented their return in the following year ?—they had the command of the sea.   The country had been so much depopulated by the wars, that the settlement of the Danes did not straiten the East Anglians ; and Guthrun, as long as he lived, appears to have continued in peace and friendship with his godfather, rendering to him that subjection which was due from a vassal to his lord.

After the death of Halfdane, the "host" of Danes who had conquered Northumbria continued without a leader. The Northmen were much at variance amongst themselves.   Several years before, the sons of Regner Lodbrok had seized upon Guthred, the son of Hardacnute, the king of Lethra, in Sweden (A.D. 803) : they sold him as a slave or thrall ; and, at the period concerning which I am now writing, Hardacnute's son was in servitude, the property of an old widow in Northumberland.   Guthred's lineage, however, was known : he was marked as one of royal race, and he was raised to the supreme authority in a very singular manner.   Eadred, Bishop of Lindisfairne, acting, as it is said, under the direction of St. Cuthbert, who had appeared to him in a dream, proceeded to the host of the Danes, and persuaded them, as well as the English, to accept Guthred as their sovereign. He was conducted to "Oswin's Dune," or the hill of

Oswin, and invested with the golden bracelets, the ensigns of royal dignity, and solemnly inaugurated as King of the Northumbrians, though in vassalage to Alfred as his superior. Guthred was deeply indebted to Bishop Eadred; and following the hint given by a second vision of St. Cuthbert, he paid his debt of gratitude by granting and confirming to the bishop, not only the lands between Tyne and Wear, the ancient endowment of Lindisfairne, but the royal dominion over all the land between Tyne and Tees. Alfred assented to this donation: perhaps he directed it should be made; and he probably saw the advantage which would result from the grant. Covered for the greater part with wood and forests, the country in itself was of little value. In the possession of the Church, the soil would be improved, and brought into cultivation; and the respect rendered to St. Cuthbert might perhaps contribute to protect his *Franchise* from hostile invasion. From this ancient donation arose the *Palatinate* rights of the prelates of Durham, which the modern bishops still, in part, retain. All the ultimate property, or dominion of the land in the county palatine, is vested in the bishop, and to him it reverts if the freeholder dies without an heir, or incurs a legal forfeiture. The gift made by the royal donor was so expressed as to convey a complete jurisdiction, and the bishop became a kind of prince within his franchise. He exercised the power of life and death. Like a king, he could **pardon** and condemn; and even now, the Bishop of Durham may, if he chooses, sit on the bench in his scarlet robes when the judges try a criminal within his palatinate.

Guthred, like Guthrun, continued true and faithful to Alfred; and the English began to enjoy a respite from their enemies. With the Britons, Alfred never was engaged in war: they seemed, indeed, to consider his government as their best protection, and they submitted completely to his supremacy. In Mercia, where the old royal line had been extinguished, the people whom he had delivered were too happy to hail him as their lord. But, according to the constitution of the Anglo-Saxon states, it was desirable that they should have a ruler of their own; and this authority Alfred bestowed upon his son-in-law, Ethelred (about A.D. 883), who, under the title of Alderman, governed the country with royal power. In the course of seven years after his restoration, Alfred was acknowledged as the paramount monarch of Britain south of the Humber; for, though the Danes were not always obedient, still the theory of their government imported that they were his vassals. Wessex, with its dependencies, the most opulent and favoured portion of the island, was entirely, in fact as well as in name, under Alfred's royal authority. Mercia was virtually under his dominion; and wherever his power extended, he applied himself, with all his heart and soul, to promote the welfare of the community.

England was like a country which had been visited with a destructive inundation. The flood had subsided, but the face of the land was covered with desolation and ruin. Alfred's labours will be detailed hereafter: successful as they were, he was compelled to prosecute them during a period of hostility, scarcely less obstinate and harassing than that series of attacks which had nearly destroyed the independence of his kingdoms.

The Scandinavian pirates had acquired so much fierceness and activity, that they seemed to have planned the subjugation of the whole of Europe. Whether they plundered the northern or the southern shores of the

Channel, their movements constituted but part of one
great scheme. It was Scandinavian heathendom, against
all Christendom. Hence, if they were defeated, it was
considered, and truly, that the advantage was for all the
civilized nations of Europe; whilst every success which
they gained was felt as a common disaster. And upon
this ground the Scots claimed and earned the gratitude
and friendship of Charlemagne (A.D. 848), for a victory
which they obtained over the Northmen. The balance
of success, on the whole, was in favour of the heathens:
and they were often really victors when they appeared
to be vanquished; for even if dispersed, after plundering a city, they were able to carry off as much booty
as repaid them for the loss of life, of which they were
reckless.

The Chronicles detail a series of attacks sustained by
Alfred, after the recovery of his authority, which could
only be made intelligible by relating them as they happened, and in chronological order. Here it is sufficient
to state, that the Danes continued hovering about the
coasts; shifting their quarters from Fulham to Ghent,
from the Thames to the Maine, as best answered their
purpose. Alfred, on his part, never relaxed his vigilance; and when the armies of the Danes were blockading
Paris (A.D. 886), he availed himself of that opportunity
to fortify the city of London, which had been repeatedly
plundered and insulted by the barbarians.

The siege of Paris lasted during two entire years.
It was followed by extensive warfare in the country now
called Flanders, then a dependence upon the crown of
the Frankish Sovereigns. A great famine ensued (A.D.
893). England still offering many tempting resources,
the Danes determined to return to our island; and in

the course of a very few days, the Kentish men saw a fleet of two hundred and fifty vessels, all filled with warriors, stationed off the mouth of the Rother * and the adjoining shore, whilst another fleet of eighty vessels entered the Thames.

This squadron, formidable from its numbers, was commanded by the famous Hasting, the son of one of the most experienced Danish warriors; and he displayed his skill by forthwith casting up strong entrenchments (A.D. 893), in which his forces took up their position, and continued for about a year. Other bands overspread the country. The Danes of Northumbria and East Anglia, the latter under King Eric, violated their oaths of fealty, and joined their kinsmen in their work of desolation.

Alfred was in much perplexity, yet nothing disheartened. He had great difficulty in bringing up his forces; for the "Fyrd," or "levée-en-masse," could not be compelled to serve more than a stated time, probably forty days; and it was also necessary to provide for the defence of the towns and the cultivation of the country. He therefore adopted the plan of calling the militia out in divisions; so that one division supplied the place of the other, which continued at home. In the course of the war, Alfred's troops surprised a fortress at Benfleet, where Hasting had left his wife and children. Alfred sent back the youths and their mother to Hasting, uninjured and unharmed. This act of magnanimity did not excite any corresponding sentiment on the part of

---

* Anterior to the Conquest, the Rother fell into the sea between Romney and Lydd, or North Lade. The course of the stream has been much altered, and its channel almost wholly filled with silt and sand. In 1822 a vessel was found in the ancient bed of the river, which excited much speculation; but it appears to have been only the hulk of a Dutch or Flemish barge of the sixteenth century. (Arch. XX. p. 553.)

the Dane. He relented not; but collected his forces again, and advancing into Mercia, he carried on the war in the very heart of England.

Being surrounded, in a disadvantageous position on the banks of the Severn, the Danes could not obtain any provisions, and were nearly starved. They broke out, and suffered great loss from the Anglo-Saxon armies, which encompassed them. And yet these routed free-booters rallied again in Essex. All that they possessed, and that they valued most, their wives, their children, and their plunder, they committed to the care of their kindred, the East Anglian Danes; and then marching on the stretch, day and night, they crossed the island, and threw themselves into Chester (A.D. 895), then devoid of inhabitants. It had been very strongly fortified by the Romans; and the noble arched gateways, built by them, were standing until a recent period.* Chester, after the Roman period, was successively occupied by the Britons and Anglo-Saxons; but the city had been abandoned during the convulsions of the times. The direction of the Danes towards this distant point, shows how well they were acquainted with the military capabilities of the country. Amidst all their apparent irregularity, they made war by system. Wales was also plundered by the Danes; and the Britons found, to their cost, that the "black strangers"† were as bitter enemies as the "sassenagh." As soon as they had gathered this harvest of plunder, away again they marched. Alfred and his army were distanced by their rapid movements;

---

* They were destroyed to please the Corporation.

† By the Welsh, as also by the Irish, the Danes were called the "black men," or the "black strangers;" the origin of this appellation is not well ascertained. Perhaps it arose from the colour of their garments or armour.

and long before the winter had set in, the Danes were stationed in Essex, and in the southern parts of the kingdom.

The Danish forces pressed so close upon London, that Alfred was compelled to encamp with his army round about the city, whilst the citizens got in their harvest. London, as I have before observed, was a place of considerable trade ; but the great majority of the burgesses, as in all the Anglo-Saxon towns, were husbandmen and soldiers. The Danes, wary and considerate, had selected a station about twenty miles from London, situated on the river Lea ; and that river, then much deeper than it is at present, was filled with their vessels.   Alfred, certainly not without much danger to himself, surveyed the Danish camp, and devised a plan for preventing further annoyance from the enemy. He caused two fortifications or bulwarks to be erected on either shore of the Lea, below the Danish station ; and he also lowered the level of the river, by cutting three additional channels, which drained off the stream into the Thames. The want of water, and the fortifications cast up by Alfred, prevented the Danes from getting their vessels out. But their boldness equalled Alfred's invention. As before, they intrusted their wives and their children, and their booty, to their East Anglian brethren ; and abandoning their vessels and their entrenchmets, they stole out, crossed the land, reached " Quatbridge "* on the Severn ; and there cast up such entrenchments, as offered a formidable obstacle to all the forces which Alfred could raise.

In the following summer, the host of the Danes dispersed themselves, some into East Anglia, some into Northumbria. Hasting sailed to the Seine, and he never

* Perhaps Quatford, near Bridgenorth.

again revisited England.   Many of the Danes, who had
lost all their gains and plunder by the casualties of war,
put themselves afloat again, and carried on their attacks
with great vigour, infesting and harassing the country.
Alfred constantly sought to meet them, and he caused
" long ships " * to be constructed, steadier in their
draught, higher in their sides, and swifter in their course,
than any others.   The Danish and Frisian build appears
hitherto to have been considered as the best model of
naval architecture ; but these more serviceable ships
were after a plan of Alfred's own.

In a battle off the coast of Devonshire, the new vessels
were tried against the enemy.   Alfred's ships were
principally officered by Frieslanders, who were, perhaps,
better seamen than his own subjects, though not better
warriors.   After the battle, two of the Danish ships were
cast on shore ; their crews were conducted to Alfred at
Winchester, and he ordered that they should be hanged
—a cruel and unjustifiable act of vengeance.   The Danes
do not seem to have violated the law of nations, as such
law was then understood.   Mortal punishment, thus
inflicted upon the wretches whom misfortune had placed
in Alfred's power, was contrary to the customs of his
age, as well as irreconcileable to the dictates of mercy;
and we must acknowledge this stain upon the character
of our Anglo-Saxon king.

That he yielded to a feeling of vengeance, is, perhaps,
to be ascribed to the contemplation of the miseries which
the Danes had inflicted upon his people.   In addition to
the harm occasioned by the war, sickness had, as usual,
followed the host of the destroyers ; and very many of

* So called in the Chronicles. The term is Latin, and, as well as the model,
may have been taken by Alfred from the Romans.

the " mightiest Thanes," or people of the greatest consequence, had perished by the pestilence (Oct. 27th, 901).
Alfred died six nights before " All-Hallows Mass-day,"
in the year 901, in the fifty-third year of his age;
prematurely, if years be alone reckoned, but full of
desert and honour.

King Alfred.

Alfred's Jewel.

Anglo-Saxon Illuminated Letter.

Anglo-Saxon Ornamented Letter.

Chapter VII.

Alfred, "the wisest man in England"—Literature and Culti-
vation of the Anglo-Saxons—The Runes—The Latin Alpha-
bet introduced by the Roman Missionaries—Difficulty of
explaining Runic Inscriptions—Art of Writing not much
practised, and comparatively of small importance—Use of
Visible Symbols in Legal Transactions instead of Written
Instruments—Poetry, extemporaneous—Historical Poetry of
the Anglo-Saxons—Scarcity of Books—Printing—Possible
Decay of Literature and Science.

ALFRED, the "Shepherd of his people," the "Darling
of the English," for these were the epithets given to him
in the old time, was deemed the "wisest man" in
England. This *superlative*, however, affords no definite
means of comparison. In order to understand the real
importance of Alfred's acquirements, it will be necessary
to take a general view of the cultivation which existed
amongst the people over whom he ruled.

Before the conversion of the Anglo-Saxons, they,
like most of the Teutonic nations, employed certain
mysterious characters denominated *Runes*—mysterious,
I call them, because the name implies *secrecy*. The
heathen Teutons supposed that these letters possessed
magical powers. Some Runes, as they believed, could
stop the vessel in her course, divert the arrow in its
flight, cause love or hatred, raise the corpse from the
grave, or cast the living into death-like slumber. The
origin of these characters, which, with some variations,
were also used by the Celtic nations, ascends into the

most remote antiquity.   Many of the letters were named
after trees—

ᚪ *A*, or *Ac, Oak*.   ᛒ *B, Beorc, Birch*.   ᚦ *Th, Thorn*.

Some from other natural objects, ᚻ *H, Hagel*, or *Hail*.

ᛁ *Is*, or *Ice;* and ᛗ *M, Man*, may be instanced ; and, in
short, all the names have some meaning.

The Runes have formed the subject of many erudite
dissertations, and have been explained by the learned,
with more satisfaction to themselves than to their
readers,—who are often strangely perplexed by the most
singular conflict of opinions amongst their guides.   Thus,
an inscription upon a pillar at Bewcastle, * which, in
the eye of the renowned *Olaus Wormius*, expresses,
" *Reno satu runa stena thissa*,"—" *Reno fixed this runic
stone*,"—is interpreted by the ingenious *Grimm* (whose
clever " Nursery Tales " have perhaps amused you) as
" *Rices Drihtenes*,"—" *Of the kingdom of the Lord.*"   The
fine and perfect font still preserved in the church of
Bridekirk * has furnished still richer materials for the
inventive faculties of the antiquaries.   Attend to Olaus
Wormius, and it signifies,—" *Harold made this heap, and
raised these stones, in honour of his mother and of Mabrok.*"
Bishop Nicholson is dissatisfied with this version.
" Honoured Sir," says he, in a letter addressed to
Dugdale, " let the inscription speak for itself ;" and,
under his guidance, it speaks most loudly.   " *Here
Eckard was converted, and to this man's example were the
Danes brought.*"   Bishop Nicholson was a learned man :
many useful works have been produced by him ; and,
therefore, upon the faith of his erudition, Harold lost the

* Both in Cumberland.

font; Harold's mother and Mabrok were forgotten, and
Eckard continued in full possession of his honours,
until he was, in his turn, deprived of them by a
most worthy Warwickshire archæologist,* who reads—
" *Richard he me wrought, and to this form me diligently
brought.*" Richard, therefore, is now in possession of
the Runic font; but let him beware! According to
despatches, addressed by our Minister at Copenhagen to
the Foreign Secretary of the Antiquaries of London, the
" *Skandinaviske Selskab,*" or *Scandinavian Society*, had
nearly completed their attack upon *Richard*—begun in
1821, when Mr. Hamper's paper was received,—and by
which the said Richard was to be compelled to march
away, bag and baggage, and *Thorbrand* installed in
his stead!

It may perhaps be thought that a spell has been cast
over the learned, and that some sportive Puck yet lurks
about the Runes, and seduces the grave antiquaries into
these interminable wanderings. Let me be allowed,
however, to observe, that I doubt whether, in these and
similar instances, any true reading can ever be obtained,
unless the object itself (or a cast from it) be inspected
by those who undertake the task of interpretation. No
draughtsman's copy, however skilful he may be,. will
ever be accurate, unless he can read the inscription, and
his mind guides his pencil. If he be ignorant of its
meaning, he may mistake an accidental indentation or
flaw for a letter;—he will omit the line, nearly effaced
by time, which joined the parts,—he will lengthen a
curve that has been broken,—and shorten a limb which
has been partly filled up;—and the aggregate of these

* William Hamper, Esq., to whose very ingenious paper (Archæologia, vol.
xix. p. 379) I must refer.

errors, though each may be trifling in itself, will cast an impenetrable veil over features, which, under the most favourable circumstances, were sufficiently obscure.

Puck has caused me, also, to wander somewhat out of my course, and we must now return to our Runes. The continental Danes retained them till a very late period: they are found in sepulchral inscriptions of the fourteenth century, and on rings and cups, and ornaments perhaps of later date; and I am not quite sure whether they are not used for some purposes in the island of Rugen at the present day. It was otherwise amongst the Anglo-Saxons; for when they were converted to Christianity, the Runic characters went almost wholly out of use. Actuated by the wish of abolishing all usages which were too nearly connected with idolatry to be allowed with safety, the Roman missionaries endeavoured to introduce the Latin character amongst the nations whom they brought within the pale of Christendom. There was indeed a manifest advantage in this practice; for it enabled such as did acquire the skill of letters, to put themselves in communication with the civilized nations of Europe, by whom the same characters were used. There are fashions in writing, as in all other matters; and the Roman hand-writing in the sixth century had changed from what it was before the fall of the empire. The Roman missionaries taught their pupils to write the hand which they themselves employed; and that character constitutes what is termed the Anglo-Saxon alphabet; and I have observed thus much, because such letters as ð, ꝼ, þ, ſ, ꞇ, appear, at first, so unlike D, F, R, S, T, that you might be puzzled by my assertion of their original identity.

The Anglo-Saxon alphabet, however, contains three

letters which are really its own. The sign of the sound expressed in English by our *th* was unknown to the ancient Romans, though it had been familiar to the Greeks ; and, therefore, in order to denote the *th*, the missionaries sometimes employed the ancient rune Þ or þ. They also used another sign for the *th*, namely, a ð, with a small line drawn through the top of the letter, thus ð. And the rune ᚹ or p, was retained to denote the sound which we give to our W, a sound which, like that of the *th*, was then also foreign to those who understood only the Latin or Roman language, or those vulgar tongues called *Romance* dialects, into which it had been corrupted by the common people. I believe, however, that the use of the Runes did lurk amongst the Anglo-Saxons, and that they employed the ancient characters for magical charms. And the Danish population of Northumbria certainly retained the Runes till the Conquest, as is proved by the Bewcastle and Bridekirk monuments, and many others of a similar description.

Reading and writing, though no longer mysteries, as in the Pagan age, were still acquirements almost wholly confined to the clergy. Hence the word " Clericus," or " Clerk," became synonymous with Penman, the sense in which it is still most usually employed. If a man could write, or even read, his knowledge was considered as proof presumptive that he was in holy orders. If kings and great men had occasion to authenticate any document, they subscribed the " *sign*" of the cross opposite to the place where the " clerk" had written their name. Hence we say, to *sign* a deed or a letter. Illiterate people still make their signs or *marks*, in this manner, just as king Offa used to do, by drawing a +, by the side whereof the lawyer's clerk adds their Christian and surnames. You sometimes see the ruins of an ancient palace degraded to a hovel; and it is thus with such old customs. They sink lower and lower, as the manners or opinions of the world rise above them, till at last they can be found only amongst the humblest orders of society.

The laity, or people who were not clerks, did not feel any urgent necessity for the use of letters. Commerce was carried on principally by truck or barter, or by payments in ready money; and sums were cast up, as amongst the Romans, upon an abacus or accounting-table, the amount being denoted by *counters* or similar tokens. From the difficulty of communicating between place and place, common people had seldom any opportunity of conveying intelligence to absent friends. Many important transactions, which now require writing, could then be effected by word of mouth, or, as lawyers say, by *parole*. At the present day, if you wish to buy a horse, it is sufficient for you to pay the money to the owner: he delivers the horse to you, you ride him to the stable, and the bargain is completed. But if you wish to buy a field, a huge deed must be drawn by a solicitor, and engrossed upon a parchment, which is stamped— money being paid to government for the same. This is called a *conveyance*. Now, in early times, the horse and the field might be *conveyed* with equal simplicity, and without any writing whatever. When land was sold, the owner cut a turf from the green sward, and cast it in the lap of the purchaser, as a token that the possession of the earth was transferred; or he tore off the branch of a tree and put it in the hand of the grantee, to show that the latter was to be entitled to all the products of the soil. And when the purchaser of a house

Runic Font at Bridekirk.

Runic Ring found in Norway.
(From the Original in the Bronstedt Collection.)

The Horn of Ulphus.

Costume of a Female, exhibiting the
under and upper sleeved Tunic,
the Mantle and Hood. (Har-
leian MS.)

Anglo-Saxon Females.
The standing figure is Etheldrytha, a Princess of East
Anglia, from the Benedictional of St. Ethelwold.]

Civil Costume of the Anglo-Saxons.

received *seizin* or possession, the key of the door, or a bundle of thatch plucked from the roof, signified that the dwelling had been yielded up to him. These symbols were sometimes varied by the fancy of the grantor. One delivered a knife, with a hair of his beard; another, a glove; a third, a curry-comb; a fourth, his drinking-horn. Ulfus, a noble of Northumbria, disinherited his sons, and granted his lands to the Archbishopric of York, in this manner, by laying his mighty ivory drinking-horn upon the altar, at the same time that he declared his intention; and the horn of Ulfus is yet kept in the minster; for such tokens being the testimonies of the right to property, were preserved with as much care as title-deeds or charters; and a part of the " Terra Ulfi" is yet in the possession of the chapter of the cathedral. And the intent of these visible symbols was also to supply the place of writing, by impressing the transaction upon the recollection of the witnesses, who were called together upon the occasion.

No small share of such knowledge as was both useful and entertaining, might be learned without book; for many matters now consigned to writing, were then oral and traditionary. Poetry, to us a kind of luxury, was in those times turned to homely use. In the ruder stages of society, verse has been very generally employed as the vehicle for preserving a record of facts, or for inculcating doctrines confided to the memory; and this state of things continued to its fullest extent amongst our English ancestors, as well as amongst their Scandinavian brethren. Their legal formulæ were in verse—the achievements of their ancestors were commemorated in song. Some of these poems still exist, and others have evidently furnished materials for prose-histories or chronicles. Greatly did the Anglo-Saxons delight in rhythm and harmony. The harp was handed round at their festivals; and he who could not join in the glee (this word is pure Anglo-Saxon) was considered as unfit for respectable company. Aldhelm, Bishop of Sherbourne, could find no mode of commanding the attention of his townsmen so efficacious, as that of standing on the bridge and singing a ballad, which he had composed; and it may be interesting to add, that we owe this anecdote to Alfred himself, who preserved in in his "handbook," or manual.

Of course, all the good to be derived from recited verse was accessible to the illiterate, and letters were hardly more necessary to the poets themselves. Verse, amongst the northern nations, was often composed extemporaneously; and, according to the practice of the *improvisatori* in Italy, either to the sound of an instrument, or at least in song. Some little was reduced into writing: more was recollected, or, as we say, learnt by heart;— by heart, because it was liked and loved—because it accorded with the feelings of the hearer. Most of all was forgotten, because it was not learnt by heart. And let me tell you, if poetry is not learned by heart, all the penmen and printers in the world cannot save the verses from oblivion.

You will understand from the foregoing account, that writing was not then needed so urgently for the ordinary affairs of life, as at the present day. A man could fairly hold his station in society, without book-learning. Some, according to the usual fashion of ignorance, probably despised what they had not. Others, and more especially the nobles, whose time was divided between war and the sports of the field, had not the leisure to employ themselves in studies which were surrounded by such difficulties.

Books were extremely rare amongst the Scandinavian and northern nations. Before their communication with the Latin missionaries, wood appears to have been the material upon which their runes were chiefly written : and the verb " write," which is derived from a Teutonic root, signifying to scratch or tear,* is one of the testimonies of the usage. The Cymri adopted the same plan. Their poems were graven upon small staves or rods, one line upon each face of the rod ; and the old English word " Stave," as applied to a stanza, is probably a relic of the practice, which, in the early ages, prevailed in the west. In the east, you will find the custom still subsisting ; the slips of bamboo upon which the inhabitants of the Indian Archipelago now write or scratch their compositions with a bodkin, are substantially the same with our ancient staves. Vellum or parchment afterwards supplied the place of these materials. Real paper, manufactured from the pellicle of the Egyptian reed, or *papyrus*, was still used occasionally in Italy, but it was seldom exported to the countries beyond the Alps ; and the elaborate preparation of the vellum, upon which much greater care was bestowed than in the modern manufacture, rendered it a costly article : so much so, that a pains-taking clerk could find it worth his while to erase the writing of an old book, in order to use the blank page for another manuscript. Books thus rewritten are called " codices rescripti," or " palimpsests." The evanescent traces of the first layer of characters may occasionally be discerned beneath the more recent text which has been imposed upon them ; and some

* *Ritzen* or *reissen.*

valuable fragments of ancient classical writers have been
lately recovered from such volumes, by the patient dili-
gence of foreign antiquaries.

The works from which any useful or elegant learning
could be derived, were to be read only in the Latin language, and this tongue, though living, as far as the
clerks were concerned (for Latin was used in all documents and transactions relating to church affairs), could
not be acquired without great difficulty. Old crabbed
Priscian was the only grammatical author whom the
learner could consult; and instead of the ready aid which
we now receive from copious and critical dictionaries
and lexicons, all helps of that description were then
wholly absent. Perhaps there might be a meagre vo-
cabulary, of which three or four copies existed in a whole
kingdom; but a stock of words could only be acquired
from oral instruction. Hard drudgery this for the
unfortunate master, and still more so for the unlucky
scholars, who were treated with the most appalling severity. We are told, for instance, that the very learned
and celebrated Erigena was so harsh to his pupils, that
at last they could bear his cruelty no longer; and rebelling against him, they stabbed him to death with
their knives.

After the first portion of the laborious path of learning
had been trodden, great difficulties impeded the further
progress of the student. Books bore a large price, and
were but very few in number. It was an extensive library
which contained fifty volumes; and they could only be
multiplied by the slow process of transcription. Why
were they not printed? The most remarkable point in the
history of this art, which has been destined to change the
moral aspect of the globe, is not its so-called discovery

by Guttenbergh or Koster, but the great length of time
which elapsed before it was put in use by the nations of
Western Christendom.

The principle of printing, the employment of a solid
type or letter, for the purpose of taking an impression
by means of a coloured pigment—and which is only a
variation of the effect produced by a die or seal—was
certainly known to the Romans. Stamps, with raised
letters, exactly like our printing types, excepting that
they are not moveable, and by which the Romans produced short inscriptions, are yet extant. Common
tradesmen employed such stamps for printing the labels
of their ware . The ancient Visigoths in Spain printed
their " paraphs " or " signs," flourished with knots and
monograms, which they affixed to their deeds and charters.

These are instances upon a small scale ; but we know
of one entire and very important volume produced by
the process of printing, anterior to the fifth century. The
silver letters of the " Codex argenteus," the volume containing the version of the Gospels, made by Ulfila, bishop
of the Mæsogoths (of which I shall speak more fully
hereafter), were produced by types employed to fix the
leaf upon the purple parchment, nearly in the manner
now practised by bookbinders.

From this stage of printing, for printing it was though
tedious and operose, to our present mode, the transition
appears most easy. Yet the discovery was not made ;
and in Europe there was a barrier which could not be
passed. Not so in China, where block-printing came
into active operation within that period, which, to us, is
the darkest age. There, the practice and effects of the
art must have been witnessed by the acute and ingenious
Venetian traveller, Marco Polo. This individual was

gifted with no ordinary powers of observation; and it might have been expected that the increasing desire for learning which prevailed in his own country, would have induced him to bring back so useful and so profitable a contrivance. Roger Bacon, who had received much information concerning China, describes the process, not in obscure and mysterious terms, but with the utmost plainness and precision of language. Yet he failed to teach the lesson which he had learnt, nor was the disclosure made till the appointed time.

I have brought these facts together, because we are often disposed to consider the progress of the human mind as the result of unaided human exertion, and the fruit of mere human experience. Unquestionably these are the means; but the general march of intellect is as fully under the direction and control of Providence as any other portion of human affairs. If the knowledge which we have in any branch of those pursuits usually called science or learning, be good, it has been granted to us by the Father of lights, and may be again withheld, if he shall choose to allow us to relapse into mental darkness.

It is not unusual for us to overlook the imbecility of human wisdom, and to extol the printing-press, as defying time. We sometimes consider that the art of printing not only secures the ever-enduring possession of our present stock of worldly learning, but that we have the certain power of adding to that store to an unlimited extent. This is a fallacious assumption, grounded upon error. Mankind can only "darken counsel by words without knowledge;" and the proud empire of intellect and science may be as easily destroyed, as those temporal dominions which were scattered to the winds of Heaven.

Let it be granted that no one conflagration could destroy the myriads of volumes which have become the records of the human mind; yet it does not necessarily follow that the inhabitants of Britain, a thousand, or even a hundred years hence, will be able to profit by the lore of their ancestors. Men may be in possession of tools, and at the same time be utterly unable to use them. The cultivation of the vastly diversified field of human acquirement, depends wholly upon the supply of labourers, and the capability which they have of reaping the harvest. Learning and science are wholly sustained by our artificial and perishable state of society. If, in consequence of a total subversion of our laws and institutions, property should be so divided, that, instead of that gradation of ranks which is now established, there should be only a working class, degraded by poverty, debased by infidelity, without wealth to reward learning or leisure to enjoy inquiry, all the attainments upon which we pride ourselves may ultimately disappear. Those who are now stimulated to study by the hopes of worldly advancement, would fall off; and that class by whom learning is pursued only for its own sake, would cease to exist. With the decline of public prosperity, with the destruction of private capital, all the arts which are directly or indirectly connected with commerce or manufactures would decay. The abstract sciences would be neglected or forgotten. And though some branches might be pursued by a solitary sage, still they would be as null, to a world in which he would find none able and willing to profit by his knowledge.

Chapter VIII.

*Alfred's early Education—His want of proper Instructors—
Great Decay of Learning in England, after the Danish Invasions—Translations of the Bible in the early part of the
Middle Ages—Discouraged amongst the nations who spoke
the Romance Dialects, and encouraged by those who spoke
Teutonic—Ulfila—Cædmon—Alfred's Plans for the Restoration of Learning.*

ALFRED was wholly ignorant of letters until he attained
twelve years of age. He was greatly loved by his
parents, who fondled the boy for his beauty; but that
instruction which the poorest child can now acquire with
the greatest ease, was withheld from the son of the
Anglo-Saxon king. Alfred was taught to wind the horn
and to bend the bow, to hunt and to hawk; and he
acquired great skill in the " noble art of the chase," considered throughout the middle ages as the most necessary
accomplishment of the nobility, whilst book-learning was
thought of little use to them.

Alfred's eager mind did not, however, remain unem-
ployed. Though he could not read, he could attend, and
he listened eagerly to the verses which were recited in
his father's hall by the minstrels and the glee-men, the
masters of Anglo-Saxon song. Day and night would he
employ in hearkening to these poems; he treasured them
in his memory, and during the whole of his life, poetry
continued to be his solace and amusement in trouble and
care.

It chanced one day that Alfred's mother,—his own mother, Osburgha, and not, as some people suppose, the French woman Judith—showed to him and his brothers a volume of Anglo-Saxon poetry which she possessed. " He who first can read the book shall have it," said she. Alfred's attention was attracted by the bright gilding and colouring of one of the illuminated capital letters. He was delighted with the *gay*, and inquired of his mother, —would she really keep her word ? She confirmed the promise, and put the book into his hands ; and he applied so steadily to his task, that the book became his own.

The information which Alfred now possessed, rendered him extremely desirous of obtaining more; but his ignorance of Latin was an insuperable obstacle. Science and knowledge could not be acquired otherwise than from Latin books ; and earnestly as he sought for instruction in that language, none could be found. Sloth had overspread the land ; and there were so few " Grammarians," that is to say Latinists, in Wessex, that he was utterly unable to discover a competent teacher. In after life, Alfred was accustomed to say, that of all the hardships, privations, and misfortunes which had befallen him, there was none which he felt so grievous as this, the enforced idleness of his youth, when his intellect would have been fitted to receive the lesson, and his time was unoccupied. At a more advanced period, the arduous toils of royalty, and the pressure of most severe and unintermitting pain, interrupted the studies which he was then enabled to pursue, and harassed and disturbed his mind,—yet he persevered ;— and the unquenchable thirst for knowledge which the child had manifested, continued, without abatement, until he was removed from this stage of exertion.

In the eighth century, the age of Bede, Britain was
distinguished for learning; the rapid decline of cultivation had been occasioned by the Danish invasions. The
churches and monasteries were particularly the objects of
their attacks; these establishments, the only libraries
and schools which then existed, were burnt, or razed to
the ground; and the clergy had fallen into such a state
of deplorable ignorance, as to be utterly unfitted for the
sacred office. "South of the Humber," says Alfred, for
we can quote his own words, "there were few priests,
indeed, when I began my reign, who could understand
the meaning of their 'common prayer,' or translate a
line of Latin into English; so few, that in Wessex there
was not one."

Throughout great part of Europe, there was a strong
prejudice against the employment of the vernacular
tongues as written languages. The "Romance"*
dialects of Gaul and Spain and Italy were broken Latin,
or the dialects into which it had been corrupted, first
by the provincials, and afterwards by the barbarian
conquerors of the Roman empire. Spanish has been
described with some drollery and truth, as such Latin as
might have been heard from the mouth of a sulky Roman
slave. And the ground-work of all these Romance
languages,—French, Spanish, Portuguese, Provençal,
Italian,—is in fact only the Latin, mangled, and deprived
of its grammatical forms and grammatical construction,
and then copiously interspersed with words derived from
barbarian sources:—Teutonic, Celtic, Vascon, and even
Sclavonic, all having contributed to the compound. By

* This term was constantly applied to the languages formed as noticed in the
text; and *Romance*, in Spanish, is still employed as synonymous to Castilian,
or the vulgar tongue.

cultivation, these irregular dialects have acquired beauty and elegance; but, to the learned, who, though they may have been deficient in critical nicety, were quite familiar with the correct forms of the Latin language, these *patois* must have sounded as ludicrous as the *talkee talkee* of our negroes in the Colonies, to which they bear the closest analogy. Such a language might be, and was applied to the oral instruction of the common people, from the necessity of the case; and discourses were delivered from the pulpit in what was termed " the rustic tongue." But the employment of this jargon in a literary composition, would have seemed as derogatory to the writer. Still less could they venture to employ it in translations of the Holy Scriptures; for they feared that the dignity of the sacred writings would be profaned by the association of ideas arising from a plebeian idiom, bearing the stamp of ignorance and vulgarity.

There are few transgressions more seductive to us all, than that disrespectful treatment of the word of God which is to all intents and purposes a breach of the third Commandment; and we are therefore bound to guard ourselves against the error with the most watchful care. It is of the greatest importance that we should resist the temptation, frequently so strong, of annexing a familiar, facetious, or irreverent idea to a scriptural usage, a scriptural expression, a scripture text, or a scripture name. Nor should we hold ourselves guiltless, though we may have been misled by mere negligence or want of reflection. Every person of good taste will avoid reading a parody or a *travestie* of a beautiful poem, because the recollection of the degraded likeness will always obtrude itself upon our memories, when we wish to derive pleasure from the contemplation of the

elegance of the original.   But how much more urgent is
the duty, by which we are bound to keep the pages of
the Bible clear of any impression tending to diminish the
blessing of habitual respect and reverence towards our
Maker's law !

We must therefore admit that the general principle
which induced the clergy of Gaul and Spain and Italy,
to avoid clothing the Scriptures in what they considered
a degrading garb, was right and sound ; but the particular application of that principle was evidently incorrect.
The Romance dialects were the only languages understood by the great body of the people.   They were a
mixed race, speaking a mixed tongue.   In their ears,
the solecisms and barbarisms which offended the
grammarian, had no uncouth or unpleasing sound ; and
it was only the fastidiousness of human knowledge which
induced the clergy to contemn the language employed,
even by themselves, in all the ordinary concerns of life,
merely because it lacked the impress of refinement and
of learning.

Such was the case in the *Romanized* countries, where
the victorious races were rapidly assimilating in language
and usages to the people whom they had conquered.
But amongst the Teutonic nations, who retained their
nationality, similar feelings did not prevail.   They
delighted in their old expressive mother tongue.   Of
such national literature as they had possessed, it was the
sole vehicle.   Their speech was a token of nobility and
superiority ; and the power and regularity of its forms
enabled the writer, when he had become acquainted with
the grammarians of Greece and Rome, to treat his
Gothic or his Saxon with the same precision as the
cultivated languages.   He had nothing to shun or to

avoid. Thus, Ulfila, the Bishop of the Mæsogoths, made that singularly valuable translation of the New Testament, to which I have before alluded. The Gospels are extant in the Codex Argenteus.* Other fragments of the Acts and Epistles have been recently recovered from " palimpsests." And if you should ever feel disposed to investigate the origin and structure of the English language which you speak, you will find that Ulfila's version affords the best and most valuable materials for the inquiry.

Translations, or rather paraphrases of parts of the Bible, were not unfrequently made in verse. The Teutonic nations, as I have before observed, were so much accustomed to view poetry as the means of instruction, that such a mode of rendering the Scripture accessible and agreeable to the common people, was fit and praiseworthy. The rhythm helped the memory of the learner; and in some cases, the idiomatic freedom of the composition enabled the translator to produce a more intelligible version than he could otherwise have effected; for ancient translators often imagined that a faithful interpretation could only be effected by placing every word of the version in the exact position of the corresponding word in the original. An Anglo-Saxon translation of the Psalms upon this plan is extant ; and, with the exception of the articles and particles not employed in the Latin, each Anglo-Saxon word covers, as it were, the corresponding word in the Vulgate or Latin text.

Of the sacred poems of the Anglo-Saxons, none were more celebrated or more singular than those of Cædmon.

---

* Now preserved in the library of the University of Upsal. A palimpsest at Wolfenbuttel has furnished a small fragment of the Epistles. Many more have since been discovered in the Vatican by Maii. Ulfila's Version is supposed to have been made about 360.

Until he had attained more than the middle stage of life (about A.D. 670), Cædmon had never been able to repeat a stave. If he happened to be in a company where each guest was bound to sing in his turn, he used, when he saw that the harp was approaching him, to rise and quit the feast for very shame; so much abashed was he by his inferiority.

It chanced once upon a time, that, having thus slunk away from a banquet, because he saw the dreaded harp coming nigh to him, he was glad to take refuge in the stable. It was Cædmon's turn to tend the cattle; and thus escaping from the humiliation which would have awaited him amongst his companions, he fell asleep in the straw. In the course of the night, he dreamt that a stranger came unto him, and asked him to sing. "Nay," Cædmon answered in his dream,—"Do I know how to sing? and is not that the reason why I have left the good company?" His imaginary companion still urged him to sing, and proposed, as a subject, the Creation; and forthwith, in his sleep, Cædmon poured forth an unpremeditated song, which, when he awoke, was firmly imprinted in his memory. The following paraphrase, which we owe to one of our best Anglo-Saxon scholars,* will give you some idea of the character of Cædmon's poetry:—

> "Now should we all heaven's guardian king exalt,
>   The power and counsels of our maker's will,
>   Father of glorious works, eternal Lord,
>   He, from of old, 'stablished the origin
>   Of every varied wonder. First he shaped,
>   For us, the sons of earth, heaven's canopy,
>   Holy creator.   Next, this middle realm,
>   This earth—the bounteous guardian of mankind,
>   The everlasting Lord, for mortals framed,
>   Ruler omnipotent."

* The late Mr. J. J. Conybeare. See his Illustrations of Anglo-Saxon poetry, as edited and completed by Mr. W. D. Conybeare, the equal, in all respects, of his lamented brother.

To these lines he added many others, and the first person to whom he repeated his strain, was the Reeve or steward of his village, or township of Streoneshalch, now called Whitby, where there was a celebrated monastery.

The story, though remarkable, is neither incredible nor marvellous, and may be entirely explained by natural causes. Cædmon's nervous bashfulness shows that he possessed a quick and excitable temperament. He retired to sleep, but not to rest, with his mind full of the mortifications to which he was continually exposed, and probably with an earnest desire to avoid these vexations in future. Anglo-Saxon poetry was very simple in its construction. *End-rhymes* were not used ; the harmony of each short verse depended chiefly upon the *alliteration,* or the recurrence of the initial letters of the words, and upon a kind of loose and varying rhythm, regulated rather by the ear, than by any fixed metrical canon. The Anglo-Saxons had a great store of poetical expressions, differing from the language of common life, and forming the stock-in-trade of the bard, yet rendered very familiar to the ear by their constant and daily repetition, and therefore likely to be forcibly impressed upon the recollection. Cædmon's inability to perform his part appears to have arisen rather from his want of musical knowledge than from his dulness. And therefore, it is quite possible, that, allowing for some little exaggeration, his poetical talent may have been suddenly developed, nearly in the manner before described.

Cædmon was forthwith introduced by the Reeve, as the wonder of the village, into the abbey of St. Hilda, where a large and learned auditory had assembled. After hearing his hymn, they gave him a subject from sacred history, and required him to put it into verse, doubting, perhaps, whether, as many a poet has done, he had not decked himself in borrowed plumes. But Cædmon stood the test; and on the following day he produced his composition, which met with great applause. Cædmon readily yielded to the proposition of those who thought his talent might be well and usefully employed in versifying the Holy Scriptures. He became a monk in the monastery of Streoneshalch. Read he could not; but his more learned brethren were accustomed from time to time to teach him portions of sacred history; and when he was well grounded, he would, after much consideration and thought, sing his lesson to his teachers in a metrical form. In this manner did Cædmon complete, not indeed a version of the whole scriptures, but a selection of portions, containing the great history of the creation and redemption of mankind, besides many hymns and devotional poems. "Never," says Bede, "did Cædmon compose an idle verse." Of his paraphrase, a considerable fragment has been preserved; and it is a very singular, and, as yet, unexplained coincidence, that his narrative of the fall of man contains passages so closely resembling Milton, that they might be almost literally translated into English, by a canto of verses from the Paradise Lost, taking line for line.

At the time when Alfred began to be in earnest about his studies, such knowledge of the Bible as could be diffused by the Cædmonian versions, was familiar to the people. Venerable Bede had rendered the gospel of St. John into the speech of his countrymen, together with extracts from other portions of scripture. There were also Anglo-Saxon versions of the Psalter, as I have before noticed. The second of the books which Alfred read—

the first being the collection of poems—was a volume containing a selection from the Psalms, with the daily prayers, according to the ancient usage of the church; and during his seclusion in the isle of Athelney, the perusal of this volume, which he always treasured in his bosom, afforded him constant comfort and support.

Alfred's plans for the intellectual cultivation of his country, were directed, in the first instance, to the diffusion of knowledge amongst the great body of the people. Hence he earnestly recommended the translation of "useful books into the language which we all understand; so that all the youth of England, but more especially those who are of gentle-kind and at ease in their circumstances, may be grounded in letters,—for they cannot profit in any pursuit until they are well able to read English." This opinion is extracted from a document appearing to have been a circular letter addressed by Alfred to the bishops; and the desire which it expresses is the best proof of the sincerity of his intentions, and the grasp and comprehensiveness of his mind. Much had been done on the continent for the cultivation of learning, particularly by Charlemagne; but the munificence of the Frankish emperor, and of those who thought like him, was calculated to confine the gift within the pale of the cloister. The general tendency of the middle ages was to centre all erudition in a particular caste, severed from the rest of society. Alfred's labours, on the contrary, were directed to enable every individual to have a share, according to his station and degree, in the common inheritance of wisdom.

Alfred had taught himself Latin by translating. You will recollect his regret at the want of masters in early life. As soon as he was settled in his kingdom, he attempted to supply this deficiency, not only for himself, but also for his people, by inviting learned men from foreign parts. Asser, a native of St. David's, or Men-evia, whom he appointed Bishop of Sherbourne, was one of them. Great friendship and confidence prevailed between Alfred and the British priest; and to the pen of Asser we owe a biography of the Anglo-Saxon mon-arch, written with equal simplicity and fidelity. Grim-bald, at the invitation of Alfred, left Gaul, his own country, and settled in England. A third celebrated foreigner was called Johannes *Scotus*, from his nation, or *Erigena*, the Irishman, from the place of his birth. Athens had been visited by Erigena, and many years had he passed in Asia—years employed in arduous study. He was a deep philosopher, and soundly versed in the Greek, the Hebrew, the Syriac, the Chaldee, and the Arabic languages; acquisitions of some difficulty in any age, but singularly so in those times, when few persons in western Christendom knew more than the Greek alphabet, and perhaps a few Greek words or phrases; and no access whatever, by books, was to be attained to the languages of that class usually included amongst those called oriental, but which are more appositely dis-tinguished by the name Semitic, as being the language of the children of Shem. From these distinguished men, to whom must be added Plegmund, Archbishop of Canterbury, Alfred was enabled to acquire that learning which he had so long sought.

Asser permits us to contemplate Alfred beginning his literary labours. They were engaged in pleasant con-verse; and it chanced that Asser quoted a text or pass-age, either from the Bible, or from the works of some of the fathers. Alfred asked his friend to write it down in a blank leaf of that collection of psalms and hymns, which, as I have before mentioned, he always carried in his bosom; but not a blank could be found of sufficient magnitude. Pursuant therefore to Asser's proposal, a *quire*, or *quaternion*, that is to say, a sheet of vellum, folded into *fours*, was produced, on which these texts were written; and Alfred afterwards working upon them, translated the passages so selected into the Anglo-Saxon tongue.

He now continued the practice of writing down such remarkable passages as were quoted in conversation. His "hand-boc" or manual, however, included some matters of his own observation, anecdotes, or sayings of pious men; but the body of the collection appears to have consisted of extracts from the Scriptures, intermingled with reflections of a devotional cast.

Alfred, thus encouraged, appears to have been induced to attempt a complete version of the Bible. Some writers, and those not of a recent period, have supposed that he completed the greater portion of the task. It seems, however, that the work was prevented by his early death. But the impulse given by Alfred did not die with him. Translations were multiplied. A new version of the Pentateuch, and of some of the apocryphal books, was undertaken by Bishop Alfric, the best philologist of his age; and who, in his preface, refuted certain objections which had been raised against similar labours. These objections show, that the mistaken judgment which has since seduced the members of the Church of Rome into many errors, was then beginning to develop itself amongst individual members; but Alfric's opposition also proves how little countenance they met with in the ancient Church of England; and the rubrics prefixed to the lessons of the Anglo-Saxon version of the Gospels, leave no reason to doubt, but that they were regularly read in the churches on Sundays and festivals. Large portions of the Scripture were also introduced in the Anglo-Saxon homilies or sermons, and the study of the Holy Scriptures was most earnestly recommended both to clergy and laity, as the ground-work of their faith.* Several versions of the New Testament are still extant in manuscript. In a remote part of the country, it might sometimes be easier for a prelate to make a new translation, than to borrow a manuscript for the purpose of transcription. Other clerks may have wished to present the Scriptures to the people of a particular district in a dialect which should be thoroughly intelligible to them. The provincialisms now found in different counties of the east and west and north of England, then existed in the shape of distinct idioms, differing as much from each other as the language of Allan Ramsay does from that of Shenstone. A colloquial language, approaching nearly to modern English, seems to have existed concurrently with the more cultivated language, which we call Anglo-Saxon, at a period before the Conquest; and one of the versions of the New Testament† is in this language.

* To confirm this assertion, it is sufficient to quote the "Treatise concerning the Old and New Testament," an epistle addressed by Alfric to his friend. In this work, the writer briefly, but ably, gives a summary of the different books of the Scriptures, interspersed with reflections, of which the following may be read as an instructive specimen:—

"The two Seraphim (Isaiah iv. 2) doubtless betokened the Old and New Testaments, which give the praise both of word and work unto the Almighty, who alone reigneth in unity of Godhead, without beginning and end. All teachers who take not their doctrine and examples out of these holy books, are like those of whom Christ himself said, 'If the blind man be leader of the blind, then shall they both fall into some pit;' but such teachers as take their examples and doctrine from hence, whether it be out of the Old Testament or the New, are such as Christ himself again spake of in these words:—'Every learned scribe in the Church of God is like the master of a family, who brings forth ever out of his own treasure, things new and old.'"

† In the Bodleian Library, and commonly quoted as the "Codex Hattonianus."

It is to such causes that the existence of the different texts of the Anglo-Saxon versions may be attributed. But, at the same time, it is necessary to observe, that the subject cannot be properly investigated until the monuments and muniments of the biblical studies of our ancestors be brought to light. From the Anglo-Saxon age, down to Wickliffe, we, in England, can show such a succession of biblical versions, in metre and in prose, as are not to be equalled amongst any other nation of Europe. But we have not yet produced our stores; nay, though the greater part of the manuscripts of these versions are in the libraries of the University of Oxford, I regret to say, that they remain utterly neglected, and mouldering on their shelves.

Chapter IX.

Works translated by Alfred, or under his Direction — Bede, Orosius, Boethius, St. Augustine, &c.—Encourages Travellers—His Embassy to the Syrian Christians in Hindostan—Prudent Management of his Affairs—Alfred's Character—Its Imperfections and Merits—Alfred's Laws—His Principles of Legislation.

WE must now advert to Alfred's "Family Library," or "Library of useful Knowledge." As far as we can judge from those portions of the plan which were carried into execution, he intended to present his subjects with a complete course of such works as were then considered the most useful, and best calculated to form the groundwork of a liberal education. Amongst the books which he selected, there are some which perhaps may appear of inferior utility; yet we must not judge of them by our standard: they must be valued in relation to the opinions and wants of the age.

The Chronicle of *Orosius*, containing a clear, but succinct, History of the World to the fifth century of the Christian era, and connecting the events narrated in the sacred writings, with the rise and fall of the Roman empire, was the best compendium which had yet been composed. Alfred, in translating the work of the Spaniard—for Orosius was a native of Seville, and the name, slightly changed into *Osorio*, is still common in the Peninsula,—enlarged the text, by additions of great curiosity. He presents us with a geographical account of the natives of Germany; and the voyages of Audher towards the North Pole, and of Wulstan in the Baltic, are detailed as these travellers related them to the Anglo-Saxon King.

Orosius supplied as much information concerning general history, as an English student would usually require. The History of *Venerable Bede,* also rendered into Anglo-Saxon by Alfred, instructed the learner in the annals of his own country. In this work, Alfred did not depart from his original; and we must regret, that no such original anecdotes as diversified the pages of the king's "hand-book" have found their place in his "Ecclesiastical History." Still, considered merely as a version, the idiomatic richness of the style gives it great beauty; and as it is translated from the most trustworthy and accurate of the writers of the Middle Ages, so is it the earliest history of any of the states formed during the Middle Ages which can be read in the language of the people to whom it relates; for the "Saxon Chronicle" is of a subsequent period.

In the "Consolations of Philosophy," *Boethius* attempted, and not unsuccessfully, to adorn the lessons of revelation by the imagery of the classical age, and to imbue the doctrines of Plato with the better spirit of Christianity. Alfred appears to have delighted in his task. First, he interpreted the "Book-Latin" *word for word.* Having thoroughly mastered the meaning, he then explained the text *sense for sense,* "in the English phrase." The narratives taken from Ancient Mythology, such as the story of Orpheus and Euridice, and interspersed in the dialogue of Boethius, are expanded by Alfred into pleasing tales, such as the Glee-man recited during the intervals of his song. In expounding the "metres" of Boethius, Alfred took a wider range; and his paraphrases, though they preserve the leading thoughts of the "Book Latin," contain so many of the king's own ideas, and are adorned with so many flowers of Anglo-Saxon poetry, that if we describe them as original compositions, we shall only assign to them the rank which they deserve.

A selection of extracts from the "*Confessions of St. Augustine*," the "*Pastoral Instructions of St. Gregory*," and the Dialogues composed by that Pope, also form a portion of the Latin Library translated by Alfred, and are yet existing. His other works are no longer extant; and we must lament the loss of his Apologues, of "wonderful sweetness," which seem to have been a collection of Esopian Fables, imitated from Phædrus, or perhaps from some other of the collections into which these Eastern parables had been transfused.

Oxford claims, or rather has claimed, Alfred as the founder of her University. This pretension cannot be established by satisfactory evidence, though the crypt or vaulting under the church of St. Peter bears the name of the learned Grimbald, by whom it is said to have been constructed. Schools, however, were founded and endowed by Alfred. But his own example, and his own authority, were more efficacious than any other teacher's could have been. He insisted that his "Ministers," or the persons whom he employed, should endeavour to obtain due knowledge; and, in case of non-compliance, he deprived them of the offices which they held. Aldermen and mayors and governors were forced to go to school, to them a grievous penance, rather than give up their emoluments and their command. Those who were too old to learn, or so utterly unfit for letters as to render

Tower of Oxford Castle.

Abbot Elfnoth and St. Augustine, Archbishop of Canterbury.

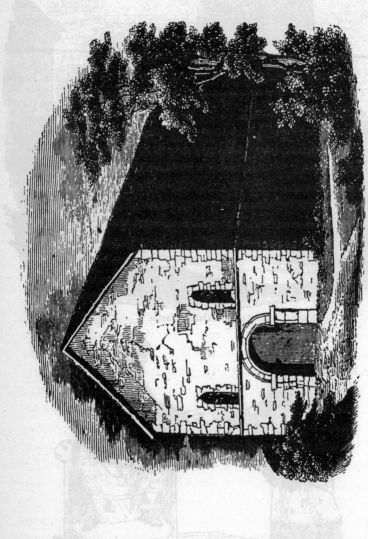

Kingston Chapel, St. Mary.

Abbot Ælfnoth and St. Augustine, Archbishop of Canterbury.

their case hopeless, were allowed to find substitutes; a son, or a near kinsman, or, failing both, a vassal, or even a slave, who was to learn in the place of his principal. This appears, at first, to be a whimsical, and somewhat despotic regulation : but if we consider it as intended to supply a succession of persons, qualified by education to render themselves useful to the community, we may have reason to admire his liberality and his wisdom.

Travelling, in ancient times, was very different from what it is at the present day; coaches and carriages were not invented, and the only vehicles which went upon wheels were carts and waggons; and these so heavy and clumsy, that there is not a farmer in the country who would use the like of them.   When people wished to go any distance, they were forced to ride all the way upon horseback; so those who were sick or infirm could hardly ever leave their houses.   You could not even change your horse at different stages; when the animal was tired, you were obliged to stop till he had rested; and if he fell lame, or died, then you were forced to buy another—that is, if you could,—for sometimes the inhabitants would refuse to deal with you, and then you could not get on at all.   Perhaps you would think, " Well, but at all events, a strong healthy man, with a good horse, could travel very pleasantly, and go a long way without encountering much difficulty."   And so he might, provided he could always be sure of finding a good road; but that was not by any means certain,—in those times there were very few roads upon which one could travel with safety.   The wise Romans made excellent roads, extending through all parts of their empire; and some of them can yet be traced in England, running along as straight as an arrow; one of these is Watling-street, so often mentioned in history: but after the fall of the Roman empire, their roads were neglected, and they fell into decay, and the traveller could hardly proceed without great danger, or, at least, without great fatigue. All at once your horse plunged into a marsh, or you came to a river, and the bridge was broken down; and when you tried to ford the stream, your horse might get out of his depth, and then he and his rider would be nearly drowned. Sometimes the traveller had to pass through a dark forest, full of ravenous bears and wolves; and, when he came to the end of his day's journey, instead of putting up at a comfortable inn, he was often compelled to stretch his cloak on the damp earth, in some wretched hut, or on the broken pavement of a haunted, ruined temple, open to the starless sky. And, what was worst, the kings and princes were almost always at war with each other, and a stranger was constantly liable to be plundered and seized, or put to death by the contending parties.

Such were the dangers of the land. Those of the sea were equally appalling, though of another kind. The ancient vessels were not fine large ships, floating like castles on the sea; but small, frail barks, with one deck, and incapable of containing any great stores. The navigators had no notion of geography: if, by any accident, the voyage was of protracted length, the crew might be starved. But the chief difficulty arose from their ignorance of the compass. Although it was well known that the magnet attracted iron, yet the property which the magnetized needle possesses, of constantly turning towards the north, was not then discovered. The mariners, if they once lost sight of the coast, could only guide themselves by the position of the sun, and of the fixed stars; and a cloudy day, followed by a cloudy night, would utterly confound them in their path over the trackless ocean. Under such circumstances, the intercourse of the Anglo-Saxons with foreign nations was necessarily very limited; and countries to which we can now transport ourselves with great ease, could not then be visited, unless the traveller was prepared to encounter much hardship and peril.

King Alfred was very desirous to encourage the resort, to England, of foreigners, from whom he could obtain any important information. One of these was Audher. He had attempted to ascertain how far the continent of Europe extended towards the North Pole; in his "skiff," he had coasted all along the northern coast of Lapland, and ventured among the wild men of Finland; and when he came to England, he related all that he had seen; and Alfred, as I have observed, inserted the narrative of this voyage in his translation of Orosius, in which we may read it at the present day. Another of Alfred's subjects, whose name was Wulstan, undertook a voyage to the Baltic, and sailed round that sea: and when he returned, he also gave an account to Alfred of all the strange nations whom he had visited, and this account the king inserted in the same volume. Other persons were sent by Alfred to distant countries, and from them he obtained a description of Bulgaria, and Sclavonia, and Bohemia, and Germany, and of the mountains and rivers of these countries, and of the nations by whom they were inhabited.

In this manner did Alfred satisfy his desire for knowledge; but he made greater exertions for a higher object, and in order to help those who were in need. You must know, that in India, on the coasts of Malabar and Coromandel, there were many towns and districts peopled

by Syrians, who, though living under the government of
the heathen Rajahs, were Christians, and whose ancestors
had been settled there from time immemorial.   How,
and in what manner they first came there, is not exactly
ascertained.   It is believed by some, that, when the
command of preaching the Gospel to all nations was
given to the Apostles, St. Thomas fulfilled this precept
by journeying to Hindostan ; and that these Syrians are
descended from the disciples and the faithful by whom
he was accompanied.   But, at whatever period they may
have been placed in India, they continued true and
steadfast in the faith.   The Hindoos, amongst whom
they dwelt, worshipped their hideous idols with many
heads and arms, and surrounded by serpents and skulls ;
but the Syrians had preserved the word of God ; and it
was a great delight to them, amidst the darkness of
surrounding nations, to be able to read the Bible in their
own forefathers' language—the same which Christ spoke
when he was upon earth,—and which they still continue
to employ.

From the many travellers who visited the court of
Alfred, he had heard of the existence of these Syrian
Christians ; and he determined to send the Bishop of
Sherburn, whose name was Swithelm, to give them help.
The Chronicles do not tell us what was the precise
distress which the Syrians then sustained.   Perhaps they
were oppressed by the heathen ; but however that may
be, Alfred despatched Swithelm on this very long
pilgrimage.   When we wish to go to India, our ships
double the Cape of Good Hope, and so proceed to Hindostan : but in the time of Alfred this passage was
unknown, because sailors believed that the Continent of
Africa extended to the South Pole ; and travellers were,

therefore, compelled to journey the whole way by land —a long and toilsome road it must have been. But Swithelm was stout-hearted, and not only bore King Alfred's gifts to India, but returned in safety with the presents which the Hindo-Syrians had sent as tokens of their gratitude; gems, and precious spices of sweet odour. And Alfred's fame was greatly increased by this enterprise.

We are told by Alfred's biographer, that his activity pervaded every department of his government. If it became necessary to provide a fleet fit to encounter the Danish pirates, Alfred's skill improved the building of the vessels. Cities were founded and fortified by Alfred; castles and palaces raised; and whatever, in his estimation, could tend to the comfort, the civilization, or the defence of his people, he sedulously fostered and maintained.

Alfred managed his affairs with much regularity. His revenue was exactly apportioned and allotted; and one clear moiety of the money paid into his treasury was applied in works of charity and piety. He gave eight hours in each day to sleep and refreshment, eight to the affairs of his kingdom, and eight to study and prayer. This arrangement, however, can only have been applicable to the intervals of peace; and few were the years during which he enjoyed such leisure as might enable him to follow the tranquil employments which gladdened his heart. Alfred's body never enjoyed rest or ease. He was afflicted with an excruciating internal disease, which the medical skill of his "leeches" could neither alleviate nor heal. Very frequently he endured the most intense torment; and if the pain chanced to slumber, the transient interval of diminished suffering was embittered by the fear and horror of impending agony. And yet, thus racked and tortured, he was so supported by the hand which afflicted him, that he never lost the strength of his spirit, or desisted from the task to which he had been called.

Alfred's character, with all these virtues, did not approach to that ideal perfection, which has been sometimes pourtrayed by his panegyrists. Certainly, he began with good intentions, but he did not always bear them in mind; and during the first portion of his reign he was proud, tyrannical, and almost as much hated as he was afterwards beloved. Still, he possessed within him the only germ of real improvement—the consciousness of his own entire insufficiency;—and the same tendency, which, before he yielded to the temptations of authority, had rendered him unwilling to accept the throne, enabled him afterwards to reform from his errors. The adventures and misfortunes which he sustained during his seclusion in the Isle of Athelney, appear to have been the means of bringing him to a lively sense of his faults and a better faith in the protection of Providence. Many failings, however, adhered to him. He continued more fond of warfare than was consistent with the duty of a Christian monarch. Though chastened and subdued, his temper occasionally led him to despotism; and his love of order and justice sometimes degenerated almost into cruelty. Yet, after making every allowance for such of Alfred's faults as may be discovered in the accounts which we possess, and still greater deductions for the faults and sins of which the memory has been buried with him, we are justified in asserting that he affords a brighter model for the character of a good king, than can be found in any other age or realm.

It is one of the most instructive lessons to be deduced from Alfred's life, to remark that he did not fall into the snares prepared for him by his taste and intellectual talents.   Carried but one step further, his love for splendour might have rendered him an oppressive ruler, grinding the faces of his subjects for the purpose of ministering to his rude magnificence.   His poetical taste was as likely to have misled him in various ways.   When the harp went round at a festival, the horn of mead or metheglin circulated quite as freely, and the song of the Northmen often became the pretext for intoxication or worse vices.   In like manner, the king's great affection for "book latin" might, if unwisely indulged, have induced him to neglect the needful toils of his station, for the baneful luxury of idle study.   But Alfred really and truly sought wisdom from her only source; and her varied gifts were employed by him in strict and conscientious furtherance of the duties which he was bound to perform.

The first and most imperative of these duties he well knew to be the establishment of good laws, and the administration of justice.   Ethelbert had reduced the traditionary legal customs of the Kentish Jutes into writing.   Ina, a king of Wessex, Offa, of Mercia, and other Anglo-Saxon monarchs, had also from time to time promulgated their "Dooms" or Judgments, which they established, fixing definite rules and regulations in the place of uncertain usage.   From these statutes, Alfred selected such articles or chapters as appeared most eligible, others he amended, and some were wholly rejected.

Alfred's code, thus produced, differs in no essential respect from the jurisprudence of his predecessors.   On this head we can speak positively; for the greater part of the laws from whence it was compiled are yet extant; and all the variations arising from insertion, alteration, or omission, do not, when taken together, afford any peculiar characteristic. Nor can we, upon mere perusal of the text, discover those excellences which so endeared Alfred to the English, that, in after times, all the more important legal institutions were ascribed to his wisdom. The division of England into shires and hundreds,— Trial by Jury,—the *Frankpledge*, or the regulation by which the lower orders of people were formed into companies or bands of ten or more, mutually responsible for each other's appearance, in case any one was accused of a crime—have all been considered as established by Alfred, though he really had no claim to their invention. But the fact is, that if any part of the legal fabric, of which the origin was unknown, possessed peculiar utility, it was supposed to be Alfred's, on the mere strength of his general reputation; just as virtuosi fancy they trace the hand of Phidias or Praxiteles in a statue of peculiar beauty, but of which the history cannot be ascertained.

Alfred did not make any alteration whatever in the laws and usages of his realms. He abstained from introducing novelties; he durst not venture to do so; and, as he tells us himself, he was afraid to innovate, lest the new laws enacted by him might, in their turn, be rejected by posterity. Without doubt, Alfred must have seen that many portions of the laws of the Anglo-Saxons were defective; but he judged—and we have his own words before us, grounded upon such judgment—that it was better to permit the continuance of a defective law, than to destroy the foundation upon which all laws depend—respect for established authority—which sudden changes, even for the better, are apt to undermine.

The first principle which appears to have guided Alfred, was a tolerant endurance of institutions, not theoretically perfect, but which could not be altered without the chance of greater evil. He willingly sacrificed the credit of seeming to be wiser than his ancestors. And, instead of confiding in his own talent for legislation, he shrunk from the endeavour of imposing his opinions upon posterity.

The second principle which guided Alfred in his legal government, was an unremitting endeavour to supply any deficiency in the theory of his laws, by the equitable and ready dispensation of them in practice. He directed all his efforts to the just and proper administration of the law in court, rather than to its amendment in the "Doom-book." Alfred was the defender of the fatherless and the widow, protecting the poor against all rapine and oppression. All judgments given by the magistrates, to whom he delegated the power of judicature, were carefully reviewed and examined by him. If he discovered that judgment had been perverted by hatred or malice, or that the scales of justice had been swayed by bribes, he punished the offender with great severity. According to the ancient tradition of London, he even caused forty-four judges, who had given false judgments, to be hanged in one year as murderers. This fact, perhaps, is not warranted by Anglo-Saxon authority, but the vigilance which he exercised is fully testified by Asser, his affectionate biographer; and if the judge had erred, not wilfully and corruptly, but merely from ignorance and neglect, Alfred then reproved him for his fault, and warned him that such conduct would risk the loss of the authority which he had abused. Thus, instead of introducing new machinery, which, however improved, would not have answered in ignorant hands, he made that which he had work well, by his unremitting care and vigilance.

The third and chief principle which actuated Alfred, was his endeavour to impart the spirit of the law of God to the temporal legislation of his kingdom. Alfred's statutes are prefaced by the Decalogue, to which he has added a selection from the Mosaic precepts, and the canons of the first Apostolic council. "Do these," he continues; "and if these commands be obeyed, no other doom-book will be required." We commonly say that Christianity is a part of the law of the land. Alfred had a clearer perception of the station which religion should possess in a Christian commonwealth. He would have wished to render Christianity the law itself. The necessity for any human law exists simply and solely in proportion to our neglect of the Divine law; and if we were enabled to write that law in our hearts, nothing whatever would be left for human legislation to perform.

Chapter X.

Edward " the Elder"—Succession contested by Ethelwald, Son of Ethelbald—Edward prevails—Ethelfleda, the " Lady of Mercia"—Mercia occupied by Edward—Submission of North- umbria and East Anglia—Danes, Scots, Britons, acknow- ledge Edward's Supremacy—Athelstane—His Character— His Wars against the Britons—Reduction of West Wales and of the City of Exeter—All Britain south of the Humber submits to him—Sihtric, King of Northumbria, married to Athelstane's Sister—Commotions in Northumbria after the death of Sihtric—Scots and Danes unite against Athelstane —they are defeated in the great Battle of Brunnaburgh— Athelstane's reputation—Alliances of his family with foreign Princes—Edgiva married to Charles the Simple, King of France — Expulsion of the Carlovingian Dynasty by the Capets.

UPON the death of Alfred, the succession was contested between his son Edward, usually called Edward the elder, and Ethelwald, the son of Ethelbald (A.D. 901). If the law of primogeniture could have been considered as firmly established, Ethelwald, being the representative of the elder brother, would have been clearly entitled to the throne; but Edward was the son of the king last in possession, and his right was acknowledged by the West Saxons, if not by the other English and Saxon nations. The pretender, however, for so we must call Ethelwald, had a strong party; he took possession of Twineham and Wimburn, and throwing himself into the latter town, he caused the entrances to be secured, and professed that he would either conquer or die. This declaration, however, seems to have been made for the purpose of misleading

his opponents; for in the course of the night, he stole out
of the town, and bent his way towards the host of the
Danes in Northumbria.   Edward, who had encamped
with his army in the neighbourhood, pursued the pretender with all possible speed, but he escaped the chase,
and reaching the Danes in safety, they hailed him as
their king (A.D. 904-905). Ethelwald had married a nun,
contrary to the ecclesiastical law; and I think it is
implied that she had eloped with him out of her convent.
This lady, who followed her husband, was pursued with
equal pertinacity by Edward, and she also had the good
fortune to escape. Ethelwald governed with success and
power.   He sailed with his fleet unto Essex, and the
East Saxons submitted to him. The Danes of East Anglia
then joined his standard, and indeed all the English
population of "Danelagh" entered heartily into his
cause.   The Anglo-Saxons inhabiting the provinces
occupied by the Danes began to unite with their invaders.
The English, in general, had been so little accustomed to
a regular government, that such kind of lawless liberty
as they could enjoy under the protection of the Danish
"holdas," or chieftains, was more grateful to them than
any advantages arising from tranquillity.

Edward, throughout the course of his reign, gave great
proofs of warlike skill. Ethelwald, the pretender, and
his followers, invaded and plundered Mercia (A.D. 905).
Edward immediately assembled his army, and took a
strong position on the frontiers of East Anglia; but the
Kentish men, though seven times summoned to join the
troops of Wessex, refused to obey. Edward's army
was surrounded by the Danes, and a desperate conflict ensued. Ethelwald was killed, together with the
Danish king Eric, and many other Norwegian and

Danish "holdas" of fame; but the loss was greater on
the part of Wessex, and the Danes remained the masters
of the "field of slaughter." Edward, however, escaped
unhurt, and the Danes, on their part, were not unwilling
to conclude a peace, or rather a truce, which they
observed as long as it was convenient for them to do so;
that is to say, until Reginald the son of Guthred landed
in Northumbria. Niel and Sihtric, his two brothers,
appear to have continued in the country, probably as
chieftains subordinate to Alfred, after Guthred's death;
and Reginald speedily captured the city of York, and
occupied the greater part of Bernicia. Such of the
Anglian chieftains as resisted him were expelled, and the
best part of the patrimony of St. Cuthbert was divided
between Scula and Olave, the latter a "holda" of great
valour and ferocity. Concurrently with these transactions, was the invasion of Mercia by the Danes (A.D. 911),
who advanced as far as the borders of the Severn; but
they were encountered by Edward, who obtained a most
decisive and unequivocal victory.

In the following year died Ethelred, the Ealdorman of
Mercia, who had governed that kingdom with royal
power (A.D. 912). Upon his death, Edward took
possession of London and Oxford : all the other portions
of his dominions devolved upon Ethelfleda, the daughter
of Alfred. The "lady," as she was emphatically styled,
possessed the sturdy valour ascribed to the Bradamante
of Ariosto; the whole character of the "bold virago,"
as the monkish writers call her, resembles that of a
heroine of romance; and Ethelfleda's wisdom was not
inferior to her valour. The successes of the Danes had
been much facilitated by their system of fortification.
This plan Ethelfleda emulated and improved; every

point that could be rendered defensible was secured by her. Worcester, her capital, had been fortified in the life-time of Ethelred. Shiregate, Tamworth, Stafford, Eddisbury, Warwick, Cherbury, Runcorn, were successively protected by the ramparts which she raised. The attack of Breccanmere—supposed to be Brecknock,—where she captured the wife of a Welsh or British king, was an expedition displaying her singular spirit and activity. But of far more moment was her recovering of Derby and Leicester : she thus regained important members of the ancient Mercian territory ; and the submission of the Danish host, stationed in and near these towns, confirmed her authority.

Ethelfleda died soon after this last success ; and the dominion of Mercia descended to her daughter and heiress, Elfwina (A.D. 920). The Chroniclers notice the right of Elfwina so precisely, as to leave no doubt concerning her claim ; and the fact is of considerable value, in shewing, that, contrary to the practice of other Teutonic nations, the sovereign authority amongst the Anglo-Saxons might descend to a female ; or, according to the Anglo-Saxon expression, which the French have adopted, "fall to the *spindle side*." In this instance, however, the weaker heir was compelled to yield to a more powerful opponent, and one from whom no enmity could have been feared. Elfwina was conducted as a captive into Mercia, by her uncle Edward, who was engaged in a successful warfare against the Danes ; and we do not hear anything more concerning her in history.

Edward had been gaining ground against the Danes, and following Ethelfleda's example, he secured his conquests by erecting strongholds (A.D. 921-924). He

began in Essex, where, as the Chronicle tells us, he
"timbered" the Burgh of Witham.   This little, dull
town was once a Roman station : the walls of the Preto-
rium may yet be seen ; and the expressions employed by
the Chronicle seem to shew that Edward's fortifications
consisted of a strong stoccade round the ancient line of
defences.   Here the people submitted to him.   Bedford
and Northampton followed.   After some fluctuations of
fortune, he gained Colchester and Maldon ; and the
result of these conquests was, that all the Danish chiefs
south of the Welland, and of East Anglia, and of Essex,
and of the adjoining parts, became his vassals, and
submitted to him as their lord.

Mercia was equally obedient.   Ethelfleda's subjects
"turned to him," and accepted him as their sovereign ;
but the kingdom still continued as distinct from Wessex
as it had ever been, though both states were now united
under one sovereign.   All the kings of the Britons—
Howel the good—and Cledauc—and Edwall—became
Edward's liege men, and rendered homage, together
with all their people.   North of the Humber, the same
subjection was yielded to Edward by the Danes and the
Angles.   The Britons of Strathclyde and Cambria, and
the men of Galloway, gladly followed their example : the
king of the Scots, and all his people, joined in this submission.   All accepted him as their "father, lord, and
protector," and Edward was now enabled to claim the
supremacy of all the various races then inhabiting the
island of Britain.

Edward died after a successful and glorious reign,
having appointed his son Athelstane as his successor
(A.D. 925).   The mother of Athelstane was only a shepherd's daughter, and I am much afraid that she was not a

lawful wife, but only a concubine. The name of "Athelstane,"* signifies "gem," or "precious stone;" and it was, perhaps, given to him on account of his personal beauty. Athelstane was tall and comely; and when he became king, he was accustomed to plait his long flaxen tresses with threads of shining gold. He displayed talents and sense far beyond his years; and if Edward had thus elevated him to the throne, he had obeyed the wishes, or rather the directions of Alfred, who saw in Athelstane the future hopes of Britain.

At a very early age, Athelstane was ennobled by the hand of his grandfather, Alfred, from whom he received the insignia of his honours—a purple robe, a baldrick studded with gems, and the national weapon, the Saxon *seax* or falchion, in a sheath of gold; and from this time, according to the very ancient usages of the Teutons, he enjoyed the rights and privileges of an independent warrior.

About this period of his life, seeking adventures, perhaps, he sailed over the North Sea, and visited the opposite shores of the Baltic. Here he became acquainted with the old Norsk tongue, and acquired great fondness for the usages and customs of the Northmen. It is said that, during the residence of Athelstane in Scandinavia, he formed a friendship with Guthrun, which afterwards aided the latter in acquiring the kingdom of East Anglia, as a dependency of the English crown.

Athelstane was thirty years of age when his father expired; and the Mercians immediately recognised him as their king. The nobles of Wessex assembled at Winchester, followed the example of Mercia without opposition, and Athelstane was crowned with great pomp and

* *Æthel*, noble—*Stan*, stone.

splendour at Kingston-upon-Thames. Kingston was so called, because it was considered peculiarly as being the "*Cynges tun*," or the king's town; and, after the coronation of the Kings of Wessex, they took possession of their kingdom by standing upon a great stone or fragment of rock, which, at no very distant period, was preserved in the churchyard. An ancient chapel, ornamented with the statues of the Anglo-Saxon kings, was a memorial of these inaugurations; but in the last century, 1735, it fell down from sheer old age.

Athelstane encountered some opposition when the nobles of Wessex deliberated upon his recognition, pursuant to his father's will (A.D. 925-926). The leader of this sedition, as it is called, was one Alfred, probably of the royal family, who with his adherents had plotted to seize Athelstane, and to put out his eyes. The conspiracy was detected; but Alfred denied his guilt; and according to the Anglo-Saxon jurisprudence, he was allowed to clear himself by oath, of the accusations laid to his charge. Such proceedings usually took place before a bishop; in this case it was adjudged, on account of the grave nature of the crime, that Alfred should appear before the Pope of Rome, and take the oath in his presence. He did so accordingly; and in the "Basilica" of St. Peter, Alfred solemnly swore that he was innocent. Forthwith, he dropped senseless before the altar, and three days afterwards he died in the English college, a building erected for the reception of the Anglo-Saxon pilgrims or travellers, and which continued to be appropriated to the same purpose, until the sixteenth century.

The sequel of this conspiracy is more lamentable. At a considerable distance of time (A.D. 933), Edwin, the brother of Athelstane, was accused of having combined with the party or faction of Alfred against the king. In vain did he declare his innocence. Athelstane was resolved upon the death of his brother; and Edwin and his armour-bearer, the latter being also implicated in the accusation, were forced into an old leaky boat, without sail, oar, or rudder; and the crazy bark being pushed out to sea, they were exposed to the fury of the waves. Such a mode of punishment was not uncommon in the middle ages; it appears to have been one of the many modes by which people often attempt to remove from themselves the responsibility of cruel acts, by interposing an intermediate agent. By good fortune, the boat drifted on shore, and the life of the armour-bearer, or esquire, was saved, but the Atheling Edwin, unable to bear up against the horrors of his situation, and dreading the slow torture of hunger, had thrown himself into the sea. Athelstane, when it was too late, discovered that he had been deceived by false witnesses, and during seven years he did penance for his misdeed.

As the assent which the English had given to the accession of Athelstane (A.D. 926-927) was due, in great measure, to the expectations which had been formed concerning his prowess, he engaged, as soon as he was settled upon the throne, in a succession of warlike enterprises against the other nations who dwelt in Britain. Thus doing, he sustained his character, and he also gave employment to those who might otherwise have been inclined to become his enemies; many a sword which would have been raised against him, was turned against the Britons and the Scots.

You will recollect that Alfred and Edward were respectively acknowledged as the supreme sovereigns of the British chieftains. But the Britons, anxious to regain their long-lost liberty, were constantly rising against their invaders. Ill-fated was this opposition to the Saxon power. Athelstane brought all his forces against the inhabitants of Wales; and Edwall Voel, king of Gwynnedd, was soon under the necessity of surrendering his dominions to the conqueror.

Athelstane, however, had too much generosity, and perhaps too much judgment, to deprive the Briton of his dominions. " Better it is," said he, " to make a king, than to be a king;"—and Edwall was restored. But he, and all the other Welsh princes, were compelled to acknowledge themselves as the vassals of Athelstane. Assembled before him, when he held his court at Hereford, they performed homage to the Saxon monarch. A heavy tribute was imposed upon them. Twenty pounds weight of gold, and three hundred pounds of fine silver, were to be paid yearly and every year into the *Hoard* (that is the Anglo-Saxon word) or treasury of the " King of London." Five and twenty thousand beeves were to be driven annually into his pastures. To these were added the swiftest hounds and keenest hawks which a nation of huntsmen could select, as the token of honour and subjection to their superior. And furthermore, it was agreed, that all the territory between the Severn and the Wye, parts of which still appear to have been held by Welsh chieftains, should be wholly united to the Mercian kingdom.

Such was the fate of the kingdoms of Gwynnedd, Deheubarth, and Powys, the modern Principality of Wales, which the Saxons called " North Wales;"* and we must now turn to the events of " West Wales," where the Britons were still the prevailing people, at least in

* See *Map* II.

numbers. In Somerset and Dorset, and part of Damnonia,—as far as the Exe,—the state of the country was
like the Welsh Marches, which I have before described,
in which the gentry are Englishmen and speak English,
while the country-folks are Welsh and speak the Welsh
language. Hence the districts which I have mentioned
were called the "Wealh cyn," the "Welsh kind," or
"Wallish-ry."* As you approached the west, the Britons
retained more power, and the ancient city of Exeter, or
"*Caer Isc*," was inhabited jointly by Britons and by
Saxons. When I say that these nations inhabited the
city jointly, I do not suppose that Rhys the Briton dwelt
in one house in the Cheap, or High Street, and that
Brightwyn the Saxon was his next door neighbour; but
that Exeter consisted of two Wards, or Divisions, one of
which was appropriated to the English or Saxons, whilst
the other remained in the possession of the Britons.
Partitions of this nature have been, and still are, very
frequent, when a country has been conquered by a nation
which refuses to mix with the original inhabitants.
Kilkenny, in Ireland, thus consisted of two towns, an
English town and an Irish town.

As far as we can judge, the Exeter men, Britons and
Saxons, lived upon good terms with one another, and
the city was a kind of little republic, like the free cities
of Italy or Germany; or like Marseilles, which, though
enclavéed in France, had all the rights of a free state,
until it was seized by the French kings. And this, I
think, may have been the case with many of the other
great towns and cities of England, which probably enjoyed their franchises and liberties before any one of our

* I have coined this term, from the analogous one of *Irishry*, as employed
by the writers upon Ireland of the Elizabethean age.

Anglo-Saxon kings had a crown upon his head, or a sceptre in his hand.

Athelstane having reduced the Britons on the northern banks of the estuary of the Severn, now directed his attacks against the Welsh or Britons of Damnonia, or Devon and Cornwall. The Britons were easily expelled from Caer Isc; Athelstane surrounded that city with strong walls and towers built of hewn-stone; and it became a fortress to bridle and overawe his newly acquired territory. All the Damnonians of any consequence were driven beyond the Tamar, into the present county of Cornwall, where they soon sunk into entire subjection to the Anglo-Saxon power. Yet the Britons were so unmixed with their conquerors, that they kept their ancient speech until the reign of Henry VIII., when it gradually became obsolete. In the reign of Queen Anne, it was known only in a few villages near the Land's End. The children, as they grew up, learnt English; and as the old Cornish folks died off, the language gradually expired with them; so that towards the middle of the reign of King George III., one Dolly Pentrath, an old fishwife, who resided about three miles from Mousehole, near Penzance, was the only surviving individual in the world, who could converse in the tongue of the ancient Damnonian Britons; which tongue, however, she put to a very bad use, since she principally employed it in swearing and grumbling when she could not get a good price for her fish, or in scolding when she was offended.

At the present time, the names of fields and towns, hills and rivers, in Cornwall, are the only memorials of the British language, whose extinction cannot be contemplated without sentiments approaching to regret.

The most useful political virtues arise from an honest feeling of nationality ; and no badge of nationality is more innocent and efficient than the cherished possession of an ancient, and at the same time, peculiar language.

Thus did Britain, south of the Humber, become subject to Athelstane's supremacy ; and we must now view his conquests in the northern regions of the island (A.D. 925-927). Athelstane's disposition seems naturally to have inclined him to peace. He was just in judgment, affable and gracious in his manner, fond of magnificence, and probably of luxury and ease ; and by bestowed one of his sisters in marriage upon Sihtric, King of the Danes, he gave a pledge of concord and amity. In the time of Athelstane, the dominions of the Northumbrian Dane extended as far northward as Edinburgh. Beyond the Frith of Forth dwelt the Scots, whose king, Constantine, was much inclined to cast off the vassalage upon the English crown. Indeed, all the Northmen were impatient of the government of the south, and the unfortunate death of Sihtric put the whole country in commotion. The Northumbrian chieftains assembled, and urged Godfrey, the son of Sihtric, to renounce his allegiance to Athelstane (A.D. 927-934) ;—"for in the old time," said they, "we were free, and never served the southron king." And they seized on all the castles and strongholds, and cast down the Dragon of Wessex, and unfurled the Raven, the Danish banner. Constantine and the Scots immediately made common cause with the Danes; but the alliance did not avail them. The Danish chieftains were driven beyond the sea. The country of the Scots was laid waste. Athelstane's fleets plundered the shores; his troops advanced as far as Caithness; the king of Scots surrendering his crown, received it back in vassalage, and he was also compelled to deliver his son into the power of Athelstane, as a hostage for the true and faithful performance of the conditions which the conqueror imposed. Olave, or, as our historians write his name, Anlaf, another Danish chieftain, had by this time conquered the city of Dublin, and obtained the preponderance over the native chieftains of Ireland. The Eastmen, as these invaders were called by the natives, established themselves firmly on the shores, and Constantine of Scotland, eager to release himself from subjection to Athelstane, excited Anlaf to return to Britain, and regain the territories which Sihtric had held. All the *Cymri* of the north, the Britons of Strathclyde, and Reged, and Cumbria, were ruled by a Scottish prince; and little persuasion was needed to induce them to enter into the confederacy. Edwall, the king of Gwynnedd, was quite as ready. The war cry was heard on every side. The Danish and Norwegian pirates assembled from all points of the horizon, rejoicing in the anticipated slaughter; and a fleet of six hundred and twenty vessels, under the command of Anlaf, all filled with chosen warriors, entered the mouth of the Humber. The "heah-gerefas," or governors, whom Athelstane had placed in the country, were speedily defeated : one was slain, and the survivor escaping with great difficulty, bore the disastrous tidings to the Anglo-Saxon king. In this emergency, Athelstane was not deserted by his accustomed policy and courage. Like a skilful general, he opened negociations with the enemy, so as to divert their attention, at the same time that he continued his route towards the seat of war.

Athelstane's march was undertaken with such expedition and secrecy (A.D. 938), that his camp was fixed at

Brunnaburgh, in the neighbourhood of the army of Anlaf, before the latter could be aware of his approach. The Dane, thus taken by surprise, was extremely anxious to obtain some information concerning the forces of the Anglo-Saxon kings. Imitating the stratagem of Alfred, he put on the garb of a bard or scalld, and with his harp in his hand, he boldly advanced into the leaguer of the enemy. He gained access to the royal presence, without any difficulty. Athelstane was a known patron of these itinerant professors of music and song—he encouraged them with some money and much praise ; and he was then sitting at a banquet with his chieftains. Anlaf danced, and harped, and sang ; and when the feast was done, a purse well filled with silver coin was slipped into the hand of the disguised invader, as a gracious token that the king was pleased with his performance, and also as a hint that he might withdraw, for Athelstane and his generals were about to hold a council of war.

Anlaf gladly obeyed : with the quickness of a military partisan he had well noted the situation of the royal tent, and he quickly stole out of the camp. But though the Dane had not thought it beneath his dignity to array himself in the dress of a harper, yet he could not submit to retain the earnings of his assumed character. The purse of silver was odious to Anlaf; he could not bear to keep it about him ;—and as the act would have excited suspicion if he had thrown the money from him, and more, perhaps, if he had given it away, he buried all the coin in the ground.

Anlaf quitted the camp in safety, but he had been discovered, and he might have been betrayed. He had been recognised by one who, at a former time, had

fought under his standard; and when Anlaf was fairly
out of reach, this warrior repaired to Athelstane, and
disclosed the name of his recent visitor. The king re-
proached him with want of fidelity. " Nay," quoth the
honest soldier, "by the same oath of fealty which binds
me to thee, O king! was I once bound to Anlaf; and
had I betrayed him, with equal justice mightest thou
have expected treachery from me. But hear my counsel:
whilst awaiting further reinforcements, take away thy
tent from the spot upon which it now stands, and thus
mayest thou ward off the blow of thine enemy." Athelstane followed this advice, and directed his tent to be
pitched in another part of the field, but without disclos-
ing the cause of the removal. In the evening, more
troops arrived; and the tent of a bishop was raised on
the green-sward which had been occupied by the royal
pavilion.

At midnight, a bold and sudden assault was made
upon the Anglo-Saxons by the Dane and his army, who
surrounded the camp. Anlaf himself, and his most
trusty followers, directed the first attack against the tent
which had replaced the royal pavilion. The seeming
scalld had marked the fatal spot with a sure eye;—all
within were slain; and, without doubt, he thought he
had secured the victory by the death of the Anglo-Saxon
king; but the tumult spread—Athelstane sprang from
his couch, and rallied and supported the alarmed soldiery,
who gathered round him. When the sun arose, the fury
of the battle had begun; and the conflict, which lasted
throughout the entire day, terminated in the total dis-
comfiture of the enemy. Five kings, and seven northern
Iarls or earls, fell in the strife. The combined army was
entirely routed—Constantine the Scot fled to the north,

mourning his fair-haired son, who perished in the slaughter. Anlaf, with a sad and scattered remnant of his forces, escaped to Ireland. Athelstane, the "lord of the West Saxons," the "giver of bracelets," was master of the field, and long was the battle of Brunnaburgh sung by the minstrel as the greatest triumph which had been gained by the Angles and the Saxons "since they crossed the broad and stormy sea."

This victory was so decisive, that, during the remainder of the reign of Athelstane, no enemy dared to rise up against him; his supremacy was acknowledged without contest, and his glory extended to distant realms.

Indeed, Athelstane had long held a distinguished station amongst the monarchs of Europe, and his relations with the various continental powers form a very singular and interesting portion of his history. Harold of Norway anxiously sought the friendship of Athelstane, and entrusted his son to the care of the ruler of Britain. Haco was educated in England; by the aid of England he succeeded to the Norwegian throne. He was extolled, and deservedly, for his good government, and the laws of Haco, the "foster son of Athelstane," are the earliest written specimens of the legislation of Scandinavia, and the best proof of the advantages derived by the Norwegian prince from his education at the court of the Anglo-Saxon king.

If ever a national antipathy was strongly marked, it was that which subsisted,—indeed in some measure it still subsists,—between the *Celtic* or *Cymric* nations and the *Saxon* or *English;* yet Athelstane overcame this feeling. The Northmen invaded Armorica; and the Britons of Gaul, flying from their new enemies, took refuge in the land of their ancestors. By Athelstane, these fugitives were hospitably received; he became the sponsor of the infant Alan, the grandson of the Breton sovereign; and, like the Norwegian Haco, the young prince of Armorica grew up in the hall of Athelstane. When he arrived at man's estate, he assembled the emigrant Britons (A.D. 937). A successful expedition placed Alan in possession of Dol and St. Brieu, and this foster son of Athelstane, like his Norwegian contemporary, was re-established upon the throne.

The sisters of Athelstane shared in the estimation acquired by their brother's conduct and success. Otho, the son of Henry, the Emperor of Germany, sought the hand of one of these noble ladies, and another became the consort of Louis, Duke of Acquitaine. These continental Princes might have matched themselves much nearer home, so that some strong and special inducement must have led to their union with the daughters of England.

About this time, France had fallen into a state of great disorder. The descendants of Charlemagne, who still continued to rule both Germany and France, had degenerated as much as those of Clovis (A.D. 887). Charles " le Gros" (*i. e.* the fat) had shown himself so deficient in the meanest of all qualifications of royalty, personal courage, that he was solemnly deposed in the diet of the German empire, and Arnolph, his nephew, elected in his stead. The French nobles followed their example (A.D. 887); and Eudo, Count of Paris, being supported by a powerful party, assumed the royal dignity. France, however, was constituted like Anglo-Saxon England. It was not a united kingdom, but a bundle of principalities, communities, and states, governed in tranquil times by one monarch; and, in times of disturbance, by as many as

could contend for the sovereign power. Eudo was not
recognised south of the Loire; and Raoul, or Rodolph,
acquired the kingdom of Burgundy, beyond the Jura, or
modern Switzerland, and its dependencies. Charles,
called the Simple, the son of Louis the Stammerer, otherwise called Louis the Lazy,—the people of those days
gave very uncourtly epithets to their kings,—and who,
after the expulsion of " Charles le Gros," was the lineal
representative and heir of Charlemagne, had taken refuge
in England to avoid the storms of the revolution. Here
he was hospitably received, and having espoused the fair
Edgiva, daughter of Edward and sister of Athelstane,
he continued a dependant upon the kindness or bounty
of the Anglo-Saxon nation. Eudo had not reigned very
long, when great discontent against him prevailed. The
young reader, no doubt, recollects Æsop's fable of the
frogs; and human nations under similar circumstances
often find that, after all, it is easier and more comfortable to live under a *King Log* than under a *King Stork*.
A deputation was therefore sent to England, for the purpose of recalling Charles the Simple (A.D. 893) : perhaps
as yet he had not quite deserved the name. Charles and
his English wife, in consequence, quitted this country.
Being supported by a strong party of nobles, he was
crowned king at Rheims (A.D. 896-898), and a compromise having been effected between him and Eudo, the
territory between the Seine and the Rhone was assigned
as his dominion ; and on the death of Eudo he became
king of the whole realm.

Charles the Simple was no coward; nor was he
deficient in the quality sometimes called " decision of
character," which is often the accompaniment of great
want of sense. " Who so bold as blind Bayard, who

never looks before he leaps,"—says the old proverb; and
those who are least qualified to meet any real peril, are
sometimes the most eager to rush into its jaws. Charles
the Simple had a favourite minister, one Hagano, who,
whether justly or unjustly, had rendered himself, as well
as his master, exceedingly odious to the whole French
nation. Disturbances arose : Charles the Simple was
kept out of the government during full seven months
(A.D. 920) ; but in a great council held at Soissons, the
nobles, after deliberating whether they should not wholly
expel him, as they had expelled Charles le Gros, contented themselves with allowing him to resume his reign,
—provided he would alter his mode of government, and
dismiss the obnoxious Hagano. Charles submitted for
a time, but much against his will; and when he thought
he could effect his purpose, he restored his favourite to
his former place and dignity. The anger of the French
nobles now knew no bounds : they assembled a great
council (A.D. 922), and elected Robert, "Duke of France,"
the brother of Eudo, as their king. Charles the Simple
forthwith arrayed his troops, and led them against
Robert, whom he slew in battle with his own hand.
Hugh the "Great," son of Robert, rallied his followers.
Charles the Simple was entirely defeated, and he fled
from the field ; but Humbert, the Count of Vermandois,
having agreed to co-operate with Raoul, Duke of Burgundy, he was imprisoned, first at Chateau Thierry, and
afterwards at Peronne, and died in captivity.

Raoul was chosen king, principally by the influence
of Hugh the Great, his brother-in-law, and crowned at
Soissons. Edgiva, who had so joyfully quitted England
when her husband was resolved to ascend the throne of
France, returned in sadness, with her infant son Louis,

to the country of her husband's exile. Hugh the Great, by whose influence Raoul had been raised to the royal dignity, possessed so much power, that he was often called "Rex Francorum," or King of the French; though he had no real claim to such a title; and as the means of securing his authority, he anxiously sought the friendship and alliance of our Athelstane. He visited London, offering rich gifts,—the sword of Constantine the Great, and the lance of Charlemagne; by which, as it was believed, victory had always been ensured to the fabled emperor of chivalry. Hugh's main object was to obtain one of the sisters of Athelstane in marriage. Hugh probably thought that Athelstane would be inclined to support the pretensions of his nephew, Louis; but that if he, the "Rex Francorum," could have another sister of Athelstane sitting by his side as his consort, the Anglo-Saxon king might be inclined to overlook the claims of the son of Edgiva; and Athelstane acceded to his request and desire.

On the death of Raoul, the royal government ceased for a time amongst the French. Each count, and each duke, and each baron, ruled his own territories as he best might; and the ancient cities, which had been Roman colonies, seem to have administered their affairs by their own magistrates. Competitors there were for the crown, but no one in France could prevail, though a strong party inclined to the Carlovingian dynasty; that is to say, they wished to place young Louis upon the throne. Athelstane, his uncle, instantly exerted himself to improve this disposition, and the French nation agreed to recall the prince from his exile. The states of France despatched a special mission (A.D. 936), empowered to act on behalf of all the nations inhabiting that realm.

They arrived in England—in the presence of Athelstane, they took the oath of fidelity to Louis as their king;—and, accompanied by many Anglo-Saxon prelates and lords, he departed from this country, and took possession of his kingdom.   Louis, on account of his long residence in England, acquired the by-name of "*Louis d'Outremer*," or "*Louis from beyond the sea*," and Athelstane's assistance tended greatly to support him against his own people, who never cordially liked him.   Whether Athelstane acted justly or not, in thus upholding his nephew, is a question upon which there may be a diversity of opinion; at present I only desire you to consider the fact as a proof of the great power of Anglo-Saxon England.

If we are to decide by the result, the interference was imprudent and ill-judged; for the Carlovingians never really re-established themselves in France.   The tree had been torn up so often, that it could not take root again—the French would not submit to the family. And on the death of Louis the Lazy, the grandson of Louis d'Outremer, Hugh Capet, son of Hugh the Great, obtained the royal dignity (A.D. 987).

In our times, these scenes have been renewed, a Louis and a Charles, the descendants of Hugh Capet, have been dwelling amongst us, like those who were driven out by Hugh Capet's ancestors and kinsmen, nine hundred years ago; and whatever may be thought of the causes of their expulsion, it is to be hoped that England will never cease to be a place of refuge for the wanderer, and a sanctuary for misfortune.

Athelstane made many good laws, and the traditional recollections of his government seem to shew that he desired the welfare and freedom of his people.   It was

currently believed, that he bestowed great privileges and
franchises upon the town of Beverley, saying—

> " As free
> Make I thee,
> As heart may think, or eye may see."

When the good folks of the boroughs began to regard it
as conducive to their welfare and importance that they
should be able to send members to the House of Commons, Athelstane's charter was pleaded more than once,
as the foundation of their parliamentary right; and
throughout the west of England there was scarcely a
town in which the statue of Athelstane was not erected.

Athelstane's charity probably contributed to his popularity.   He directed that each of his royal manors should
be subject to an annual charge in favour of the wretched
and destitute.   The steward, or " Reeve," was once in
every year to redeem a slave from captivity.   When
criminals amongst the Anglo-Saxons could not pay the
fines imposed upon them, they were in some cases
reduced to servitude; and it was these unfortunate
individuals whom Athelstane thus intended to relieve.
Furthermore, it was his pleasure, that upon every two of
his royal manors, the stewards should feed and clothe
one poor Englishman, " if he can be found;" and from
the doubt whether such an object could be discovered,
we may infer the general prosperity which the nation
had attained.

Keep of Richmond Castle.

Dumbarton Castle Gates.

Chapter XI.

Edmund—Revolution in Northumbria, which raised Olave to the Throne—Treaty by which Britain was divided between Edmund and his Competitor—Death of Olave—Edmund reduces Northumbria—Cumbria, or Strathclyde—Retrospect of the History of the Cumbrian Britons—Donald, King of Cumbria, expelled by Edmund, and his Kingdom granted to Malcolm—Extinction of the Cumbrian Britons—Death of Edmund—Edred—Constitution of the Anglo-Saxon Empire —Revolt of Northumbria—Eric raised to the Throne—Edred reduces Northumbria, and converts the Kingdom into an Earldom.

EDMUND the Atheling, son of Edward the Elder, was only eighteen years of age when he succeeded to the throne of his brother Athelstane (A.D. 941).

The submission of the Northumbrians to the direct dominion of Athelstane, had been much against their will. They cast off their allegiance, and sent for Olave, a king of the Eastmen, or Danes, settled in Ireland, to reign over them. Olave, however, seems to have been restored by the will and wishes of the English, as well as of the Danes, for Wulstan, Archbishop of York, was his most powerful supporter, and continued a steady adherent of the independent party to the very last.

Olave immediately began offensive operations. He advanced as far as Tamworth, being supported by the inhabitants of the country adjoining to the Danish burghs (A.D. 942),—though the burghs themselves had been occupied by Edmund,—and stormed the town, losing many of his men in the battle, but gaining much plunder.

Some while afterwards, Edmund besieged Olave and his faithful counsellor Archbishop Wulstan, in the town of Leicester. Olave sallied out of the town by night; and joining some other of his troops, a great battle took place (A.D. 943). Edmund, on his part, was accompanied by Odo, the Archbishop of Canterbury; and a conference having been held between the two prelates, a treaty was effected upon the following terms. Olave was to rule all Britain north of Watling-street; Edmund was to rule the south; and upon the death of either of them, the survivor was to possess the whole empire. By this treaty, therefore, Edmund consented to disinherit his brothers; and the chance of survivorship might have placed all the English nations beneath the supremacy of the Dane. Sad terms these for a descendant of Alfred; and such as must lead us to suppose, either that Edmund was reduced to great straits, or that he was betrayed by his counsellors. Odo was a Dane by birth; the son of one of the chieftains who had invaded England under Hingwar. He was erudite in no ordinary degree, but harsh and ambitious; and it is possible that he may have been inclined to the cause of his countrymen. Considered as a matter of calculation, the chances of survivorship were, it is true, in favour of Edmund. He was the younger of the two, and the Danish kings were subject to many mischances besides the ordinary casualties of life. Olave might be killed by a brother, like Niel, who fell by the hand of Sihtric; or the Northumbrians might depose him, as they had done many of their native sovereigns. These considerations may have had their share in inclining Edmund to submit to such apparently humiliating conditions.

It happened, fortunately for the English, that Olave died in the course of the following year. Edmund im-

mediately invaded Northumbria, in which two Danish
kinglets, Anlaf and Reginald, were then reigning. How
the former had established himself does not clearly
appear—whether he had continued as a vassal under
Olave, or whether he had entered into Northumbria
upon Olave's death. As for Reginald, he had obtained
his authority by the grant or concession of Edmund.
These sovereigns could offer no resistance (A.D. 944);
and the Northumbrians passed again beneath the sceptre
of Edmund.

The Britons of Cumbria occupy a tolerably large space
on the map, but a very small one in history;—their
annals have entirely perished;—and nothing authentic
remains concerning them, except a very few passages,
wholly consisting of incidental notices relating to their
subjection and their misfortunes.   Romance would
furnish much more ; for it was in Cumbria that Rhyderc,
or Roderic the Magnificent, is therein represented to
have reigned, and Merlin to have prophesied. Arthur
held his court in merry Carlisle ; and Peredur, the
Prince of Sunshine, whose name we find amongst the
princes of Strathclyde, is one of the great heroes of the
" Mabinogion," or tales of youth, long preserved by
tradition amongst the *Cymri*.   These fantastic personages, however, are of importance in one point of view,
because they show, what we might otherwise forget—
that from the Ribble in Lancashire, or thereabouts, up
to the Clyde, there existed a dense population, composed
of Britons, who preserved their national language and
customs, agreeing in all respects with the Welsh of the
present day. So that, even in the tenth century, the
ancient Britons still inhabited the greater part of the
western coast of the island, however much they had been

compelled to yield to the political supremacy of the
Saxon invaders.

The "Regnum Cumbrense" comprehended many
districts, probably governed by petty princes or *Reguli*,
in subordination to a chief monarch, or *Pendragon*.
Reged appears to have been somewhere in the vicinity
of Annandale. Strathclyde* is, of course, the district
or vale of Clydesdale. In this district, or state, was
situated Alcluyd, or Dunbritton, now Dumbarton, where
the British kings usually resided; and the whole Cumbrian kingdom was not unfrequently called "Strathclyde," from the ruling or principal state; just as the
United Kingdom of Great Britain and Ireland is often
designated in common language as "England," because
England is the portion where the monarch and legislature are found. Many dependencies of the Cumbrian
kingdom extended into modern Yorkshire, and Leeds
was the frontier town between the Britons and the
Angles; but the former were always giving way, and
their territory was broken and intersected by English
settlements. Carlisle had been conquered by the Angles
at a very early period; and Egfrith of Northumbria
bestowed that city upon the see of Lindisfairne. He
extended his conquests into that district now called
Furness, in Lancashire. Kyle, in Cunningham, was
reduced by Edbert. Alcluyd, "the strong city," was
besieged and taken by the same monarch (A.D. 685 to
756), aided by Unnust, King of the Picts, and afterwards
wholly destroyed by Olave and Ingvar. Many Cumbrian
tribes, harassed by the Northmen and also by the Saxons,
wholly abandoned their country, and found shelter and

---

* The word *strath* is still universally used all over Scotland, highland and
lowland, for *valley*.

protection in Wales or the marches, where, as it is said, they regained some of the lands which had been occupied by the Mercians. After the destruction of Alcluyd, these Britons were governed by kings of the Scottish line, who, probably, acquired their rights by intermarriage with a British princess; and Eugenius, or Owen, one of these rulers, was engaged, together with Constantine, King of the Scots, against Athelstane, in the great battle of Brunnaburgh.

The Kings of Cumbria became the vassals, or " men," of the Anglo-Saxon kings. Eugenius had thus submitted to Athelstane. Of the nature of the obligation, I shall speak hereafter. The Anglo-Saxon kings appear to have been anxious to extend and confirm their supremacy; Edmund proceeded against Donald, or Dumhnail, the Scottish King of Cumbria (A.D. 945), with the most inveterate and implacable hostility. He called to his aid his other vassal, Leoline, or Llewellyn, King of South Wales; and leading this British force against other Britons, he expelled Donald, their Scottish prince, from his Cumbrian kingdom. The sons of Donald were blinded by the command of Edmund; and a cairn, still called " Dumnail Raise," on the borders of Westmoreland and Cumberland, is supposed to mark the spot where the battle was decided, and the victory abused. Possibly the conqueror may have been exasperated by some recent act of treachery on the part of Donald; perhaps the violation of the fealty which the vassal had formerly promised may have been the alleged cause of the war. Edmund having thus obtained possession of Cumbria, granted the country to Malcolm, King of the Scots, upon condition, as the chronicles say, of being his co-operator, both by sea and by land. In other words,

Malcolm was bound to fight Edmund's battles, and to assist him with his forces whenever required; it being an old usage in diplomacy, even amongst rude nations, to conceal any onerous or disagreeable stipulation by civil and courtly language.

Fordun, the ancient Scottish chronicler, adds, that Malcolm, by the assent of Edmund, immediately made a *subinfeudation* or grant of Cumbria to Indulf, the "Tanaist" or heir-apparent of the Scottish crown, to the intent that the province should be governed as an apanage, until the prince should be called to the throne; and that it should thus descend from heir to heir—due fealty being rendered for the same to the English crown. And the Scottish chronicler also states, that when Constantine bestowed Cumbria upon Eugenius, this mode of succession had been established by his decree. The relations between the Kings of the Scots and the Kings of England are amongst the most litigated portions of our history. Englishmen and Scotsmen have long been at *drawn pens*, if not at drawn daggers, with one another upon this subject; and, therefore, all the details which affect or relate to the Scottish homages are to be considered as of great historical curiosity. The general question is involved in many difficulties; but from this period the right of the Scottish kings or princes to the kingdom of Cumbria, as vassals of the English crown, seems to have been fully admitted: and the rights of the Scottish kings to the "Earldom of Cumberland"—for such it was afterwards termed—were founded upon Edmund's grant.

The Britons of Strathclyde, and Ryed, and Cumbria, gradually melted away into the surrounding population; and, losing their language, ceased to be discernible as a

separate race.   Yet it is most probable that this process
was not wholly completed until a comparatively recent
period.   The " Wallenses," or Welsh, are enumerated
by David the Lion amongst his subjects ; and the laws
or usages of the *Brets* or Britons continued in use until
abolished by Edward I., at the period when Scotland,
by his command, appeared, by her representatives, in
the English parliament at Westminster (A.D. 1304).   In
the bishopric of Glasgow, comprehending the greatest
portion of the ancient Cumbrian kingdom, the " barbarous" British speech generally gave way to that dialect
of the Saxon English, which is called lowland Scottish,
about the thirteenth century ; but in some secluded districts the language is thought to have lingered until the
Reformation, when it was possibly destroyed by the
ministration of the protestant clergy.   In our English
Cumberland and the adjoining Westmoreland, a few
British traditions yet survive among the people.   Pendragon Castle reminds the traveller of the fabled Uther.
Some of the mountains which adorn the landscape retain
the appellations given to them by the original population ; and " Skiddaw" and " Helvellyn" now rise, as
the sepulchral monuments of a race which has passed
away.

Edmund " the Magnificent" would probably have
equalled the fame of his progenitors ; but in the year
which ensued after the conquest of Cumbria, he fell by
the hands of an assassin.   The anniversary, or mass-day,
of St. Augustine, was a great festival amongst the English ; and then (A.D. 946), as now, according to a habit
which is not the more praiseworthy because it is ancient,
the holyday was rendered unholy by debauch and revelry.
Edmund and his company being hot with wine, he dis-

cerned amongst the guests one Leof, who had been banished or outlawed for some offence. The sight of this man roused the king to extreme anger. Edmund started from his seat, threw himself upon Leof, and clutching him by his long hair, flung him to the ground. Leof grappled with the king, and drawing his dagger, stabbed his opponent with a mortal thrust.

Upon the death of Edmund, his brother Edred succeeded to the "fourfold empire of the Anglo-Saxons and Northumbrians, Pagans and Britons." This is the style which Edred assumes in his charters; and the titles are important, as showing the form into which the government had settled. Mercia and Wessex, with their dependencies, composed a dominion now considered as the proper state of the Anglo-Saxons or English. Northumbria constituted another kingdom. The pagan kingdom must be sought in the dominions possessed by such of the Danish chieftains as had not embraced Christianity; and, as ruler of the Britons, Edred was king of the kings and kinglets of West Wales and Cornwall, Gwent or Monmouth, Brecknock, Powys, Gwynneddh and Deheubarth, and the other territories now included in modern Wales; as well as of the Scottish princes who held Strathclyde and Cumbria, by virtue of the grants which Edmund had made.

Over the Scots themselves, Edred claimed the same supremacy; and, as the chronicle says, "they gave him oaths," or became his vassals, with the usual and accustomed formalities of the law.

This species of government was specious and imposing in appearance, but it did not possess sufficient union or stability. Every one of the larger states—nay, every one of the smaller communities included in the larger

states, was virtually independent of the other members.
They were aggregated under one crown, but they were
not welded together; and, with the exception of Wessex,
all were more or less hostile to the "Basileus"—for the
Anglo-Saxon monarchs assumed this Byzantian title—
who asserted his authority over the heterogeneous assemblage of tribes and nations forming his empire.

The theory of the constitution, such as it was, appears
to have required that the "Basileus" should receive a
distinct recognition of his authority in each of the leading or dominant states. The minor states tacitly consented to be bound by the acts of the more important
powers; and, on the whole, after deducting the differences between a rude and disturbed people, and a more
settled and civilized country, Britain was not unlike
Spain at the accession of Charles V.—Castile was the
more important and leading state; but the rights of the
monarch to the crown of Aragon and the seignory of
Biscay were distinct from the title to Castile; and the
recognition by the Cortes of each of these ancient states,
was the legal foundation of the authority which the king
enjoyed. I bring these facts before you as clearly as I
can, because nothing is so common as the supposition
that the kingdoms of the so-called *Heptarchy* became
thoroughly incorporated into one kingdom, before the
Conquest. But this theory is erroneous. It was not
until after the Conquest that England really became one
kingdom, governed by one king, and possessing one
supreme legislature; and the false consequences deduced
from the mistaken supposition of their earlier union per-
plex the whole course of our history.

Edred's empire thus consisted, not of a united kingdom, but of an aggregate of states, standing side by side

under his authority; and he was inaugurated as King of Northumbria, in a Great Council, or *Witenagemot*, held at Taddenscliff. Wulstan, the archbishop, and all the *Witan*, or members of the assembly, took the oaths of fealty, and Edred was accepted and acknowledged as monarch, from the Humber to the Tweed.

These oaths, however, were taken without the slightest intention of adhering to the obligation; and, as soon as Edred had quitted the country, a general revolt took place (A.D. 947). If Archbishop Wulstan did not head this conspiracy, he fomented and encouraged it; and Eric, the Northman, was elevated to the throne.

Edred, wasting away under the influence of the disease which brought him to an early grave (A.D. 948-949), was weak and puny in body, but he was resolute and vigorous in mind. He raised his forces and overran Northumbria. The country was plundered and ravaged without pity or mercy; and amongst other acts of devastation, the Minster which good St. Wilfred had built at Ripon, was set on fire and destroyed. This incident is important, because it shows the fierceness of Edred's hostility; the "pagans" could not have done worse. When Edred returned homewards from this expedition, the Anglo-Saxon army was attacked by the Northumbrians. Eric, by a secret and rapid movement, divided the van-guard of the English army from the rear-guard. Edred sustained a considerable loss; he became extremely angry, and declared that he would speedily return, and utterly ruin the land and the people.

The Northumbrian nobles were much alarmed at this menace: they had experienced the weight of his hand; and in order to make their peace with Edred, they rose against Eric, deprived him of the throne, and assassinated the deposed monarch, together with his son and brother. This murder took place at Steinmore, and Eric fell by the hands, or at least by the contrivance, of Maccus, a Norwegian chieftain, and of Osulf, an earl, who must have been among the chief of those by whose suffrages Eric had been promoted to the royal dignity. Edred was now again King of Northumbria, but the country continued as unsettled as before. Another Danish chieftain assumed the royal title (A.D. 952-954), and Archbishop Wulstan continued to plot against the government of Wessex. Edred acted with his usual decision and promptitude. Archbishop Wulstan's clerical dignity might protect him against capital punishment, but his person was not sacred against the law; he was arrested, and cast into prison at Jedburgh, and ultimately removed from Northumbria. Wulstan was translated to a lower step in the hierarcy, and the unruly Archbishop of York passed the remainder of his life as Bishop of Dorchester, in Oxfordshire, where he could do no further harm. The Danish rulers of Northumbria had hitherto been allowed to use the title of "king," and the rebellions which I have briefly noticed were principally excited by the efforts made by these kings to throw off the allegiance due to the crown of Wessex. This form of government was abolished by Edred; and, instead of creating a king, and allowing the country to subsist as a *kingdom*, the name of the dominion was altered, and the *earldom* of Northumbria was intrusted to Osulf, by whom Eric had been slain.

Chapter XII.

Accession of Edwy—Alteration in the aspect of Anglo-Saxon History—Dunstan—His Character and Influence—Celibacy of the Clergy—Establishment of the Benedictine Order—Dissensions between the partisans of the Monks and the Secular or married Clergy—Elgiva—Dunstan's intemperate conduct —He is banished from England—The Monkish Factions occasion a Revolt in favour of Edgar—Edwy deprived of his Dominions north of the Thames—Cruel treatment of Elgiva— Death of Edwy—Accession of Edgar—Promotion of Dunstan to the Archbishopric of Canterbury—Edgar's bounty to the Clergy—His Government—Edgar's Triumph on the Dee— Origin of the Feudal System—Tenures of Land—Earls— Aldermen—Edgar's Feudal Supremacy—Division of Northumbria—Lothian granted to Kenneth—Defects of Edgar's Character.

EDRED, who had been rapidly declining in strength, died soon after the reduction of Northumbria (A.D. 955), without leaving any children; and his nephew, the young Edwy, then not exceeding fifteen years of age, succeeded to the Empire. He was speedily "chosen," as the phrase ran, in Wessex, his own proper dominion. Mercia also acknowledged him, and the "Emperor of the Anglo-Saxons and Northumbrians, Ruler of the Pagans, and Protector of the Britons," appears to have been recognised without opposition in the other states of the empire. At the same time, Edgar, the brother of Edwy, became a sub-regulus, or vassal-king, under his supremacy. This fact, which is of some importance, is proved, like many other points of a similar description,

Cup found in the Ruins of Glastonbury Abbey.

Saxon Lantern (from Strutt's Chronicles of England).

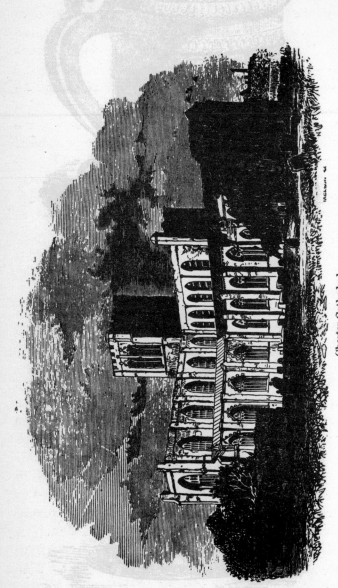

Saxon Lantern (from Strutt's Chronicles of England).

Chester Cathedral.

not by historians, but by a charter. The document does not designate the locality of the dominions assigned to Edgar, but it is most probable that Mercia was thus bestowed upon him as an apanage.

In the earlier portions of our history, if we except the kings, we have little personal acquaintance with any of the actors who appear on the scene. In a monarchy, the king is naturally considered as the most prominent personage; but those who stand beside the throne, and still more those who are concealed behind it, are very frequently of much more real importance than the prince arrayed in all the insignia of royalty; and the annals of the era into which we have now entered, furnish us with a satisfactory portrait of the individual who, throughout many reigns, must be considered as the leading and master spirit of the Anglo-Saxon empire.

Dunstan, Abbot of Glastonbury, had, at an early period of his life, been admitted into that ancient monastery, which was then also a school or college. Glastonbury was principally filled by Scots, or monks from Ireland. They were the most learned men of the age; but the defects of the stern and moody Celtic spirit were enhanced rather than regulated by mystic and ascetic piety: and the place itself was such as to encourage every dream of devotion or romance. Joseph of Arimathea, as the legends taught, had founded the holy fane in the fated isle of Avalon. Here was the burial-place of Arthur, the last of the British monarchs—if indeed Arthur was dead, and not entranced in fairy bower. A British population still lingered in the surrounding country; the inmates had repaired to the Abbey from the remotest parts of the west; and Glastonbury was the central point, which commanded the veneration of the Scots, the Cymri, and the English, the three great nations of the isle of Britain.

The poetical legends which Dunstan heard in this domicile became so familiar to him, that, in after life, he was accused of too great a proficiency in the magical songs of the olden time. As a child, he was singularly weak and delicate in body, but his talent was almost preternaturally active.

When very young, his intense application to study brought on an attack of fever : his strength failed, and his companions and teachers thought they beheld him on the bed of death. Suddenly Dunstan arose, apparently entranced, and directed his steps towards the church of the monastery ; the great doors were closed : but by some other entrance he ascended a flight of stairs which led to the roof. He proceeded cautiously along the beams, and dropped unhurt into the aisle below. Dunstan recovered, and when restored to health, he related that he had risen from his bed by the command of an angel—fiends had encountered him in his path—but he had put them to flight ; and, borne on the wings of a protecting spirit, he was wafted down from the fearful height, to the pavement of the building.

This was the first of Dunstan's visions. Of the many others which are found in his biography, it were useless to tell. If repeated in seriousness, no instruction is derived from them ; and I would not sport with the greatest affliction which can befal human nature ; for it is quite evident that they resulted from partial insanity. The " monomania" of Dunstan, as is frequently the case, was consistent with perfect good sense on all points, save that which became the subject of his delusions ; nor did his madness in the slightest degree diminish his singular and almost unexampled acuteness, activity, and industry. Dunstan possessed not only all the learning and all the science, but all the accomplishments of the age. In the arts—a Royal Academician of the present day will smile if I call them the *fine* arts— he particularly excelled : Dunstan was a sculptor, a painter, and a calligraphist : he could work with equal facility in the hardest and most ductile metals, in steel or in gold. But music constituted his chief delight : he struck the harp which he had made : and if, as we are told in the legend, the strain burst forth from its chords when untouched by hand, we may suppose that his mechanical skill had enabled him to produce the melody, by some of those contrivances now familiar to us, but of which the effect might then be ascribed to supernatural power.

In his earlier youth, Dunstan had been introduced at the court of Athelstane by his uncle, Athelm, Archbishop of Canterbury. Dunstan was of noble, or rather of royal lineage, for he was related to the king, and he won great favour by his musical talent and general knowledge.

His growing favour excited the enmity of some of the courtiers. They defamed him to Athelstane, and insinuated that the young student of Glastonbury was a sorcerer. Dunstan soon perceived that he had lost the good-will and favour of his sovereign—his high spirit could not brook any affront : and rather than be warned away from court by the knitted brow of Athelstane, he determined at once to quit the palace. The disgrace and departure of the favourite did not satisfy his enemies. They plotted against Dunstan, and lay in ambush for him ; when he came up, they surrounded him, drove away his servants, pulled him off his horse, bound him hand and foot, trampled on him, and threw him into a marshy pool. Here Dunstan was found by some passengers, who carried him to an adjoining village, where he was nursed until he recovered from the effects of the assault which he had sustained.

Dunstan repaired to his uncle, the archbishop, who exhorted him to become a monk. This the young man resolutely refused. He had become attached to a very beautiful maiden, his equal in rank and station, and whom he wished to marry. In this wish there was nothing but what was honourable and good. Had Dunstan followed his inclination, had he wedded his beloved, and settled in his paternal halls, the weakness of his constitution would have prevented him from following the trade of war. His knowledge and love of art, affording him sufficient resources within himself, would have preserved him from the ruder vices of his contemporaries, and he would have presented an example, most rare in those days, of a layman usefully and happily employing a life of ease and literary leisure.

This lot was denied to Dunstan. The archbishop incessantly represented that his pure attachment was an evil temptation. Dunstan resisted the importunities of his uncle, and argued fairly and reasonably in support of his own views. Athelm, at length, prayed loudly that some affliction might fall upon his nephew, and bring him to a sense of his duty. Dunstan was seized with a violent fever, probably the result of mental anxiety. The disease increased, and he was in the greatest danger; but he recovered from the attack; and being taught to consider the illness and the recovery as equally intended for heavenly warnings, he at length took upon himself the obligations of the monastic vow.

The young monk had nothing left in life, and he sought a living grave. The ordinary austerities of the cloister did not suffice to Dunstan, for the miserable man was in that state of affliction when corporal sufferings relieve the agony of the mind; the stimulus of bodily pain diverting the attention from the more intense torture of the soul. Dunstan built a hut by the side of the church, in which he enclosed himself. The cell was five feet in length, and two and a half wide, and it only rose four feet above the ground; but he had excavated the earth so far, as to enable himself to stand upright, though he could never lie down. In this sepulchre he abode, denying himself rest as well as needful food. He fasted to the point of starvation, constantly working at his forge when not employed in prayer. The hammer was always sounding, except when silenced by his orisons.

There is little reason to marvel at the return of Dunstan's partial insanity during his seclusion. He imagined himself assailed by the foul fiend, and he related his adventures; but in all other matters he was as shrewd and sensible as ever. His fame spread, and votaries from far and wide flocked to him. Dunstan now occasionally came out of his sooty den; and when Edmund ascended the throne, he invited Dunstan to court, in order that he might be at the head of the peers and palatine officers—or, as we should say, that he might be prime minister of the kingdom.

Dunstan immediately accepted the offer, or rather obeyed the command. He thus acted, as he said, in conformity with the precept of the apostle, " Let every soul be subject unto the higher powers;" and to the end that he might be enabled to establish the empire of righteousness and justice.

We may fully admit Dunstan's sincerity. Riches he utterly despised—when in his cell, he bestowed the whole of his ample patrimony, as well as the other great property which he acquired by bequests, upon the monastery. He had mortified his flesh, subdued his appetites and passions; and, from a deep sense of duty, however mistaken, he had abandoned that which was dearest to him in the world. But this painful process had left terrible effects behind; his heart was now seared against all those affections and feelings of humanity, which connect us with our fellow creatures, and afford the best means of testifying our love toward our common father. His mind was narrowed to the compass of his order; and the single object of his existence was, the establishment of the Benedictine rule and the extension of the Papal power.

The Popes of Rome were, about this time, most earnest in compelling the celibacy of the clergy. In the Anglo-Saxon empire, this regulation had never yet been enforced upon the inferior orders of the hierarchy. The principle upon which the prohibition was founded, arose from a mistaken application of passages of scripture, appearing, when separated from their context, to justify a restriction, which, if imposed as a yoke upon men's consciences, was wholly in contradiction to the spirit of the gospel. Considered, however, as a matter of discipline and expediency, there were reasons of policy which might then render it in some degree advisable. In the middle ages, when all the institutions of society had a strong tendency to the establishment of hereditary right, and when there was little written law, any usage or custom which had subsisted for two or three generations, easily acquired the validity of positive legislation.

Lands had been granted to the clergy for their maintenance. A married priesthood would soon have degenerated into a caste of sacerdotal nobility, holding their
lands as a patrimonial inheritance, by the nominal condition of serving at the altar, but neglecting, in fact,
every duty which they were charged to perform.

At an earlier period, this state of things had been
sufficiently realised in Northumbria, to show the nature
and extent of the imminent danger by which the church
was threatened. If the system had prevailed, the spiritual ministration of religion would have been debased;
the temporal advantages resulting to the community
from the establishment of Christianity would have been
wholly destroyed; therefore, we can well suppose, that
many thinking men, honestly anxious for the real in-
terests of religion, would labour for the prevention of
such an abuse. Most closely connected with this question of celibacy, was the introduction of the Benedictine
rule among the monks of England. Before Dunstan's
time, each congregation of recluses lived according to
its own internal regulations, nor were the several monasteries consolidated into one community. A Roman of
the name of Benedict, a man of sincere piety, had introduced a new code into the monastery which he founded
upon Monte Cassino, in the ancient territory of the
Samnites (A.D. 529). Amongst much that was trifling,
it contained more that was well adapted to increase the
utility of the monastic life, and to restrain its vices,
being particularly adapted to prevent the cloister from
becoming a nestling place of sloth and profligacy. These
monasteries, upon the continent, had united into one
corporation. The Benedictines of Italy were members
of the same body as the Benedictines of Gaul. They

were exempted from the jurisdiction of the bishops, and placed under a "general" of their own; and they soon became the ready instruments of papal ambition.

The great object sought by the Popes was the suppression of the independence of the different national churches of Christendom; and the celibacy of the clergy became a party badge—a pledge of submission to the Church of Rome, if yielded,—a token of hostility, if refused. And in this spirit of conquest did Dunstan, and those who co-operated with him, engage in the plans which they pursued.

The Scottish or Irish, and Pictish and British churches, though in communion with Rome, were still independent of the Papal See. The Anglo-Saxon church was more inclined towards subjection, and the Benedictine rule had been introduced at Glastonbury. Yet the opposition was very strong: all dissension is contagious —the disputes amongst the clergy were espoused by the laity; the secular priests found many powerful protectors; and the schisms in the church, as is too often the case, became factions in the nation.

Dunstan was compelled to fight with every weapon which he could seize : the monk became a statesman and an intriguer; and he constantly exerted all the power which he derived from his rank, and all the influence resulting from his character, for the main and single purpose of promoting his party views.

Dunstan had entirely gained the confidence of Edred : in the words of his ancient biographer, he was, during that reign, "King and the King's commander"—"Rex et Regis Imperator." In all things was Edred obedient to Dunstan; and every part and portion of the government had been entirely under his control and power.

The king could not nominate the abbot as heir to the throne; but Edred could bequeath all his property and treasures to Dunstan.   Edwy, on the other hand, who had been taught to consider himself as having been unjustly excluded from the throne during the reign of his uncle, was naturally disinclined towards Edred's counsellors, and Dunstan was very soon placed in collision with the new king.

Edwy was a youth of singular beauty, but vain, rash, petulant, profligate, and surrounded by a host of young courtiers, all encouraging and emulating the vices of their master.   Acting by their advice, Edwy imposed unjust taxes upon his subjects (A.D. 957) : he spoiled the clergy, and treated his own grandmother with great contumely.   Edwy was married to a very lovely woman, named Elgiva.   On the day of his coronation, whilst the nobles were banquetting and carousing, the king quitted the hall, and retired to an inner chamber with his wife and her mother Ethelgiva.   There was some real or supposed stain upon the character of Elgiva; and Dunstan, deputed by the nobles for the purpose of inducing Edwy to rejoin the revellers, rushed into the chamber, and addressed the queen and her mother in the most brutal language, threatening the latter with the gallows.   The ancient biographers of Dunstan, who extol him as a faultless hero, do not give the slightest intimation that this lady, whatever her demerits may have been, had been guilty of any crime punishable by the temporal law ; we are, therefore, fully justified in asserting that Dunstan's language was merely the ebullition of rage and passion, and his conduct towards Edwy was of the same tenor.   The monk dragged his sovereign by main force off his seat, and led him into the hall; and thus, shamed and disgraced, was Edwy compelled to reappear before his assembled nobility.

The insulted youth, however, was still a king: he could avenge himself upon the man by whom he had been thus outraged. Dunstan was banished from Britain; and the monks of whom he was the leader shared in his proscription: they were driven out of their monasteries and exiled like their patron. This act, without doubt, rendered Edwy the protector of the secular clergy, and the married clerks entered in triumph into Dunstan's own monastery of Glastonbury. Dunstan fled to Ghent, and took refuge in the monastery of St. Peter in that city, even thus escaping with difficulty from the vengeance of Ethelgiva, for she despatched emissaries after him, who, if they had caught him, would have put out his eyes.

It is said in Dunstan's legend, that when he was compelled to quit his abbey, a loud fiendish laugh resounded through the sacred building. "Thou shalt have more sorrow at my return, than thou now hast joy at my departure," — exclaimed Dunstan, addressing himself to the unseen demon. It is very possible that the hallucination under which he laboured may have drawn forth these words; but it is equally probable that the incident is merely a legendary fiction, founded upon the language which he used when he was expelled. He had left behind him those who possessed full inclination to sustain his cause. Scarcely had Dunstan quitted the country, when a general rising of the people (A.D. 957-959), instigated by Archbishop Odo, took place, and the Mercians and Northumbrians accepted Edgar as their king, not as a vassal-king beneath his brother, but in full supremacy; and from the Thames to the "Castle

of Maidens," the modern Edinburgh, Edwy was deprived
of all authority.

The fate of Edwy in his own kingdom of Wessex remains to be told. By the command of Archbishop Odo he
was compelled to abandon Elgiva. She was seized in the
king's palace by the knights and soldiers of the prelate.
They branded and scarred her face with a red-hot iron,
and caused her to be transported to Ireland, probably as
a slave.   From this wretched exile she returned to
Edwy.   They were pursued by their armed adversaries,
and were taken near Gloucester.   By the retainers of
Odo she was cruelly mangled, so that within a few days
afterwards she expired in great torture.   Edwy soon
afterwards died by the sword, or by the effects of sorrow
and despair (A.D. 958) ; and Edgar was now accepted as
monarch of Wessex, and as ruler of the whole empire.

Dunstan had already returned in triumph, as soon as
Mercia and Northumbria separated from Wessex ; and
Edgar, then sixteen years of age, placed himself entirely
in the hands of the party by whom he had been raised
to the throne.   Dunstan was promoted to the sees of
Worcester and London, which he held conjointly, and
soon afterwards to the primacy of Canterbury.   In the
latter see, there had been a quick succession.   Odo died
soon after the accession of Edgar : his successor, Elsy,
was frozen to death whilst crossing the Alps.   In the
place of the latter, one Brithelm, Bishop of Sherborne,
was elected, a man of singular humility, gentleness, and
modesty.   It is stated that he was deficient in proper
energy for the correction of the clergy, or, in other
words, that he did not cordially enter into the plans of
Dunstan.   Edgar compelled Brithelm to resign the archbishopric and go back to Dorsetshire,—and who could

be the new Archbishop but the learned Dunstan ?—With the Archbishopric of Canterbury Dunstan retained the Bishopric of London ; Rochester was added. Nothing could be more incompatible with the proper spirit of the church than such an accumulation of pluralities ; but the ambition which prompted Dunstan to solicit them, enabled him to retain his preferments, and to avail himself of all the influence which they bestowed.

Dunstan, the Wolsey of his age in power, but not like Wolsey in his fall, became the chief of the counsellors of the young king. Another was Oswald, a Dane by birth, the nephew of Odo, and who obtained the Bishopric of Worcester by the influence of Dunstan ; for he had been contented to resign this see, upon his promotion to the archbishopric. The third was Bishop Athelwold, equally the creature of Dunstan, who promoted him to the see of Winchester.

Unquestionably these were all men of talent, and under their guidance, Edgar attained great temporal prosperity. The successes of his reign may fairly be ascribed to their counsels; for, considering Edgar's youth, we must in great measure attribute his acts to the suggestion of Dunstan and of the cabinet which Dunstan had formed. Hence, we may judge that, as ministers, they executed their office with honesty and ability; and the reputation which they thus fairly earned, enabled them the better to carry into effect their plans for the reformation of the clergy. Armed with the delegated authority of the head of the Latin Church, supported and defended by the king,—for Edgar was entirely one with them in heart and hand,—they proceeded with the utmost energy and decision.

The married clergymen, who refused to separate from

their wives, were driven out by main force. Some, perhaps, were bribed into compliance by the king's bounty.
As soon as a body of monks was established in any given
church, large and ample donations were bestowed upon
the new colony. Such of the old English monks as had
not yet received the Benedictine rule, were induced to
fraternize with Monte Cassino, either by approbation of
the real merits of the system—for merits it certainly
had—or in order to conciliate the king. During
the Danish invasions and the consequent troubles,
many of the endowments of the monasteries had been
seized or acquired by the nobles and other laymen.
Edgar often succeeded in persuading these persons
to restore the property, which they could not hold
with a good conscience. In other instances, if a stubborn "Thane" resisted the persuasions of the monarch,
and had made up his mind to despise the anathemas
denounced against the usurpers of church property,
Edgar purchased the land with his own money, and
restored it to the church. By these means, before the
close of the reign of Edgar, forty-eight opulent Benedictine monasteries of monks and nuns were established
in Anglo-Saxon Britain; and these subsisted until the
era fatal to all similar foundations.

Edgar the Pacific, as he was called, gave a greater
extent and majesty to the Anglo-Saxon dominion than
any Bretwalda had hitherto obtained. Peace, it was
believed, had been prophesied to him by Dunstan, and
peace certainly prevailed. A combat with the Britons,
faintly indicated, is the only sign of war which can be
traced in the annals of his reign. Yet such obedience
was rendered to Edgar as no sovereign of Britain had
ever claimed before. Circumnavigating the island with

a fleet, whose numbers are said to have amounted to five thousand vessels, he led his mighty force to the city of Chester, where the vassals of the Anglo-Saxon crown had assembled pursuant to his behest.

And who are these who come before the throne of Edgar, the "Basileus," or "Emperor" of Albion? Kenneth, King of the Scots; Malcolm, the son of Kenneth, King of the Cumbrians; Maccus the Dane, King of Mona, and of the Southern Isles, or Hebrides. These are followed by the kings of the Britons, Dyfnwall, Siferth, and Edwall; the train continues to approach, and the kings of Galloway and "Westmere" stand amidst their compeers. Kenneth kneels before Edgar— he joins his hands in the humble attitude which, in the present day, is considered as denoting supplication or prayer; and by repeating the declaration,—"I become your man,"—he acknowledges his subjection to the Anglo-Saxon sovereign. The oath of fealty must now be taken by Kenneth—"Lord, I will be faithful and true to thee. All whom thou dost love, will I love. All that thou dost shun, will I shun; never wittingly or willingly will I do aught that is hurtful to thee." And further, declaring that he submitted to Edgar, and "chose his will," he affirmed that he would "co-operate with him by sea and land," or, in other words, that he would render such military service as the "Basileus" should need or require. All the other kings successively perform the same homage, take the same oath, and confess the same obligation. A banquet is held, and the day concludes with loud festivity.

On the following morning, Edgar, the Basileus, and his homagers, enter the royal barge, moored in the Dee, which flows by the palace walls. Edgar grasps the

Norman Vessel.

Roman Gates of Chester

Entrance to Rochester Castle

helm : each of the royal vassals plies at his oar; and, with Edgar as steersman, they reach the adjoining monastery of St. John's.   Mass is sung : after divine service has been celebrated, the barge rows down the Dee to the palace; and Edgar, when he enters his hall, addresses his nobles, and exclaims, that his successors may hereafter well call themselves kings, since he will bequeath to them such honour and glory.

The triumph of Edgar belonged to himself alone; it was never repeated,—but the oaths of fidelity thus taken by the vassals, and their military obligations, constitute two of the elements of *feudality*—an institution of a very complex nature, and of which the origin must be sought in the union of Teutonic custom and Roman law.

Upon this subject I must offer a few observations. The Feudal System is one of the most important passages in the history of the middle ages.   Feudality became so interwoven with the policy of the principal kingdoms, that, unless the student understand its nature, he cannot advance a step in historical knowledge.   And the state of landed property, in general, must be considered literally, as the ground upon which the real history of nations is founded.

In the Anglo-Saxon treatise of Elfric, before noticed, a passage occurs, to the following effect : " Every throne which standeth aright, standeth upon three pillars—the Priest, the Warrior, and the Labourer.   The priest prayeth day and night for the welfare of the people; the warrior defendeth the people with his sword; the labourer tilleth the earth, and worketh for the livelihood of all.   And if any one of these three pillars be broken, the throne will be overturned."   From the nature of the materials of history, the palace, the cathedral, and

the castle, will always be the most prominent features
in the picture; and we are therefore apt to forget, that
the indwellers of these proud and towering structures,
ultimately depend upon the cottage and the barn. All
worldly wealth is derived from the fulness of the earth;
and it is by the weal or woe of the peasant, that the
prosperity of nations is principally to be defined. The
importance of appreciating the real situation of the
cultivator may be best illustrated by very homely imagery. Supposing that to-morrow, each and every man
in England, from the queen downwards, were to be
deprived, by the wand of a magician, of breakfast,
dinner and supper, without a coat to his back, or a bed
to lie on; in this case, it is very certain that all affairs
would come to a stand. Of course such a state of
things, as to the whole nation, is impossible: but it
always must exist with respect to a part of the community. So long as the hungry bellies are in the
minority, there will be general peace and tranquillity,
whatever the individual privations of those hungry
bellies may be; but if, unluckily, the hungry happen to
be in the majority, the country will always be disturbed
and unhappy, notwithstanding the goodness of its constitution, or the excellence of its laws. And whatever
may be the importance possessed by the intriguer of the
cabinet, or the successes of the tented field, the cause
which operates most steadily, is the course of the plough.
I have enlarged upon this subject, because, in various
parts of this history, I shall enter more fully into the
ancient relations of landlord and tenant than is usual in
works of this description. But I must not forget that
I am the teacher of a family; and I can confidently
assure my younger readers, that if they live to grow

older and wiser, they will find more real pleasure in such facts, than in the most brilliant fictions of romance. I must now return to feudality.

The homage, or "becoming your man," was an obligation which the Germans brought with them from their forests.   It was a fruit of the old oak, though somewhat matured, if 1 may use the expression, by cultivation.   The lord was the protector of the "man," who, on his part, was bound to attend the superior to whom he had "commended" himself, both in peace and in war.   The price of this engagement might be a steed or a helmet, a shield of silver, or a purse of gold; and its duration was originally limited to the joint lives of the contracting parties.   If the lord died, his son could not claim the submission of the vassal.   On the other hand, if the vassal died, his child might choose any other lord.   But he was bound, whilst the compact subsisted, to take his place in the hall of his superior, and to fight beneath his banner when it was unfurled; and so imperative was this obligation, that the vassal who abandoned his sovereign in the conflict, rendered himself liable to capital punishment.

As society advanced, and its different relations became more firmly established, there was a strong tendency to render this kind of obligation hereditary.   The son of the lord endeavoured to stand in the place of his father, and the son of the vassal often found it convenient to claim the protection which his ancestor had received. And this tendency was much increased, when the remuneration, by which the lord purchased the services of his vassal, was made, not in moveables or personal property, but in land.   Amongst the "old Saxons" and other Teutonic nations, so long as they continued in their primitive state, such a price could not have been paid, because land was an article in which no one man had a distinct and separate property. The district inhabited by each sept or clan, which in the Alemannic language was called the *" Gau,"* * belonged to the people collectively, or in a body, exactly in the same manner as the hunting-grounds of the Red Men of America are held by each tribe. This mode of possession does not by any means exclude the strict idea of property; for every one of the miserable Cherokees and Osages who have been devoured by the grasping tyranny of the white aristocracy of the United States, is as sensible that he is entitled to the land of his fathers, as is the citizen of New York that he has the lawful property of his store in the Broadway. But at the same time, such an occupation of the soil does not afford to any one individual the means of retaining or enjoying any portion of land, apart from the rest.

The first steps adopted by the Germans for the encouragement of agriculture, are noticed by the Roman historians. The chieftains, every year, allotted a plot of land to each clansman. He ploughed the field and reaped the harvest, and then the land reverted to the community; and thus a fresh division was annually made. The most noble of the clan had the greatest share, which they probably subdivided amongst their dependants. But, even under this arrangement, much of the territory of the *Gau* remained as common land, into which every clansman could drive his sheep or his kine. These, or analogous customs, deduced from remote antiquity, subsisted in England till a recent period; and perhaps still linger in some of the few parishes which

* Probably from the same root with γη.

have escaped enclosure. In some parts of the country there were "shifting acres." John Spring was entitled to an acre in Cowholme mead: but this year he has it by the river side; and next year, by the side of the parson's close. In other manors, the plots of land in the common field were pointed out by mere-stones, and each was known by its peculiar mark. On some particular anniversary, a number of apples, each scored with a field-mark, were put into a hat, and drawn out by a boy on behalf of the several tenants, entitled by custom to the land; and each took his share according to the lot. In Norfolk, there was a custom, that after harvest, and until sowing-time in the following year, all the fields were thrown into common; the cattle ranging in full freedom over the whole township, without impediment or counter-claim.

Further lessons were soon learnt. The *Liuti* took their donations, as the lands were measured out by the Cæsar whom they served. And when the Germanic nations, such as the Franks, became the conquerors of a Roman province, they availed themselves of all the advantages of civilization. The Roman senator slunk out of his villa, and was contented to vegetate in the portion of the estate, usually one third, which was left to him by his ugly guest; and the "guest,"—for thus these unwelcome visitors civilly called themselves—plucked the grapes, and reaped the corn upon the remainder. The history of landed property is a subject of much perplexity, and very mainly so, in consequence of the great difficulty of disentangling the Teutonic customs from the Roman laws. It is sufficient to observe, that whatever the Germanic nations adopted, they adopted coarsely and clumsily. To repeat my architectural simile, they confused the details, and frequently connected discordant members. These are so jumbled and so rudely copied, that at first sight they appear to constitute an original style; but, if minutely examined, we can easily detect their prototype. This clumsy billited moulding has been suggested by the dentals of the Vitruvian cornice; for that thistle-capped capital, the pattern must be sought in the Corinthian Acanthus—that disproportioned base has been chiselled from the Doric of the Colosseum; and all are arranged upon a ground plan, of which no Roman would have dreamed.

Thus, the grants of land to the Roman veterans, of which I have before spoken, and sometimes called "Benefices," furnished one of the leading principles which the barbarians adopted; namely, that the soldier was to be rewarded by a territorial donation; and from the first establishment of the Franks in Gaul, we find that grants of this description were made out of the lands which constituted the royal domains. We have not equally full proof of the same practice in Britain; still we know from Bede that the land was considered as the public stock from which the soldier was to be remunerated. And when such land was appropriated to other purposes, so that the State was unable to bestow sufficient rewards upon the military, it was considered as a waste and spoil of the public treasury. This fact rests upon the authority of Bede; and although we have no particulars of the mode in which the grants were made, still we can plainly understand how numerous and important they must have been. The word "benefice" continued in general use till the ninth century, when it gradually went out of fashion; but we have retained the term as applied to the temporal possessions granted to the clergy upon condition of performing divine service in the chancel, just as the soldier obtained his "benefice" upon condition of performing military service in the field.

Lands which the barbarians held freed and discharged from all conditions, were called *Allodes.** Their jurisprudence always inclined in favour of possession, which, according to the common proverb, is nine points of the law ; and when Good Title has to recover his lands from Holdfast, Holdfast has always the best chance of remaining *in statu quo.* And it seems to have been a general principle, that if a father, and his son, and his grandson, were able to maintain possession of the land, free of rents or services, they were entitled to keep it against all the world. In a "benefice," however, it was considered that the person who held the territory, and whom we therefore call the tenant, had only the use and enjoyment of the lands, whilst the absolute property was always in the lord or the person by whom the benefit was granted. As a benefice was frequently prayed for by the dependant, it was also called a *Precaria;* and since the enjoyment only was granted, it was said to be land lent, or shortly, a *Præstita,* that is to say, a loan,— according to the old Anglo-Saxon and German spelling, a *Læn,* or *Lehn*—and what we, following the French, call the "feudal system," is denominated *Lehnwesen* in German ; and by some analogous name in all the northern tongues.

All this subject of tenures will be easily understood by the following comparison. A gentleman now lets a farm to his tenant, upon condition that the latter shall

* A word of dubious and contested origin. In the Scandinavian dialects, such possessions were called *Odal* land ; and, perhaps, the word in question was formed from *Odal* by a metathesis, or transposition of syllables.

pay him so much money every year. If the rent be not paid, the landlord seizes his tenant's stock, or ejects or drives him away from his farm. The squire reserves to himself the right of sporting over the fields; and there is an understanding that the tenant will do his best to preserve the game. The landlord also expects that the tenant should vote in his interest at the county election: if a body of yeomanry be raised, he considers that the tenant is bound to join the troop under his command. And, lastly, supposing that the tenant should not only pay his rent punctually, but duly perform his honorary engagements, and then die, leaving a son old enough to carry on the business of the farm, the landlord will probably renew his lease upon nearly the same terms.

In a similar transaction during the early ages of the feudal system, the landlord would have allowed the tenant to hold the farm, not upon condition of paying a money-rent, but of following him to the wars, at his (the tenant's) expense, for a certain number of days in the year. Instead of trusting to the honour or feeling of the tenant to obey his wishes, he would have secured the fidelity of the vassal by a solemn oath. Still the essence of the arrangement is not dissimilar: the landlord has parted with the possession of the land upon conditions; but the farm itself continues to be his property, and the tenant has only the right of enjoying that property. By the Roman lawyers, an agreement nearly of this nature was called an "*Emphyteusis*," pronounced *Emphytefsis*. This seems to have been shortened or corrupted into "*Phitef*," or *Fitef;* and ultimately into *Fief, Fevd,* or *Feud;* and about the eleventh century the latter word wholly supplanted the term *benefice*, in France and Italy. But the Teutonic nations never called their benefices by any name excepting that of loans, as I have before observed. *

This is the mere outline of an institution which gradually expanded so as to embrace the entire policy of the most flourishing nations of Western Christendom. Here, it will be sufficient to observe, that upon receiving the benefice according to the rough copy of the Roman law, the vassal always performed homage according to the Teutonic law : the one appeared the necessary consequence of the other.   And the class of persons thus benefited or *beneficed* increased very rapidly, both on the continent and in Britain.   We are compelled to help ourselves, in the history of the Anglo-Saxon tenures, by borrowing a few pages from the continental historians ; but we may do so with confidence.   The general features of the law were similar on either side of the channel.   Morally speaking, the different kingdoms of Christendom formed but one commonwealth; the " Clerks," who were almost the only lawyers, constituted one corporation, and were in constant intercourse with each other, and their management of legal business tended greatly to increase the uniformity which prevailed.

At the mention of a " knight," we immediately see a noble and gallant warrior, mounted on a prancing steed, his shield decorated with blazonry, and his plumed helmet adorned with the favour bestowed upon him by the fair "ladye" whom he has left in her summer bower. Such was the aspect of the feudal tenantry of the middle ages, after the institution had been adorned by the spirit of Gothic chivalry.   But originally the Anglo-Saxon

---

* For the proofs of this etymology, see Rise and Progress, &c. p. ccv., &c.

Knight* was merely the servant of his lord, whom he
followed to battle, in order that he might work out, by
the hard dints of his sword, the service for which his five
hydes of land had been granted to him.   These Knights
were also called *Thegns* or Thanes,† which means the
same thing, Servants.   The title of thane, however, soon
became an honour, when applied to those who attended
upon the sovereign.   Terms denoting the most humble
offices, acquire pride and honour when brought within
the sphere of royalty, and gilt by the splendour of the
rays which dart from the crown; and when, for instance,
we know how well it sounds, at this day, to be *Groom
of the Stole*, or *Lord of the Bedchamber*, we may easily
understand that the serving-men of Ethelbert or Redwald
would hold their heads much above their fellow-country-
men, who did not sit in the king's hall.

At the period when we can obtain any clear insight
into the history of the country, the thanes had already
become the main landed interest of the Anglo-Saxon
kingdoms.   But the application of the feudal principle,
as applied to the sovereigns, whether kings or " aldermen," who appear as vassals of the Anglo-Saxon crown,
cannot be distinctly traced higher than the reign of
Egbert; and I suspect that he learned the advantages
resulting from the doctrine, when he resided in the
dominions of the Frankish sovereigns.   It will be recollected, that the court of Charlemagne, in which Egbert

* *Cnicht* (A. S.), in German, *Knecht*, both signifying servant, as noticed in
the text.   About the time of the Conquest, the term *Cnicht* had acquired nearly
its modern signification.   In Germany, such are the changes of language, it
dropped as low as possible, so that *Knecht* designated a retainer or villain, and
was put in opposition to *Ritter* or *Eques*.
† From *Thegnian*, or *Thenian*, to serve.   German, *Dienen*.   In the Latin
Charters, the Thanes were usually called *Ministri ;* sometimes, but more rarely,
Milites.   A hyde of land contained from 100 to 120 acres.

had been taught and disciplined during his banishment, was considered as the very model of good government and policy, and feudal subjection was now becoming one of the main supports of the power of the Carlovingian dynasty. As an example of the policy thus pursued, let us read the history of the restless Tassilo, the representative of the *Agilofings*, the ancient chieftains of the Bavarian nation. Defeated by Pepin (A.D. 748), he received back from the victor the territory upon which the Bavarians dwelt, to be held as a benefice: he took the oath of fealty; and the obligations to which he had subjected himself are soon afterwards displayed. Tassilo appears as one of the vassals of Pepin's crown; and Tassilo and his followers increase the host which Pepin leads against the Lombard enemy. His subjection is again solemnly confirmed. Appearing in the *Cour Plenière* at Compiegne (A.D. 757), amongst the nobles of the Frankish crown, he humbly "commends" himself as the vassal of Pepin, and of his sons, Charles and Carloman : his oath is renewed upon the relics of the apostles of the Gauls; and all the great men and nobles of the Bavarians assent, on their part, to the bond which Tassilo has thus incurred. But neither the promise, nor the oath, nor the obligation, could ensure the obedience of Tassilo. The Bavarian withdrew his allegiance from Pepin, nor was the latter ever able to regain his supremacy.

The power of Charlemagne at length visited the rebel who contemned his summons. His armies advance to the banks of the Lech (A.D. 788); and Tassilo, surrounded by the troops of Charlemagne, humbly draws near to the emperor, and surrenders up his Duchy of Bavaria, by delivering his sceptre or staff. But the benefice was immediately regranted to him; and Tassilo, in addition to the usual forms of homage, delivered his son and twelve other hostages into the power of his sovereign.

The lieges of Charlemagne assemble from all parts of the empire, in the imperial palace of Ingelheim (A.D. 789)—Tassilo amongst the rest. He is accused of treason, or rather, of desertion from the army. Sentence of death is passed upon him; but, by the sagacious clemency of Charlemagne, the rebel vassal is clad in the monkish cowl, and the punishment is commuted into the perpetual imprisonment of a monastery.

I have chosen this example of Tassilo, as one of which we possess the most ample details, and by which the bearing of these transactions may be best understood. Charlemagne, by compelling a conquered chieftain to become his "man," acquired a much firmer hold upon Tassilo than by merely demanding tribute from an inferior or weaker chieftain. A legal obligation was created; and, if this were violated, there was established a pretence for inflicting a legal punishment. The act which might appear as vengeance, if directed against a vanquished sovereign, assumed the specious character of strict justice, if it took the shape of the solemn sentence pronounced by a competent tribunal. The vassal, on his part, obtained some compensations for the surrender of his independence. Protection against an enemy was not the least of these advantages, for the obligation between the lord and his vassal was mutual; and the submission which the latter rendered, gave him a full right to demand the assistance of his lord.

But the greatest of the benefits resulting to the vassal from this relationship seems to have consisted in the increase of power which he gained over his own subjects.

An ancient Teutonic chieftain, like Tassilo, before he performed homage, was only the leader of his people, not the lord of the land.   He commanded the men, but he did not own the soil.   This, to my Scottish readers, will be perfectly intelligible.   The " *Cean-Cinne*,"—the king of the kin, the head of the lineage—or chieftain, who possessed the most absolute power over his clan, had not necessarily any claim to the superiority of the country of the clan; whilst the feudal superior had not, as such, any authority over the clansmen.* The au- thorities of chieftain, and of feudal lord or baron, might be united, but they were frequently quite distinct.   By the compact with his sovereign, Tassilo acquired a new right; and, from being merely the Duke of the Bava- rians, he became Duke of Bavaria.   It is true that the transactions between Tassilo and Pepin and Charlemagne could not, according to strict justice, divest the people of their franchises; but might, in all cases, overcomes right; and, as the Bavarians in general participated in the protection afforded to their sovereign, they might be the less impatient of the change.   Over the minor chieftains of his nation, Tassilo would equally gain in authority.   He would attempt to impose upon them the same obligations to which he had submitted; and, if they rebelled, the ready hand of his liege lord would surely aid him, in suppressing any example of resistance likely to prove a dangerous precedent for the vassals of the crown.

The two elements of feudality—namely, the donation of land as the price of military service, and the tie of

* Thus the late Duke of Gordon, as feudal superior of the lands and estates held by the Camerons, Macphersons, and Macdonnels of Keppoch, had no vassalage or command over these clans, who only obeyed their patriarchal chieftains, Lochiel, Clunie, and Keppoch.

vassalage, appear to have grown up with the Anglo-Saxon kingdoms, and we may consider them as coeval with the kingdoms themselves. But, as a political institution, or as applied to the relation between an Anglo-Saxon Bretwalda and his subordinate sovereigns, we do not find that at any time, anterior to the reign of Egbert, they were clearly connected. Oswald, for instance, in obtaining the superiority over the Picts and the Scots, did not thereby claim any dominion over the land upon which they dwelt. The vassalage was personal: it was like one army surrendering to another. The Picts and the Scots submitted to the Angles, but the land was not considered; and I am not prepared to say, that if the Scots or the Picts threw off their allegiance, the Bretwalda could treat them as rebels in the legal sense of the word. He would attack them in their fastnesses; burn their huts; carry off their cattle; and put men, women, and children to the sword, and do them the utmost harm. All this, however, was according to the ordinary rules of war, and not by any pretence of lawful authority; nor did he claim any kind of right to adjudicate concerning the Pictish or Scottish territory. But in the reign of Egbert, as I have observed, the constitution of the government had altered; and we may discern that, to a considerable extent, Britain was approaching to the state of the Carlovingian empire. The submission of the East Anglians to Egbert was a clear act of homage; and, as we descend in the Anglo-Saxon history, the institutions of feudality become more and more apparent.

Perhaps you will already have remarked that the donation of Cumbria by Edward the elder to Malcolm, was a feudal grant, such as might have been made by Pepin or Charlemagne. Edward had also established the same jurisdiction over the Britons, and we possess the documents which show that the Prince of South Wales, Howell, the Good, submitted to the judgment of Edward's court (A.D. 922) concerning two " *Commots* " of Brecknock,* claimed by Morgan Hên, who, like himself, was a vassal of Edward's. Under Edgar the feudal system was carried to its full extent; and the vassalage of his allies was obtained, not by force, but by milder means. " Kings and earls repaired to him, submitting to his will without strife or battle." Perhaps no one of them, singly, was strong enough to resist him. Hence he was enabled to reduce them all to a uniform rule, and it is to this uniformity of policy that we must apply the language used by the chroniclers, who extol him as the restorer, or rather the founder of the state, the " Charlemagne, the Cyrus, and the Romulus of Britain."

The royal title had been lost by all the subordinate chieftains of the Anglo-Saxon or Anglo-Danish states. They continued, however, very powerful. Athelstane, Alderman or Duke of the East Angles, was called " semi-rex," or, " half-king." His wife, Alfwina, much praised for her piety, was the nurse of Edgar; and Aylwin, his son and successor, obtained the title of Alderman of all England. It is difficult to define the exact signification of these titles; and I am inclined to think that the latter, inscribed upon Aylwin's tomb, only referred to East Anglia. But be that as it may, they were tokens of the great power which these rulers possessed. Northumbria, since the submission of the country to Edred, had been governed by *Jarls* or Earls

---

* The Commots of *Ystradwy* and *Ewias*—the latter is now included in the county of Hereford.

(A.D. 950-952). The word Earl was not unknown to the
Anglo-Saxons; but they employed it as a generic term,
to denote a person of noble race, who was said to be
Earl-cund, or of Earl-kind. The Danes applied it abso-
lutely, to designate any great man or leader, until, by
usage, it was more particularly given to the rulers who
governed the provinces or shires under the king, and at
length it wholly supplanted the old English title of
Alderman, as applied to such high dignitaries. Our
aldermen, therefore, are now in Guildhall, feasting with
my Lord Mayor; but our earls are in the Parliament
House, by the side of the king; for the Danish title has
adhered to the successors of the Anglo-Saxon " witan,"
through all the vicissitudes of subsequent ages.

The earls, or aldermen—for in the reign of Edgar we
may consider the titles as nearly synonymous—had
many royal rights, though, of course, inferior to the king
in degree. One third of the revenues of the earldom
belonged to them: hence such earls were sometimes
called " Earls of the third penny." Their other prerogatives varied in different parts of the empire; but so
did the prerogatives of the Anglo-Saxon kings, and we
may easily suppose that the farther they were from the
seat of government, the more would they assume. " Give
him an inch and he will take an ell," may be fairly
applied to all mankind, and I do not see any reason for
excepting an earl—I mean a Danish or Anglo-Saxon
earl—from the general rule. Hence, upon the death of
Osulf, Earl of all Northumbria (A.D. 971), Edgar, the
wise Edgar, did not think it expedient to allow this
kingdom to remain unbroken. A great council of the
Northumbrian thanes—in the chronicle they are called
" barons"—was assembled. Deira, or Yorkshire, was

assigned to Earl Oslac. Another dismemberment was bestowed upon Eadulf Evilchild; and these chieftains were "girt with the swords" of the earldoms which they had obtained. This mode of inauguration, it may be remarked, was usual in cases where the ruler of a country had no right to the prouder distinction of a crown. The Duke of Normandy was girt with the sword of the Duchy. Even when the title of earl became merely nominal, and a shadow of its former dignity, this ancient ceremony was retained. As late as the reign of James I., the newly-created earl, when he was introduced into Parliament, was girt with his sword by the king, in presence of the peers.

Lothian, or the part of Bernicia which lies between the Tweed and the Frith of Forth, was constantly exposed to the incursions of the Picts and the Scots (between A.D. 953 and A.D. 961). On account of the great difficulty of defending this remote part of the empire, it had been much neglected by the Anglo-Saxon kings; and the king of the Scots, Indulf, had taken possession of the "Castle of Maidens." This fortress was also called Edwin's burgh, probably because it had been built or restored by Edwin of Northumbria, and it is hardly necessary to observe, that it is the modern Edinburgh.

Kenneth M'Alpine, King of the Scots, had destroyed the Pictish monarchy. Even the Picts themselves almost disappear from history (A.D. 836-859); and our older historians used to believe that the whole nation had been extirpated by Kenneth, the victor. This is certainly an exaggeration; but the Scots subverted the Pictish power; and the people became so absorbed amongst the Scots, that the latter, instead of being con-

fined to the western coast, became the possessors of the
Pictish territory, bounded on the south by the Frith of
Forth, and on the north by Scandinavian settlements,
in the present shires of Caithness and Sutherland, but
whose boundary is ill defined. Kenneth, the son of
Malcolm, whom I have already mentioned, claimed some
right to Lothian, upon what ground we know not; and
we can only understand that the claim was contested,
and that it involved the performance of homage to the
superior sovereign.

Yielding to the persuasion, or, perhaps, we should
rather say to the mediation, of Earls Oslac and Eadulf,
and of Eadsi, Bishop of Durham, Kenneth repaired to
the court of Edgar. The son of Alpine was kindly and
hospitably received by the " Basileus of Britain" (about
A.D. 971); and when engaged in familiar and pleasant
conversation, Kenneth contrived to solicit that he might
be restored to Lothian, which, as he alleged, ought to be
held, as an inheritance, by the Scottish kings. Edgar
listened courteously to the demand; yet he was on his
guard, and instead of yielding an immediate assent, he
referred the " petition of right " to the judgment of his
tribunal. The " Witan " decided in favour of Kenneth;
but the claim was only admitted upon condition of homage; and Kenneth was also obliged to promise that he
would maintain the English inhabitants in the enjoyment
of their language, their customs, and their laws. The
territory thus granted, now called the Lothians and the
Merse, may be considered as the nucleus of the modern
kingdom of Scotland. The attention of the Scottish
monarchs was drawn to the richest part of their dominions, in which they ultimately placed the seat of
government. The policy of a more cultivated people

prevailed over the ruder tribes. The Scottish monarchs became Saxonized; and the Gael were virtually conquered by the strangers over whom their sovereign had acquired dominion.

It is probable that the homage rendered by Kenneth at Chester, may have been merely due in respect of Lothian. But the rulers of England interpreted the act in their own favour; and the ancient subjection of the Scots to the Anglo-Saxon Empire became the basis of the supposed feudal rights of Edward I., and the primary cause of those bloody wars which desolated both countries until the union of the crowns. Even after that event, pretensions were urged on the one side, and denied on the other, with so much heat and contention, as to keep alive the angry feelings of the elder time. And at the present day, there is more than one true Scot, who thinks himself bound to live and die in the belief, that every charter which attests the attendance of a Scottish prince at the court of the Saxon "Basileus" is a monkish forgery.

Such feelings ought to be regretted rather than encouraged. The real credit and glory of Scotland consists, not in the turbulent independence of the early inhabitants of that country, with whom the present Scots have nothing whatever in common but the name; but in the steadiness and good principle which has enabled them to overcome all the evil tendencies resulting from a weak, factious, and divided government; and to settle into their present state, of a religious, prosperous, and well-ordered community. These are the real glories of Scotland; and they would not be tarnished if every king of the line of Fergus had been dragged in chains at the chariot of the conqueror. Scot-

land is now united to Middlesex by the same ties as
Yorkshire. And it would be as unreasonable for the
good folks of Leeds to rebel against Queen Victoria, in
defence of the prerogatives of King Oswald, as it is
for the Edinburghers to make themselves unhappy
because King Kenneth was subjected to Edgar's supremacy.

But the question, though utterly unimportant as the
object of national pride, is of great importance as a
matter of history. By affording a clear and distinct
view of the obligations incurred by Kenneth as a member of one of the orders or " Estates " of the great
Council or Witenagemot of Edgar, we are enabled to
judge concerning the others who sat and acted as his
compeers, and to obtain a distinct idea of the nature of
the assembly.

Under Edgar, as under the earlier Bretwaldas, the
states governed by the Basileus, or Emperor, continued
as distinct provinces or kingdoms, each preserving its
own individual existence—one sovereign, one empire—
many kingdoms and provinces, many customs and laws.
Edgar attended diligently to the administration of justice.
In the character of supreme judge of his people, he made
frequent circuits for the purpose of redressing those
wrongs which could not be remedied by the inferior
tribunals. Theft was punished by him with peculiar and
almost savage severity. He certainly succeeded in preserving the public tranquillity. To use the figurative
expressions of his historians, the earth seemed to be more
fertile, and the sun to shine brighter, under Edgar, than
in the reign of any other king.

But there were great defects in Edgar's character.
The monks have made the best of their protector ; but

some anecdotes have escaped them affording us a hint of the matters contained in the popular ballads, by which, as Malmesbury says, Edgar was much defamed. These ancient satiric ballads, specimens of which still remain, though of a later period, were, comparing poetry to painting, similar to the political caricatures of the present day. Addressed to the vulgar, they exhibited a distorted and degraded likeness of the features of the original. Edgar's chroniclers have embellished these features; but they intimate that he incurred great blame for the encouragement which he gave to foreigners— Germans, who uncivilized the English,—Flemings, who corrupted their simplicity of manners, and Danes, by whose example they became drunkards.

I am afraid that all these vices, said to be imported, were indigenous to the soil; but they seem to have received encouragement from the king.

One of Edgar's many concubines was the beautiful Wulfreda, whom he had carried off from the monastery of Wilton. Whether she was a nun or not is uncertain; for the monasteries, as is yet the case, were places of education for females; and some writers assert that Wulfreda had not taken the veil. For this offence Edgar was punished severely. He did penance for seven years, fasting twice a-week. In the Anglo-Saxon age, such a mortification of the flesh was a real *bona fide* bread and water diet, with the addition, perhaps, of a few green herbs and a little salt. Furthermore, the penitent was compelled, during such abstinence, to renounce all the luxuries, and even the comforts of life. Soft beds and the warm bath were denied; and Edgar, as an additional token of repentance, put off his crown, and did not resume it till the expiration of the term of his humiliation

(A.D. 973-974), when he was crowned, or perhaps re-crowned, with great solemnity, at Bath, or "Ake-man-nes-ceastre," as it was called by the Anglo-Saxons,—literally, the city of aching men, or invalids—the year preceding his triumph on the Dee.

Chapter XIII.

Death of Edgar—State of Parties—Edward the Martyr and Ethelred respectively supported by the partizans and adversaries of Dunstan — Edward's party prevail—Dunstan's opponents killed by the falling of the building at Calne— Murder of Edward by Elfrida—Accession of Ethelred the Unready — Danes renew their attacks—The Dane-geld — Ethelred marries Emma of Normandy— Massacre of the Danes on St. Brice's Day—Sweyne's Invasion—Ethelred abandons England to him—Death of Sweyne—Restoration of Ethelred—Canute continues to occupy the North—Death of Ethelred—Division of the Country between Canute and Edmund Ironside—Murder of the latter—Reign of Canute— Succession of Harold Harefoot and Hardicanute.

EDGAR departed this life just at the period when he had attained the summit of his power (A.D. 975). In the words of the Anglo-Saxon ode by which his deeds are commemorated, he " chose a brighter light, and ended his earthly joys." He left two sons, the eldest named Edward, son of Elfleda the Fair, and Ethelred, the youngest, the child of his second wife Elfrida. This last-named queen had been the wife of Ethelbald, Alderman of the East Angles. Edgar had slain Ethelbald, in order to obtain the hand of his widow ; and this wicked woman appears to have connived at the crime.

The right of directing the succession to the throne appears to have been still inherent in the king ; and Edgar, in exercise of this power, had nominated his eldest son Edward as his heir. But the " Atheling," or Prince Royal, and his brother, were both mere children ;

Edward was fifteen, and Ethelred only seven years old; and the parties who divided the nation, and whom for shortness sake I will call the Dunstanites and Anti-Dunstanites, were each equally anxious to rule in the name of a minor, and great dissensions arose between them. The whole nation was involved in contention, but the particulars of the disputes are lost. The chronicles describe the events very briefly : they are mentioned with more force, but with great obscurity, in the ode to which I have alluded, and from which we learn that Oslac, the great Earl of Northumbria, was banished, and compelled to fly beyond the "gannet's bath," "the inheritance of the whale," the periphrases by which the Anglo-Saxon scallds designate the sea.

Alfere, the Ealdorman of Mercia, was the chief leader of the Anti-Dunstanites, or the party supporting the seculars. Throughout the whole of his extensive dominions, the monks were instantly expelled. All that the Dunstanites had inflicted upon the seculars, was now retaliated upon them in return. Aylwin, the Alderman of East Anglia, on the contrary, was equally zealous on behalf of the monkish party. Force was opposed to force, and the country was in a state approaching to civil war. A great council, or witenagemot, was summoned to meet at Winchester; and the influence and activity of the two archbishops, Dunstan and Oswald, enabled them to place the young Edward upon the throne, in conformity to his father's will.

Dunstan had obtained a victory, but not an easy one ; and his enemies were not disposed to retire from the conflict (A.D. 977-978). Against him stood Alfere, and a very powerful confederacy of nobles, aided by Elfrida, the mother of the candidate for the crown. The seculars gathered strength; and Dunstan was now compelled to submit to the humiliation of meeting his adversaries in the synods, held for the purpose of deciding the momentous questions by which church and state were divided.

The seculars made every effort to defend themselves by argument; and they expected to derive great advantage from the talent and eloquence of a Scottish or Irish bishop named Beornhelm, whom they had invited from his own country, to aid them in the discussion, and stand forward as their champion against Dunstan. The choice of this advocate is a remarkable fact in ecclesiastical history, because it tends to prove that, at this period, the church of the Scots—probably in Ireland—was not entirely subjected to Rome.

A meeting was appointed at Calne, in Wiltshire, and the council, or witenagemot, which included the best part of the nobility of England, assembled in a large upper chamber. Beornhelm addressed this meeting at length. His speech exhibited all the fire and eloquence which could have been expected from his fame. Dunstan now rose, slowly and deliberately, and, as it were, oppressed by age. He avoided entering into any argument, declaring that his time of labour was past;—he sought no conflict,—no—he desired to end the remainder of his life in peace,—but as to his cause, the cause of the church, he trusted that the power of Heaven would be displayed against the enemies of Heaven.

Dunstan had scarcely closed his lips when the edifice shook, the timbers cracked, the floor gave way on the opposite side of the chamber. All those who came together against the Monkish party, were precipitated into the depth below, and maimed or killed amidst the

falling beams. But the end of the floor on which Dunstan and his friends stood, remained quite steady and
firm ; and none of them were in the least degree hurt or
harmed. Was this the result of a fraudulent device ?
Had Dunstan so caused the chamber to be prepared,
that he might entrap his adversaries to their destruction ?
This question has been much mooted in our days ; and
the balance of probabilities must be left to the reader's
judgment. The moody zeal of Dunstan, heightened and
inflamed by mental aberration, may perhaps be thought
to have suggested this murderous artifice ; but it must
be admitted that the difficulty of carrying such a plot
into execution with secrecy and safety, must have been
very great ; and this consideration may serve to diminish
the force of our suspicions.

But we must now pass to an undoubted crime : " the
foulest deed," as the chronicles say, which ever stained
the English name (A.D. 978). Edward and Ethelred,
though their partisans might strive to render them
enemies to each other, were united by brotherly affection.
Elfrida, however, entertained extreme aversion towards
her son-in-law ; and a plot was formed, at her instigation, to deprive him of life. The "nobles" who were
engaged in this conspiracy are not mentioned ; but the
expressions employed in the Saxon chronicle imply that
Alfere was deeply implicated in the scheme. An opportunity to effect their intentions soon offered. Edward,
having hunted the deer at Wareham, proceeded to the
royal town or manor of Corfe, where Elfrida and Ethelred then resided. It is said that, with youthful curiosity,
he was allured to the spot, by little *Wulstan*, the clever
cankered dwarf of the queen. Edward's companions
were dispersed, and he had advanced alone to the lofty

hall of his mother-in-law. She received him at the doorway, and kissed him. Before the young king alighted, a cup was offered, and as he was quaffing the draught, one of Elfrida's attendants instantly stabbed him in the back. The wounded prince had yet strength enough to give spurs to his horse, and to attempt to rejoin his companions; but he expired on the road; and the bloody corpse, dragged in the stirrups by the affrighted animal, revealed the fate which "Edward the Martyr" had sustained.

Ethelred came to the throne with a bad name. He was called "the Unready;" and this appellation appears to have been suggested almost as soon as he was born, by Dunstan's ill-will. When he took Ethelred from the font, he exclaimed, with his usual vehemence, that "the babe would prove a man of nought;" and he never concealed the dislike which he entertained towards the son of Elfrida.

The nobles, prelates, and great men of England being assembled, according to the usages of the constitution, Ethelred was acknowledged as king (A.D. 979). Dunstan was compelled to assist at the ceremony. Probably he would have set up a pretender, if any could have been found; but Ethelred was the sole scion of the royal stem. Dunstan, however, did his worst: when he placed the crown upon the head of Ethelred, he accompanied it by a curse. "Even as, by the death of thy brother, thou didst aspire to the kingdom, hear the decree of heaven. The sin of thy wicked mother and of her accomplices shall rest upon thy head; and such evils shall fall upon the English as they have never yet suffered, from the days when they first came into the isle of Britain, even until the present time."

There is no reason to suppose that Ethelred, a child of eleven years of age, had, in any way, assented to the murder of Edward. An anecdote is related concerning him, so trivial in itself that I shall not repeat it, but important as showing that Ethelred was strongly attached to his brother; and even in the course of Dunstan's invective it may be observed that all the sin is laid to Elfrida's charge. Dunstan's imprecations, however, arising out of his aversion towards the prevailing party, bore most heavily upon the nation; and his prophecy was, like many others, excellently well calculated to insure its own accomplishment. By inducing the people to attribute their misfortunes to the government, he weakened their powers of resistance, so long as Ethelred was on the throne; and he also directly instigated them to desert their monarch as the cause of the evils to which they were exposed. England was prepared to succumb to any foreign enemy. Englishmen were prompted to civil war and treachery; and the calamities and miseries which ensued, and which, in fact, opened the way for the entire subjugation of the country by the Normans, if not occasioned by the very words of Dunstan, were yet extremely enhanced by the effect of his denunciations. Ethelred, deprived of the confidence of his subjects, could not lead them to their own defence; and their distrust of their sovereign involved the whole state in confusion.

Dunstan just lived to see the dawning of the wretchedness, which, in the bitterness of his heart, he had desired should fall upon his countrymen because he hated their king (A.D. 980-981). The Danes, since the reign of Athelstane, had abstained their attacks upon Britain; but, in the third year after the boy Ethelred's accession,

the dreaded banner of the raven was again unfurled, and
the Danish vessels approached the shore.   Sweyne, the
son of the King of Denmark, appears to have been the
leader of the army.   Banished from home by his father,
he was in the full vigour of youth ; and the assistance
which he had received from Palnatoke, one of the wisest
and bravest of the Danish chieftains, rendered him a
fearful invader of a country unprepared for defence,
either in the council-hall or in the field.

Fiery clouds and meteors had overspread the sky;
and the coincidence between these appearances and the
changes of fortune on the earth, contributed to dishearten
those upon whom the burden of calamity had fallen.
The strong burgh of Southampton was plundered, and
the inhabitants carried into slavery.   At the very same
time, other detachments of the " host," the pirate army
of the north, invaded Mercia (A.D. 982) ; Chester was
taken, and London was burnt, and the whole of the coast
from the Mersey to the Thames was ravaged by these
insatiate plunderers.   The Danes did not act in combi-
nation with each other ; and their fleets, or rather their
squadrons, were frequently very small.   Thus, Dorsetshire was invaded by three ships ; and if we estimate
their crews at six hundred men, we shall probably over-
rate their numbers.   Any reasonable degree of vigour
would have been sufficient to repel the enemy ; but at
this very period, when unanimity was requisite, great
dissensions prevailed.

Disputes arose between the government and the Bishop
of Rochester.   Ethelred ravaged the lands of the bishopric, and laid siege to Rochester (A.D. 985-986) ; but,
upon payment of a sum of money, he desisted from his
hostility.   It is probable that the quarrel between the

young king and the bishop arose out of some legal demand, with which the latter refused to comply. But at
such a season, when the country was yet smoking with
the fires kindled by the Danes, the contest, whatever
might have been the strict rights of the parties, was
peculiarly unfortunate ; and Dunstan, then almost upon
his death-bed, laboured in every way to asperse the conduct of the king.

About the same time, Alfric, the son of Alfere, who
had succeeded to the earldom of Mercia, having engaged
in a conspiracy against Ethelred, was condemned by the
witenagemot. His property was confiscated, and he
himself, being outlawed, was banished from the country.
Such an event is an indication of the internal dissensions
which prevailed. But if the banishment of Alfric be a
proof of the rebellious spirit of Ethelred's nobles, the
speedy restoration of the Earl of Mercia to his former
honours is a still greater proof of the disorders of the
government, and of the weakness of the executive
power.

The only part of England in which the Danes met
with any effectual resistance was, where such patriotism
might have been least expected, in East Anglia. Here
the host of the "Vikingar," commanded by Justin and
Gruthmund, was encountered by Earl Brithnoth and his
warriors. The earl was, perhaps, himself of Danish
blood ; but, if so, the lapse of a century had obliterated
in this district the distinction between those of that
lineage and the older inhabitants (A.D. 991). The pious
warrior had no communion with the heathen bands.
His loyalty was unimpeachable ; and he was most
strenuous in defending his sovereign Ethelred, and
Ethelred's subjects and kingdom. But the "noble

Thane of Ethelred" fell by the *hassagay*,* which the Danish pirates had probably brought from the Saracen realms.

Brithnoth's achievements have been commemorated in an historical poem of no ordinary merit. And though we may not perhaps agree with the antiquary, who considers the lay as approaching to the simplicity and fire of Homer, still it must be considered a singular and valuable relic of the poesy of the olden time.†

Brithnoth was thus celebrated by the bard, but no others were incited to follow his example, or emulate his fame; and the subsequent invasions of the Danes showed how completely all courage had departed from England. The Danes threatened the southern coast. The Witan assembled; the baneful counsel given by Sigeric, Archbishop of Canterbury, Alphage, Bishop of Winchester, the Ealdorman Ethelward, and the factious Alfric, induced the king and nation to adopt the old and fatal expedient of attempting to appease the invaders by the tribute of the "Dane-geld;" and the sum of ten thousand pounds was the first payment which they exacted from the cowardice of England.

At this price did the English, in the words of the treaty, attempt to "buy peace" of Olave and Justin, and Gurthmund the son of Stegetan. Yet even the payment of the "Geld," raised by direct taxation upon the land, was, perhaps, less humiliating than another condition imposed upon the English. The Danes were fed by the country which they had impoverished, and

* In Anglo-Saxon, *Ategar* or *Hategar*, evidently the same with the Spanish Acagaya. I do not know the root of the word, but it seems to be found also in *attaghan*.

† A translation of this poem may be found in Mr. Conybeare's most valuable work,—a publication which affords a general view of the whole body of Anglo-Saxon poetry.

the people were compelled to pamper their fiercest
enemies. In the advice which prompted this submission
there was both weakness and treachery. Alfric had
been in secret league with the Danes; and a defeat was
occasioned by his treason. A large fleet had assembled
for the defence of London; Alfric sent secret intelligence
to the enemy, and went over to them on the eve of the
battle. He escaped unpunished by Ethelred, who caused
his son, Elfgar, to be blinded—a savage and unpardon-
able revenge for the misdeeds of his father.

The punishment inflicted upon Elfgar could not repel
the Danes. They were not to be scared by such a
vengeance (A.D. 994). Sweyne, accompanied by Olave,
King of Norway, advanced with redoubled force and
fury. London was spared; but the whole of the south
of England received " unspeakable harm;" and sixteen
thousand pounds were paid to the Danes, literally for
the purpose of inviting them to further mischiefs. Every
payment thus made, told them, that a repetition of the
same aggressions on their part, would lead to the same
compliance.

It was part of the treaty that Olave should be baptized, and he swore that he would never again act in
hostility against the English, a covenant which he duly
performed. But the treaty did not import that the
Danish host should quit the English waters. They continued stationary about the coast—further invasions
ensued—their depredations were incessant—almost the
whole of England was laid waste (A.D. 997-998), and
another precarious truce was purchased by payment of
twenty-four thousand pounds, together with the usual
engagement of " feeding " these unwelcome visitants
(A.D. 999-1002). Fifty thousand pounds had now been

paid as Dane-geld. Each pound was then equivalent, in weight of silver, to somewhat more than three pounds of our nominal currency. But the intrinsic worth of the coin affords no adequate measure of its value. And the worth of fifty thousand pounds in the reign of Ethelred will be understood, by knowing that this sum would have purchased about one million two hundred thousand acres of arable land, together with such rights and privileges in the common lands and woods appertaining to the inclosed land, as may be considered to have trebled the superficial admeasurement.*

The success of the Danes was much facilitated by the extreme want of steadiness on the part of the English. When the enemy was in the field, the king and his witan ordained to proceed against them " by sea " and " by land." But when the ships were prepared, delays arose, and thus, in the words of the chronicle, " the forwarder the expedition should have been, the later it was ; and from one time to another they still suffered the army of the enemies to increase." The Danes continually retreated from the sea-coast, and the English pursued them in vain. And, in the end, no other consequences were produced, excepting " vexation to the people, waste of money, and increase of strength to the enemies." Even when the king summoned the whole power of Wessex and of Mercia, the Danes went wheresoever they would, whilst the undisciplined English militia, raised for the defence of the country, did more harm to the people than any external foe.

Hostilities had prevailed between Ethelred and Richard

---

* The ordinary price of land was about five pounds of silver per hyde. The calculation must not be considered as precise, but I could not find any better mode of showing the value of money, than by taking the price of land as the standard.

II., or the Good, Duke of Normandy, son of Richard
" *Sanz-peur*," the grandson of Rollo the " *Ganger*" (A.D.
991). These disputes were terminated by the mediation
of the Pope; and it was particularly agreed that neither
party should harbour any individual suspicious to the
other potentate (A.D. 1002). This pacification was
followed by a marriage between Ethelred and Emma,
the sister of the Duke of Normandy. Ethelred proposed
thereby to increase his power, and to protect his kingdom.
But this eventful union, which ultimately afforded the
pretext for the Norman claims, seemed, from the first,
to bode ill to the English nation. Emma was accompanied by a train of favourites and dependants. One
of them, " the French Earl Hugh," was appointed
" Gerefa," or Sheriff of Exeter, and his negligence or
treachery afterwards surrendered the city as a prey to
the Danish enemy.

Ethelred's government was much disturbed: he
quarrelled again with Duke Richard, and prepared to
invade Normandy. The Normans say, that Ethelred
behaved with great arrogance. He gave orders that
Richard's hands should be tied behind his back, and the
captive thus conducted before his conqueror, and that
every building in the country should be burnt to the
ground, the monastery of Mount Saint Michael only
excepted. The English troops effected a landing not far
from Coutances, but they were entirely defeated, and the
crew of a single vessel, who returned home, declared to
Ethelred—this is the Norman story—that the women of
Normandy alone would have been sufficient to extermi-
nate the English army.

On the "mass day," or feast of St. Brice, immediately
following Ethelred's marriage with the lady Emma,

(13th Nov. 1002), he gave the fatal order for the massacre of all such Danes, within his dominions, as were subjected to his power.   This wicked act arose out of a most mischievous policy.   From the reign of Athelstane, the Kings of Wessex had been accustomed to encourage the resort of Danish adventurers, whom they retained as their own body-guard, or household troops.   It is said that the kings exerted the prerogative of quartering one of these satellites in every house.   Such, indeed, were the "guests" of the despotic monarchs of Norway, who were placed by the king's command, as the inmates of his subjects, quite at his will and pleasure; and the constant resort of the Norwegians to the courts of the opulent and munificent Kings of England, so often commemorated in the Icelandic "sagas," may be considered as one of the evidences of the favour shown to the "heathen thieves."   That these stipendiary bravoes, the "huscarls," placed under the immediate protection of the sovereign, should have conducted themselves with great insolence towards the natives, may be easily credited; and it is equally possible that a formidable body of soldiery, feeling no tie of allegiance or affection towards the monarch who had purchased their mercenary aid, may have conspired to slay him and his witan, and to usurp, or to assist their brethren in usurping the kingdom.

Numbers, however, of the murdered Danes had become quiet and peaceable settlers in England.   Many had intermarried with the hosts who received them, and the Danish women and children were included in this inhuman proscription.   Gunhilda, the sister of Sweyne, a woman of high spirit and great beauty, had embraced Christianity; but neither her sex nor her faith could protect her.   She was compelled to witness the death

of her husband, and of her son; and she was then beheaded by the express direction of Edric Streone—of
whom more anon—who appears to have been the chief
instigator of this massacre.

This is not one of those stories of atrocity concerning
which we can indulge in scepticism. We cannot escape
from the conviction of the entire truth. So much
abhorrence did the deed excite, that William the Conqueror afterwards employed the " murder of St. Brice's
day" as an incentive to his Norman nobles, in urging
them to avenge the blood of their kinsman. A nearer
punishment was at hand. Gunhilda, in the hour of
death, exclaimed, rather with a prophetic spirit of sorrow
than of anger, that the shedding of her blood would
bring the greatest evils upon England; and Sweyne her
brother, whose greediness had now received the additional stimulus of revenge, attacked the island, with
greater inveteracy than at any former period (A.D. 1003-
1004 to 1007). His repeated invasions reduced the
country to the extreme of misery. Every shire of
Wessex was " marked with fire and flame and desolation." In this emergency a great council of the witan
assembled by Ethelred's commands. Was it possible to
save the land before it should be utterly undone? Loth
as they were to adopt the expedient, there appeared no
other mode of mitigating the evil except by again rendering a tribute. An embassy was sent to the " Danish
host," offering money, and praying for a respite: the
enemies accepted the terms. Provisions were furnished
to the Danes from all parts of " Angel Cyn," and thirty
thousand pounds of silver,—or the worth of seven
hundred and twenty thousand acres of land—purchased
the truce which was sought.

It appears from the expressions used by the chroniclers, that the pride of the English nation was deeply wounded by the payment of " geld," or tribute, to the enemy.   Tribute was the mark of subjection which the Kings of Wessex had so long exacted from the subject states of the Cymri; and the stipend was as prejudicial to the honour of the crown as it was burdensome to the people at large.   Under these circumstances Ethelred adopted a new policy.   In addition to the ancient national militia, an armed host was raised by the landholders in proportion to their property (A.D. 1008). Every nine hides of land were bound to find one man armed with a hauberk and helmet.   A naval force was raised in the same manner; every three hundred and ten hides being charged to provide one vessel for the defence of the kingdom.*   This imposition is the remote origin of the well-known tax of " ship money;" and according to the dependence of the mystic chain by which human events are linked and bound together, we may view, in Ethelred's regulations, the cause of the expulsion of the Stuarts from the throne.   By means of these measures, a formidable fleet was equipped.   " Never were so many ships gathered together in England before, as in this king's day, as the books tell us ;"—if the land north of the Humber furnished its due contingent, the fleet may have amounted to one thousand vessels, and the men at arms to upwards of forty thousand men—a force which, properly directed, might, with the aid of the " fyrd," or militia, might have been sufficient to drive the Danes for ever from the British shores.   But the account of the armament is concluded by lamentations for its inutility.

* The Chroniclers vary in the particulars of the assessment.

Ethelred's reign began with ill omens. Dunstan's curse hung heavy upon him. He had lost his character as a king; and the vices of the man did not redeem the defects of the sovereign. Ethelred neglected his Norman queen; and whilst his subjects at large suffered from his injustice, his nearest kindred dreaded his violence and rapacity. The moral defects and transgressions of Ethelred may be admitted; but the facts disclosed by his history do not altogether justify the charge of incapacity which has been brought against him by the chroniclers. Treachery, and the misplaced confidence by which he sought to counteract that treachery, contributed to paralyze his efforts. The success of Sweyne's predatory invasions is attributable to the falsehood and craft of Elfric, who continued high in office and power, notwithstanding his declared and notorious treasons. His faithlessness was most evident—he might have prevented the loss of Exeter, to which I have before alluded. The forces of Wilts and Hampshire were under his command. But when he should have led them on—" he brought forth his old wiles again,"—by pretending sickness, he avoided battle; and allowed Sweyne to plunder and ravage the shores with entire impunity. A hurried narrative of judicial sentences pronounced at this period betrays the discovery and punishment of some real or supposed offences against the state. " Wulfgeat" forfeited all his property; " Wulfheah" and " Uffigeat" were blinded: of their guilt or innocence we cannot judge. But at the same time, the Ealdorman Ælfhelm was unjustly slain by the commands of Edric Streone, who, as far as one individual can affect the destiny of a nation, was the chief cause of the calamities of England.

Edric was a man of low birth, but extremely eloquent,

possessing abilities equal to his wickedness; and he soon acquired the highest favour.   The favourite became the relative of the king; he obtained the hand of Edgitha, the daughter of Ethelred, and was soon afterwards appointed Ealdorman of the whole kingdom of Mercia, or the dominion which Elfric had held.   Elfric was yet alive, and it is uncertain whether he was again deprived of his hereditary dominions, or whether the appointment of Edric was in the nature of a viceroyalty.   I incline, however, to the latter opinion, and I think that Edric obtained a delegated authority which enabled him to exercise the royal functions, and to demand such obedience and services from the nobles of Mercia as the king himself might have claimed.   This promotion, and still more, this mis-alliance of a daughter of Odin, constituted an entire departure from the ancient principles of the Anglo-Saxon government.

Edric was the head of a numerous and ambitious family, who seem all to have participated in his good fortune.   Great dissensions, however, existed amongst them (A.D. 1009).   Brihtric, the brother of Edric, conspired against Wulfnoth, his nephew, who bore the ambiguous title of "child" of the South Saxons.   In other documents he was called the "minister," or the Thane of Sussex.   Wulfnoth fled the country, but he contrived to induce twenty of the king's ships to join him, and with this force he plundered the southern coast, and wrought every kind of mischief, even as the Danes themselves would have done.   Brihtric obtained the command of eighty vessels, and with this fleet cruized against Wulfnoth.   But a tempest drove Brihtric's vessels on shore.   The "child" of Sussex profited by this mischance, and attacked the king's fleet, which he burnt. From some cause, which is not clearly explained, but which probably is to be traced to the influence of Edric, Ethelred appeared panic-struck, and returned home with his ealdormen and " heah witan," or great councillors, and the fleet was dispersed. In this miserable civil war, the forces intended to guard the coasts were dissipated and lost.

Immediately after this disaster, about Lammas (A.D. 1009), arrived a large army of Danes called " Thurkill's host," surpassing all previous foes in ferocity. Earl Thurkill was one of the pirates of Jomsburgh, so celebrated in northern story for their invincible courage and hardihood, no less than for their inveterate hatred of the Christian name. Thurkill's expedition was taken for the purpose of avenging the death of his brother, Earl Sigwald, and his vessels were filled with the flower of the Scandinavian youth. A sum of three thousand pounds, paid by the men of East Kent, purchased a temporary respite. After which, " as their custom is," the Danes plundered the Isle of Wight, and many of the shores of the south and west, cruizing about as best suited their plans, but keeping their chief station in the port of the river Thames. It is remarkable, however, that they could not make any impression upon London, which appears to have been strongly fortified towards the river. " God be praised," says the chronicle,—in this portion a contemporary history—" the city yet stands firm ;" and had it not been for the treachery of Edric, adds the chronicler, it is possible that the Danes might have been prevented from advancing into the country.

In the following spring the Danes invaded East Anglia, and a fearful battle took place near Ipswich (A.D. 1010).

As soon as the armies were opposed to each other, an East Anglian Dane, Thurkill Myrenheafod, either from cowardice, or, as is more probable, from treachery, took flight,—all the East Anglians followed, and the English army was defeated with great slaughter. Here perished the noble Wulfric, "the consul of the Mercians," whose dominions appear to have been afterwards known as the earldom of Lancaster; Athelstane, the king's kinsman; and many other good thanes. It is noticed in the account of the battle, that "Cambridgeshire stood firm," —a mode of expression which shows how the levies were identified with the districts from whence they proceeded.

This victory seemed to place the whole country in the power of the Danes. All the witan were summoned to meet the king, to concert measures of defence; but the members of the legislature were utterly confounded. No good counsel could be given or adopted. Whatsoever was advised, "it stood not a month, until at length there was not a captain left, who could or would assemble any troops; each fled as he could, and no shire, moreover, could stand by the other." The spirit of the English was wholly broken. If two or three pirates appeared, they drove the whole country before them. The chronicler enumerates, with doleful precision, the districts which they had reduced to the last stage of misery and desolation, and then, by way of climax, exclaims, these disasters "befel us by bad counsels, because we would neither offer tribute nor fight with the enemy." But the evil lay in the first of the alternatives—for it was the submission to the Danegeld which had wholly ruined the strength and heart of England.

The Danes had now overrun almost the whole of Mercia and of Wessex, and the mischief being done, Ethelred and his counsellors resorted to their old dastardly policy. Tribute was offered, as usual; and the Danes were bought off, for a short period, by the offer of money and of provisions. It should seem that a vigorous effort might yet have rescued the country; but Ethelred was so perplexed by domestic treachery, as to render resistance impossible. Edric Streone had prevented any effectual opposition to Thurkill in the first instance, and he was now about to cause still greater evil. A brother of Edric had been appointed governor, perhaps sheriff, of Kent. He acted with great tyranny towards the people, and deprived the nobles of their inheritance. These haughty and ferocious people avenged themselves, and Edric's brother perished in his dwelling, which was burnt in a popular tumult.

Edric demanded vengeance; Ethelred refused, alleging that the misdeeds of him who had been slain justified the act. Edric quitted the council hall, pale with anger. The Danish fleet was now stationed off Sandwich (A.D. 1012). The army had not yet ventured to attack Canterbury— one of the many proofs of the numerical smallness of their forces, as compared with the English. Edric joined the enemy with all his power, amounting to upwards of ten thousand men, and the united forces marched to the attack of the Kentish metropolis. The citizens were appalled. Archbishop Alphege, whose courage never failed him, exhorted them to defence. He reminded them of the constancy of the primitive saints and martyrs; the assembled multitude received his blessing, and prepared for the advance of the Danes with constancy and fortitude.

Chapel in Canterbury Cathedral.

Monk Bar, York.

During twenty days, the Danes besieged Canterbury without effect, when that faithlessness, which seems to have been the bane of England, delivered the city into their power. Elfmar, the traitor, who secretly admitted the Danes into Canterbury, was doubly guilty, for his life had been saved by the intercession of the prelate whom he betrayed. The city was burnt, the inhabitants slaughtered or carried away as slaves. As for the archbishop, the Danes kept him in cruel and squalid captivity. They offered to allow him to ransom his life, and even urged the acceptance of the offer. The old man steadily refused. He had no worldly goods of his own, he said, nor would he waste the possessions of the church, which belonged not to him, but to the poor and needy, for whose benefit they were given. At length the Danes, incensed beyond measure by his firmness, condemned him to death. They still thought they could obtain their wishes; and as they brought him out, they cried out, " Gold, Bishop, give us gold, gold !" Alphege was calm and unmoved. The Danes were assembled in a drunken banquet; they threw their battleaxes at him, cast the horns and bones of oxen at him, and stoned him until he fell to the ground, desperately bruised and hurt, yet not dead. At length one of the Danes, whom Alphege had baptized, put an end to his agony.

Edric, and all the chief witan of " Angel Cyn," now assembled at London, and continued their session until a tribute of forty-eight thousand pounds, being the price of one million one hundred and fifty-two thousand acres of land, was paid to the enemy. No mention is made of the king, and it is not certain that he was present; but after the money had been received by the Danes, " oaths of peace" were sworn, and he appears to have regained his authority. Earl Thurkill and a large detachment of the Danes became his soldiers, and undertook to defend the country; and an earldom—probably of East Anglia —conferred upon the pirate, rendered him the vassal of the English king. It has been said that Thurkill's submission was intended to be deceptive, and that he entered Ethelred's service merely for the purpose of being enabled to betray the English to the Danes, his countrymen. The subsequent transactions in which he was engaged might appear to countenance this opinion; yet the conduct of the earl was represented to Sweyne as an act of rebellion against his authority. Sweyne had already become jealous of the warlike and impatient Thurkill; and the advice given by his retainers, who urged him to attack the English and their new adherent, was gladly received and speedily adopted.

A mighty fleet was assembled by Sweyne, glittering with gold and silver—the vessels were adorned with bright and fantastic imagery. Lions, dolphins, eagles, and dragons rose above the prows, and the sea foamed beneath the oars of the ships which, vieing with the gay and splendid barks of eastern seas, seemed rather prepared for festal triumph than for battle. But this barbaric splendour, like the trappings of the war-horse, excited the pride and energy of the rude warriors who manned the vessels, and, by displaying the wealth and power of the leader, added to the panic of his enemies.

Sweyne sailed up the mouth of the Humber, and landed at or near the city of York. The greater portion of the inhabitants of the "Danelagh" joined him without hesitation or delay. Earl Uchtred and the Northumbrians, Lindesey, the Five Burghs, were up in arms, and lastly, all the "host" north of Watling-street. The

Walmsgate Barbican, York.

Ely Cathedral.

Silver Coin of Canute.

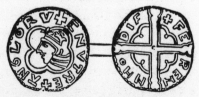

Silver Penny of Canute, struck in Dublin.

term "host," used in this place, cannot be well applied to the old descendants of the Danish settlers; and it must designate a fresh floating population of Danes by which the country had been occupied during the disturbances.

Committing his fleet to the command of his son Canute, Sweyne marched to the south, with his main army. According to the usual scheme of operations adopted by the Danes, they had compelled the inhabitants of the provinces which submitted to them, to supply horses and provisions, and thus they were enabled to proceed with the greatest rapidity. Oxford and Winchester surrendered, and probably escaped further harm.

Northumbria had been spared, the south was abandoned to desolation. The country was wasted far and wide by fire and sword. London, which was occupied by Ethelred and Thurkill, held out against the Dane. The citizens were pre-eminently distinguished for their martial spirit. Malmesbury, in a strain of monastic eloquence, exclaims that Mars himself would not have disdained them; and they either gave battle to Sweyne, or made such a show of resistance as compelled him to retreat. But the Danes did not meet with any effectual opposition in Wessex; and Sweyne having established his head-quarters at Bath, he received the homage of Ethelmar, Ealdorman of Devonshire, and of all the thanes of the west. The people of the north confirmed their previous submission. Ethelred abandoned London; and like King John, under circumstances not entirely dissimilar, he took refuge in the Isle of Wight. The burgesses of London, who had hitherto defended themselves so stoutly, now opened their gates to the invader (A.D.

1013). "They feared lest he might undo them," spoil their wealth, and deprive them of their eyes and limbs. Sweyne was now considered as "full King of England," or rather of the several kingdoms and earldoms of which it was composed. Some portions, however, of the Anglo-Saxon dominions refused their homage, nor did the Scottish Prince of Cumbria acknowledge the supremacy of the Dane.

London, it is stated, would not have surrendered, had Ethelred encouraged the burgesses to defend themselves. His own courage, as Malmesbury informs us, was broken by the consciousness of his own misdeeds. This is the usual tone which has been adopted towards Ethelred by the ancient historians; but when Ethelred addresses the few faithful prelates and thanes who had followed him to the Isle of Wight, we hear him disclose another cause. "He had been banished," he declared, "by the treachery of his generals — abandoned, deserted, and betrayed. The country was subdued, the coast narrowly watched, and greater peril was to be apprehended to his followers from their own countrymen, than from their enemies." Ethelred described and confessed the perils in which he and his adherents were placed, but concluded by stating his intention of sending Emma and his children to the court of Richard, Duke of Normandy. "His favour shown to my wife," continued Ethelred,—"will be the pledge of my own security. Should he oppose me, I am confident I shall not want spirit to die here with honour, in preference to living in Normandy with infamy."

Emma was received with great affection by her brother. The same kindness was shortly afterwards extended by Richard to Ethelred (A.D. 1014-1015), who found a secure and hospitable home in the palace of the

Duke of Normandy, till he was recalled by the sudden and unexpected death of Sweyne. According to the legends, the pagan was slain by the anger of St. Edmund, whose possessions he invaded.

Upon the death of Sweyne, the warriors who manned the fleet, and the Danish "Thingmanna," whom we may call the household troops, accepted Canute as their king—an act of authority which they were perhaps empowered to exercise, as representing the Danish community. But the "witan" of "Angel Cyn," or the English legislature, unanimously resolved to restore the line of Cerdic, and deputies were sent to Ethelred accordingly, to inform him of their resolution, which was in substance, that the English would prefer their legitimate sovereign to any other lord,—*provided that he would govern them better than he did before.* In consequence of this address, Ethelred despatched his son, Edmund the Atheling, with his reply; and the expressions employed in the Saxon chronicle seems to be the very words of the writ or letter which Ethelred addressed to the nation by whom he had been recalled. "He would be a good lord to them—amend those matters which, as all agreed, required reform—and grant a general amnesty for all that had been said and done against him; *provided nevertheless that they should submit to his royal authority without fraud or treachery.*" These conditions were gladly accepted. The compact was confirmed by the legislature; and it was "given for doom," that all Danish kings should from henceforth be outlaws in England.

This remarkable transaction laid the foundations for the greatest alterations in the principles of the constitution. With the full acknowledgment of hereditary right, the nation stipulated that the king should not abuse his power. They imposed terms upon Ethelred, they vindicated their national liberty, at the same time that they respected the sanctity of the crown; and in the concessions made by Ethelred, we may discern the germ of Magna Charta, and of all the subsequent compacts between the king and people of England.

Ethelred returned and took possession of the realm. But the decree of the witan was fulminated in vain against Canute. It does not appear that the Northumbrian Earldoms had concurred in recalling Ethelred; and the inhabitants of Lindesey continued, if not under the lawful government of Canute, yet under his power. But he was exceedingly incensed. Hostages had been given to Sweyne; these Canute sent on shore, cruelly and miserably mutilated. And the sum of twenty-one thousand pounds, as the price of one million and eight thousand acres of land, which Ethelred was compelled to pay to the " host " at Greenwich, shows that they continued in undiminished strength and hostility.

Through all these revolutions, Edric Streone retained his power. He was always the second man in the country, let who might be the first. A great council of the witan of the Danish and English nations was held at Oxford (A.D. 1015). This was one of the political congresses which were assuming the place of the earlier witenagemots. Sigferth and Morcar, the chief thanes of the Danish burghs, attended the convention,—in modern language, we may say that they were the virtual representatives of the communities to which they belonged. By the guile of Edric, and with the assent, as it is said, of Ethelred, these nobles were slain in the banquet chamber, when they were so drunken as to be

unable to defend themselves. Their retainers sought
refuge in the Tower of St. Frideswide's, now Christ's
Church Cathedral, which was burnt by the assailants.
The widow of Sigferth, distinguished for her beauty, was
borne as a captive to Malmsbury. Thence she was
carried off by Edmund the Atheling—Edmund *Ironside*
—as he was called by the English, and he was equally
strong in body and energetic in mind. The young
widow, nothing loth, became the wife of sturdy *Ironside*;
and Edmund, by force, obtained possession of the territory which had belonged to Sigferth and his brother.
It does not clearly appear that the murder of Sigferth
and Morcar was intended to answer any political
purpose; but, in its consequence, it enabled Edmund
Ironside to obtain a power in opposition to the plans of
Edric Streone.

Ethelred was sorely stricken by infirmity, and Canute
continued to harass and plunder the western parts of
Wessex. Edric and Edmund respectively raised all their
forces; and the commanders assembled their troops at
Corsham, where Ethelred was confined to his bed by
illness. It was intended to attack Canute with their
united armies; but Edric was now plotting to betray
Ironside into the hands of his enemies. The armies
separated, and Edric, together with forty ships, joined
the Danes. The greater part of Wessex followed the same
example. Mercia continued true to Ethelred, though
many districts were shortly afterwards plundered by
Canute, with the help of the traitor Edric.

Ethelred was now in London, where his authority was
scarcely acknowledged; for when Edmund the Atheling
began to collect another army, which the Mercians were
willing to furnish, he could not act with effect, because

the "burgesses" did not assist him—a remarkable proof of their military importance. Another general array of the country, or of such parts as were not in Canute's power, was then summoned, under penalty of the highest mulct which the law imposed for neglect of this duty. Ethelred, however, would not take the command; he had secret information of some conspiracy that was hatching against him, and he returned to London.

Uchtred, the Earl of Northumbria, had begun to carry on a predatory war on his own account. It was expected that he would assist Ethelred; but he marched with his army into the Mercian Earldom of Chester, which he ravaged without opposition. Canute, on his part, employed himself in wasting the eastern parts of Mercia, plundering the country as he advanced, until he reached York. Uchtred was then much alarmed, and returning to Northumbria, he submitted to Canute, giving hostages for the performance of his engagements. But this could not save his life; he was slain by the instigation of the traitor Edric; and Canute, who appears throughout to have constantly asserted the full rights of sovereignty, bestowed Northumbria upon Earl Eric, his brother-in-law. Eric held great part of Norway as a loan or feud, but he surrendered this territory to his son Haco, being contented to abandon the rocks and forests of the north, and seek his fortune in England.

On St. George's day, Ethelred died. Edmund appears to have been in London; and the citizens, together with such of the witan as were assembled there, forthwith accepted Edmund as lawful king in the place of his father (April, 1016). It may be perhaps supposed, that those influential nobles who assembled in London were the members of the great council of Mercia; but at the same time another rival convention was sitting at Southampton. It is described as composed of the bishops, abbots, dukes, and chief nobles of all England. This is the expression of an ancient, though not of a contemporary writer; but as it is evidently incorrect, we can only conjecture that the witan of Wessex constituted this assembly, which assumed the entire disposition of the crown.

The members of the Anglo-Saxon parliament accommodated themselves to circumstances with the most admirable and edifying facility. But a little while since, they had recalled Ethelred and outlawed the Danes for ever—now they again declared that they withdrew all allegiance from the children of Ethelred; they accepted Canute as king, and took the oath of fidelity to him; and Canute, on his part, promised that he would govern the English according to law, human and divine. No feeling of personal dislike could exist towards Edmund Ironside, who on all occasions is mentioned with praise. This proceeding, therefore, of the English legislature shows that Ethelred's constant suspicions of treachery, or, to use a milder term, of disaffection, were not unfounded. But the compact itself, irregular as the mode may have been in which it was effected, exhibits the progress of new ideas of government in the monarchy. The witan considered themselves as competent to alter the succession, to expel the ancient line, and to transfer the crown to another dynasty; demanding at the same time a promise from the new sovereign, that he would rule according to law and justice.

It might be very difficult to decide who was legitimate king and who pretender; and, as usual in such cases, the question was referred to the decision of the sword.

Canute assembled a formidable fleet, and the Thames
was covered by his vessels; but Edmund possessed all
the qualifications of an ancient chieftain. He was subtle
and valiant, and escaping through the very midst of the
hostile squadrons, his prowess compelled the men of
Wessex to annul their declaration in favour of Canute,
and confess that the son of Ethelred was the legitimate
heir. At Sherston, Edmund was nearly routed by the
stratagem of Edric the traitor. His courage, however,
prevailed, and he was enabled to muster such a force as
to raise the siege of London, which had been again
attempted by Canute; the aid which he gave being,
however, nobly supported by the strenuous courage of
the inhabitants of this "most populous city."

Other victories succeeded, and Edmund, if Canute had
trusted only to strength, would have cleared the land of
the Danish enemy. But the crafty Canute, whose virtues
were deeply stained by the cunning of the savage, conquered his opponent by intrigue. At a previous junc-
ture, when the rapid advance of Ethelred would have
destroyed the Danish army, Edric Streone, assuming the
haracter of a repentant and submissive subject, had
joined the host of Ethelred with his followers; by his
persuasion he induced the king to desist from improving
his victory, and thus afforded to Canute the opportunity of
reorganizing his power, and of obtaining the advantages
which I have detailed.

It was strange that Edmund should place any trust in
this caitiff; yet he not only followed the advice of Edric,
but allowed him to marshal his forces amongst the ranks
of the English army; and thus accompanied, he encountered the Danes at Assingdune. Canute unfurled
the banner of the raven. Edmund headed his troops,

and displayed all the valour and energy of his character.
It was the fifth time that he had assembled all the English nation against the enemy.   The defeat of the Danes
would have been inevitable, when Edric suddenly raised
the cry that Edmund had fallen.   "Flee, English! flee,
English!" exclaimed he, "dead is Edmund!"   I quote
the words exactly as they have been preserved.   Edric
had slain a thane, whose countenance greatly resembled
that of Edmund, and holding the bloody head aloft, at
the same time that he cast away the dragon, the standard
of Wessex, he and his troops took flight, and abandoned
the field.   The whole army was thrown into confusion,
and entirely routed; and thus did Canute gain the
victory, though all the English nation fought against
him.   The consequences were most disastrous: and, as
it is expressed in the Anglo-Saxon chronicle, all the
nobility of England were undone.

Canute marched with great rapidity towards Gloucestershire, following Edmund, who had retreated in that
direction.   Ironside reassembled his forces, and when
the armies were arrayed against each other, he stepped
forward and challenged Canute to single combat, "for
it was pity," he said, "that so many lives should be put
in jeopardy to satisfy their ambition."*   Canute declined the duel; alleging that he, a man of small stature,
would have no chance if opposed to the stalwart Edmund.
There was prudence in this determination; and he added,
that it would be better that they two should divide the
realms between them, even as their fathers had done
before.

* According to Ethelred, Abbot of Rivaulx, this mode of ending the differences
between the monarchs, was directed by the acclamation of the leaders of both
armies, who declared that the kings should either settle their differences by single
combat, or agree to a pacification.   There are other variations in the narratives.

When this proposal was made known to the respective armies, they hailed it with gladness. Edmund was compelled to yield to the clamour; and Edric Streone, always ready and alert to act against his natural sovereign, was at the head of a party of counsellors, or "witan," by whom the partition was negotiated. Wessex, Essex, East-Anglia, and London were assigned to Edmund, with a nominal superiority over the remaining dominions, which were allotted to the Dane—thus, to use the expression of the chroniclers, the crown remained to Edmund Ironside.

Soon afterwards Edmund ceased to live. The manner in which he met with his death was never exactly known, yet no one seems to have doubted but that Edric Streone was the perpetrator of the deed. The evidence that the crime was committed is satisfactory; that Canute was strictly an accessory, cannot be distinctly proved; but he reaped all the profit of the murder, and became sovereign of the whole empire.

He began, however, with a colour of law and a pretence of legitimacy. A great council of the bishops, duces, and "optimates," was convened at London (A.D. 1017); and in this assembly Canute appealed to those who had been witnesses to the convention between him and Edmund, as to the terms upon which the compact was concluded. They all loudly testified that Edmund had not intended to reserve any right of succession to his brothers, and that it was his wish that Canute should be the guardian of his own children during their infancy. This was a falsehood extorted partly by force, and partly for the purpose of conciliating the favour of the monarch. Canute did not stop here; he urged the witan to take the oath of fealty to him, the members of the assembly yielded, and acknowledged him, not as regent, but as king; he gave them his "handselled" pledge of peace and protection; all old enmities were to be buried in oblivion. Full amnesty was granted for all that had been said and done. Ethelred's descendants were outlawed, and for ever excluded from the throne; and a payment of "geld" to the "host" ratified the compact, and purchased the gratitude or mercy of the Danish sovereign.

Canute, by dividing England into four distinct governments, made an important alteration in the administration of the country. Wessex, as the chief and predominant state, he retained under his own immediate sway. Thurkill obtained the earldom of East Anglia, the jealousies which had arisen between him and Canute having been appeased. Edric and Eric were respectively confirmed as earls in Mercia and Northumbria. But it must be recollected that these great earls were of the nature of viceroys, and the ancient territorial earls and ealdormen retained their old authority. Leofric in particular, the Earl of Mercian-Chester, ruled in his dominions with so much energy, as to render him one of the most influential nobles in England.

By the legislative proceedings of the witenagemot, or parliament, the descendants of Ethelred were again excluded from the throne. But the pretensions of these Princes were sufficiently strong to excite the apprehensions of Canute, and he was tempted to a repetition of those crimes by which his character, otherwise deserving of no ordinary praise, was so deeply stained. Edwy, the brother of Ironside, was declared an outlaw in the witenagemot, and afterwards slain, according to the advice of Edric, and by Canute's express command.

Edwy bore the singular title of "King of the Churls, or Peasantry." This designation cannot have had any relation to a real dignity, and we can only conjecture that it was a name given to him on account of his popularity among the villainage, and which would be the more likely to excite the jealousy of the Danish sovereign.

Edric Streone, who pursued the family of his late sovereign with fanatic hatred, gave counsel that Edmund and Edward, the two sons of Ironside, should be sacrificed. A feeling of shame, rather than of compunction, withheld Canute from perpetrating this deed in Britain ; and he sent the babes to the King of the Swedes, his ally and vassal, requesting him to remove these objects of suspicion. The children's innocence moved the pity of the Scandinavian chieftain ; he placed the infants quite out of the reach of Canute, under the care of the King of Hungary, by whom they were treated with affection and honour. Edmund died without issue. Edward espoused the kinswoman of the Emperor of Germany, and the fruits of the union were, Edgar Atheling, Christina, and Margaret, the latter of whom afterwards became the wife of Malcolm, King of Scots ; and through her, the rights of the line of Cerdic were transmitted to Malcolm's progeny, after the conquest of England.

There were two other claimants, equally young in years, but more formidable from the power of their maternal relation. Edward and Alfred, the sons of Ethelred by Emma, had continued in Normandy, and Duke Robert, their cousin, treated them with all brotherly kindness. His ambassadors were sent to Canute, demanding, on their behalf, the restoration of the kingdom. Canute offered to surrender a moiety of

his dominions. But we hear nothing more of the treaty;
and instead of restoring the inheritance of the children,
he wooed their widowed mother, the thoughtless, heart-
less Emma, who bestowed her hand without reluctance
upon the murderer of her husband. According to the
well-known legend, she proved her innocence, when
accused of incontinence, by walking unhurt over seven
burning ploughshares : but it would be difficult to find a
test by which she should be exonerated from great moral
guilt, in contracting this most unnatural union.

About the same time Edric met with his merited fate.
It is said, that an angry discussion arose upon his claiming some further reward for his good services. Mercia
he continued to hold; but he desired a further addition
of wealth and power; and he urged upon Canute, how,
by quitting the ranks of Edmund, he had contributed to
that very victory which had secured the crown to the
Dane (A.D. 1017). Canute tauntingly replied, that the
murderer of an old master would show little fealty to his
new liege lord. The tone or the gesture of Canute indicated his wishes.   Eric of Northumbria was present;
and conformably, as it should seem, to a preconcerted
plan, the Danish earl stepped forward, and cut down
Edric with his battle-axe : the carcass of the wretch was
thrown into the Thames; and the ghastly head, spiked upon the highest gate of London, announced to the people
that the felon had now paid the penalty of his misdeeds.

We seem to be reading the history of Turkey, when
we are told by a contemporary, that Canute caused
Edric to be put to death quietly, and in his palace, in
order to prevent any disturbance in the city.   But
despotism bears the same shape in all climates and ages;
and Canute, at this period of his reign, had no law but

his will. The punishment of such a signal traitor as
Edric might wear an appearance of equity; but the
other assassinations which took place at the same time
have not that excuse. Northman, the son of the Ealdorman Leofwine, Athelward, the son of Ethelmar the
Great, Brithnoth, the son of Alphage, and Edwy the
Atheling, were all involved in one common proscription.
It does not appear that any judicial proceedings took
place, when these victims were sacrificed to the policy of
the Danish king. But other English nobles are said to
have been proscribed by his sentence, on the charge of
having conspired against the Danish kings, his predecessors. Their lands were forfeited, and bestowed upon
Canute's Danish followers.

All these proceedings created great discontent amongst
the English, who felt that they were really treated as a
conquered people. The Danes, proud in the protection
of their king, behaved with great haughtiness. According to popular traditions, if an Englishman and a Dane
met on a bridge, the native was compelled to dismount
from his horse, and make way for the victor. We know
from more authentic sources, that the Danish possessors
of the forfeited property were in constant danger from
an irritated people, who saw their lands taken from them
and given to strangers—new lords, who, tyrannizing
over the villainage, increased their toil—and the new
landlords were themselves harassed by constant apprehensions of revenge. The Northman could not sleep in
quietness. The hall which he had usurped was garrisoned like a fortress in the country of an enemy: and
the law which imposed a fine upon the township in
which a Dane was slain, attests the general insecurity
which prevailed.

Canute, the king of six realms, did not desire to retain all his stipendiary soldiery in England, and a large body of these dangerous followers departed from the island; but this measure scarcely relieved the English from their oppressions. The Danish thanes continued as an unblended class of population in the English cities, even far out of the boundaries of the Danelagh. In London, the citizens adopted much of the barbarity of the Danes. Here also a great influx of the Danish population may be apprehended, for at the present day, the principal municipal court of London, the "husting," bears a Danish name.

The first "geld," or tribute, paid pursuant to the treaty which placed Canute upon the throne, amounted to seventy-two thousand pounds, or the price of full one million seven hundred and twenty-eight thousand acres of land, a tribute almost insupportable; ten thousand five hundred pounds fell upon the city of London. This levy was paid to the "host," and the share which fell to Canute was received by him, as a military commander (A.D. 1018). Throughout his reign the territorial taxes continued to be levied with great vigour. If the owner of the land could not pay his assessment by the end of the third day, the land itself was seized by the officers of the revenue, and sold forthwith for the benefit of the "hoard," or exchequer of the Danish king.

Canute, King of the "Danes, and of the Swedes, and of the Northmen," appears to have considered the opulent realm of England as the chief of the states over which he ruled, yet he did not neglect his other dominions. His continental possessions contained many turbulent subjects, and were bordered by the fierce and hostile Sclavonian tribes, the *Wendi*, who had pushed

their conquests as far as the Elbe. Against these enemies Canute proceeded (A.D. 1017-1019), aided by a
considerable body of English troops, commanded by
Godwin — whose father, Wolnoth, nephew of Edric
Streone, may be recollected as the "child" of Sussex.
Godwin, in a night attack, surprised and defeated the
Sclavonians, and the English obtained great praises for
their valour. Canute acted wisely when he thus employed the subjects whose fidelity he might well distrust
whilst they remained in their own country ; and it was
equally a gain to him whether they slew his foes, or were
themselves slain in the field of battle.

Canute kept a strong hand over his Danish earls.
Thurkill, Earl of East Anglia, was outlawed for his non-
appearance before a synod, to which he had been
summoned by the king's writ ; the civil authority thus
coming in aid of the ecclesiastical power. The " doughty
Haco," Canute's own nephew, who had obtained the
Earldom of Worcestershire, was driven into exile ; and
met with his death, either in the Orcades or on the
coast of Norway.

The Swedes, trusting in Canute's absence from their
country, repeatedly rose against him, refused their
tribute, and defied his power ; but at last they were
thoroughly reduced, by the help of the English and of
Godwin.   And the earldom bestowed upon the English
chieftain made him one of the most powerful nobles of
the island. Towards the conclusion of his reign (A.D.
1033), Canute enforced the allegiance due from the Cumbrian and Scottish Kings. Duncan, Regulus of Cumbria,
the "gracious Duncan" of Shakspeare, had refused to
acknowledge Canute as his superior ; alleging that he
was an intruder, and, as such, had no right to demand

the homage which was due only to the lawful heir of Ethelred. Malcolm, King of Scots, equally declared his hostility; but Canute assembled all his forces, and marched forthwith against the opponents of his authority. Malcolm was compelled to submit; the light-armed Celtic tribes, and the mixed Saxon host of the Lothians, could not resist the steady ranks of the English and of the Danes: he became the "man," or vassal of Canute. The "Reguli," or minor sovereigns—Malbethe, so well known to us as Macbeth, and Jemark, called by the Scandinavians the "Kings of Fife,"—followed the example of their superior. The infeudation of the kingdom of Cumbria, as the apanage of the heir-apparent of the Scottish monarchy, completed the pacification between the vassals and the sovereign; and the "Basileus," or Emperor of the Anglo-Saxons—for this was the title which Canute assumed—could boast that six nations—the English, the Scots, and the Britons, the Swedes, the Danes, and the Norwegians, were subjected to his power.

Canute, like all sovereigns who come in by force, or by the support of a party, has been represented very differently by his friends and by his enemies. In such a case each sees the same man through a different medium. Actions, which the one set of partisans represent as just and vigorous, seem harsh and cruel to the others; and the gift which is extolled by the receiver, as a proof of generosity, is stigmatized as the prodigal bounty of a rapacious tyrant, by those whose purses have been drained to supply the bounty thus bestowed.

On the whole, however, Canute governed in England with more justice than could have been anticipated from his origin and station. He was a foreign warrior, accustomed to exercise despotic authority over the great body of his Scandinavian subjects, who had acquired the crown by force, and been compelled to propitiate his immediate followers out of the goods and lands of the conquered people.   Time, however, diminished the necessity for such exactions; age softened Canute's temper; devotion purified his heart.   He journeyed as a pilgrim to Rome; and on his return he issued a solemn address to the English people, professing repentance for the violence of his youth, and his hopes that he might be able to renew his life, and govern according to the dictates of mercy and justice (A.D. 1031).

When Canute was in the plenitude of his glory, he caused his throne to be placed on the sands of the seashore; and, addressing the ocean, he said, "Thou art my kingdom, and the dry land is also mine; rise not, obey my commands."   Canute perhaps called the sea his realm, in allusion to the maritime dominion often ascribed to the crown of England.   But the waves ascended with the swelling tide, and rolled on to his feet; and then Canute turned to his warriors and courtiers, and called upon them to confess how weak was the might of an earthly king, compared with that power by whom the elements are ruled.   After this declaration, he took off his crown; and, depositing the symbol of royalty in the cathedral of Winchester, he never again adorned himself with the diadem.

Canute was very bountiful.   On his way to Rome, we are told that he "scattered gold and silver with unparalleled liberality."   The laws and statutes which bear his name are generally founded upon the laws of his predecessors; and he administered justice with an even hand.   He was well spoken and cheerful; a liberal

Abbey Gateway, Bury St. Edmunds.

Country near Dover.

patron of the scallds and gleemen, being himself a reasonable proficient in the art of poesy. A ballad which he composed, continued long afterwards to be a favourite amongst the common people of England. It chanced that, when navigating the Nenne near the minster of Ely, the sweet and solemn tones of the choral psalmody fell on his ear; and Canute burst forth with his lay—

> " Merrily sung the monks, within Ely,
> When Cnute, king, rowed thereby.
> Row, my knights ; row near the land,
> And hear we these monkés' song."*

All the other stanzas have been lost; and we may regret that we possess no further specimens of this composition, which entitles Canute to rank as one of the royal authors of England. Amongst the few ancient public works of which the origin is known, is the *King's Delf*, a causeway connecting Peterborough and Ramsey, and raised amidst the marshes, by Canute's command. Whilst the rich monasteries erected by him, St. Bennet's in the Holme and St. Edmund's Bury, have been utterly subverted, this memorial of his reign alone remains.

Canute died at Shaftesbury, and was buried at Winchester (Nov. 12, 1035). He had one son, Hardicanute, by the lady Emma, the sister of Richard, Duke of Normandy ; and there were two other lads acknowledged by Canute as his children, but who, according to common report, were of very doubtful parentage. Their mother, or reputed mother, Alfgiva, daughter of Elf-

---

* The following is the original fragment, as preserved in the Historia Eliensis. It will be observed, that the alteration of two words only converts the stanza into modern English. **Ben**, for *binnen* or within, is still employed in the ancient Saxon dialect of modern Scotland :—

> " Merie sungen the muneches *binnen* Ely,
> *Tha* Cnut Ching, reu ther by.
> Roweth cnihtes, næer the land,
> And here we thes muneches sæng."

helm, Ealdorman of Southampton, was the acknowledged concubine of Canute; but it is said that she was barren, and that the babes, whom she called her own, were both supposititious. Sweyne, the eldest, was universally believed to be the son of a priest, whom the artful woman had presented to Canute as her own infant. Harold Harefoot, the youngest, was thought to be of still lower origin—the son of a cobbler—who had also been imposed upon the king.

These specimens of antiquated scandal may remind my readers of the opinion, so firmly maintained by the "news writers" in the reign of King William, that the poor little pretender had been smuggled into the lying-in chamber of Mary of Este, concealed in a huge royal warming-pan. But however much the stories may have been adorned by Anglo-Saxon gossip, the contemporary chronicles do certainly deny that Harold was the son of Canute and Alfgiva: " it was not sooth," are the words of the text; and upon this denial we must rest.

Canute intended to divide his dominions between Harold, Hardicanute, and Sweyne. Britain was to be ruled by the first, Denmark by the second, and Norway by the third, who had received his portion in his father's lifetime. The nomination of Harold, as King of the Anglo-Saxon realms, was much against the inclination of Earl Godwin; and the English wished to choose either one of the sons of Ethelred, or Hardicanute the son of Emma, who was at least connected with the old line. Earl Leofric of Mercia, and the thanes north of the Thames, and all the Danes, espoused the cause of Harold: the citizens of London cast their powerful influence into the scale; and in the great council or witenagemot held at Oxford, Harold was recognised as

King of Mercia and Northumbria. Earl Godwin and the nobles of Wessex resisted as long as they could— probably rather by assumption of power than by any clear constitutional right of interfering with the concerns of the other kingdoms; but they were in the minority. Yet they prevailed so far, that Earl Godwin was allowed to maintain possession of Wessex for the prince whose cause he espoused; and this kingdom was afterwards assigned to Hardicanute; whilst Mercia and Northumbria, as before mentioned, acknowledged the sovereignty of his real or supposed brother.

Hardicanute lingered in Denmark: his mother Emma acted for a time as Regent of Wessex, governing on his behalf, and holding her court at Winchester. After a short delay, however, Harold Harefoot and his party grew bolder, and he was proclaimed as "full king" over all England. But this election was not sanctioned by legislative authority. Ethelnoth, Archbishop of Canterbury, also refused to bestow the regal benediction. He placed the crown and the sceptre on the altar, and said to Harold—"I will neither give them to thee, nor prevent thee from taking the ensigns of royalty; but I will not bless thee, nor shall any prelate hallow thee on the throne." Harold tried threats, prayers, bribes—all in vain: and being unable to obtain the sanction of the church, he lived as one who had abjured Christianity.

Edward and Alfred, the children of Ethelred, were safe beyond the sea; but as soon as the news of Canute's death was known in Normandy, they, by the assistance of their friends, fitted out a fleet and sailed to England. Edward approached the port of Southampton, where he found the inhabitants in arms, not to aid him in his enterprise, but prepared for the most strenuous resistance. Either they were really hostile to the son of the unpopular Ethelred, or they feared to draw down upon themselves the vengeance of the brutal Harold. Edward, therefore, had no choice; and abandoning the inhospitable shore, he returned to his place of refuge in Normandy.

Soon afterwards, an affectionate letter was addressed, in the name of Emma, to Alfred and Edward, urging one of them, at least, to return to England for the purpose of recovering the kingdom from the tyrant. Alfred obeyed the summons; and with a few trusty followers, whom he retained in Flanders, he proceeded to England, where he was favourably received by Earl Godwin at London, and thence conducted to Guildford. The plot was now revealed. Alfred was seized by the accomplices and satellites of the tyrant, blinded, and conducted as a captive to Ely, where death soon closed his sufferings. Godwin was very generally accused of the murder. The epistle had perhaps been forged by the direction of Harold. Rumour is always busy in these foul transactions; and Emma herself does not escape vehement suspicion; but nothing is known for certain, except the fate of the miserable victim and of his companions, who suffered an agonizing death.

Harold expired after a short and inglorious reign. Upon his death, the proceres or nobles, Danes as well as English, invited Hardicanute to return to Britain, and receive the sceptre of the kingdom (A.D. 1040); and the chronicler says, that they paid dearly for their advice. He certainly appears to have been in good repute upon his accession: he was open-handed—a quality which obtains favour in all times; but he did not long retain his popularity.

Heavy Danegelds were imposed : one is noticed in particular, amounting to thirty-two thousand one hundred and forty-seven pounds, being, according to the scale which I have before used, the price of seven hundred and seventy-one thousand and fifty-six acres of arable land.   The taxes were collected by military execution.   Hardicanute employed his " huscarles," or domestic troops, for the purpose of enforcing the levies. At Worcester the citizens rose against the collectors, and slew these odious functionaries.   Hardicanute assembled all his earls, and commanded them to march with all their forces against the rebels ; and the greater part of the city was burnt.   So heavily did the burthen of taxation fall upon all ranks of the community, that the clergy were compelled to sell even their chalices to discharge their assessment.   Corn rose to an enormous price, probably in consequence of the scarcity of money.

Hardicanute affected to feel great sorrow for the death of his brother Alfred.   The corpse of Harold was torn up from the grave and cast into the Thames ; and Earl Godwin, upon the accession of the new king, purchased his friendship, or appeased his enmity, by the gift of a vessel splendidly adorned, and manned with eighty thanes, all armed and apparelled with extraordinary magnificence.   Such was the array of the crew.   Each thane was adorned with two golden armlets, severally of the weight of one pound, a triple hauberk, and a gilded helm.   A sword with a golden hilt hung by the warrior's side.   Over his shoulders was slung a Danish battle-axe, damasked with silver.   The shield was bound and embossed with gilded metal ; and in his right hand he wielded a gilded " ategar," the Moorish assagay.   The chief men and principal thanes of all England swore that

Godwin had not incurred any guilt by his participation in the death of Alfred. It seems to be admitted that he had concurred in the misdeed; but the commands of his sovereign were probably thought sufficient to absolve him of all legal as well as of all moral responsibility.

The death of Hardicanute is singularly characteristic both of the man and of the age (A.D. 1042). Goda, the daughter of Osgod Clopa or Clapa, an English thane of great wealth, was given in marriage to "Towid the Proud," a powerful Dane, the king's banner-bearer or marshal; and Hardicanute graced the banquet with his presence at Lambeth, as it is said, but more probably at Clapham or *Clapa-ham*, the *hame* or *home* of Clapa. The potations were prolonged deep into the night. In the midst of the revel, Hardicanute dropped speechless upon the ground, and a few days afterwards he expired.

Chapter XIV.

Edward the Confessor—State of Parties—Influence of Godwin and his family—Earldoms held by them—Edward's Norman favourites—Siward and Leofric, Earls of Northumbria and Mercia, oppose Godwin—Disturbances occasioned by Eustace, Count of Boulogne—Commotions in the country—Godwin takes the field against the King's party—He and his family are outlawed—Visit of William of Normandy—Godwin returns, and is restored to power—Death of Godwin—Questions concerning the Succession—Edward the " Outlaw," son of Ironside, called to England by the Confessor, and acknowledged as Heir to the Crown—His untimely Death—Edward appoints William of Normandy as his successor—Death of Edward.

EDWARD THE ATHELING, the only surviving son of Ethelred, had been invited to England by Hardicanute, from whom he received great kindness.   Hardicanute had no children, and the easy and quiet disposition of his half-brother averted all suspicion or anxiety.   As soon as Edward was informed of Hardicanute's death, he was seized with great and almost unaccountable dismay; and he immediately despatched messengers to Earl Godwin (A.D. 1042-1043), requesting his council and aid.   Neither was afforded readily.   This powerful nobleman, who had so lately been accused of the foul murder of the noble Alfred, was at first little inclined to protect his suppliant brother; and we can best understand the character, the station, and the ambitious views of Godwin, when we are told that Edward endeavoured to throw himself at the feet of the earl.   What did the Atheling ask from Godwin ? Did he claim his rightful inheritance ? No, he did not seek to ascend the throne of England. All he prayed was, that Godwin would be pleased to assist him to return to Normandy, where, under the protection of his uncle Richard, he might pass the remainder of his days in peace and obscurity.

Godwin replied in a very different tone. "Are you not," he exclaimed, " the lawful heir to the throne, the son of Ethelred, the grandson of Edgar ; and why should you prefer an inglorious exile ?" He encouraged the prince, by reminding him of his qualifications. Edward had attained mature age, had been taught in the school of adversity, and the hardships and afflictions which the Atheling had himself felt, would, as Godwin maintained, better enable him to alleviate the miseries of the people confided to his care.

Godwin, continuing to manage the discourse with great art, proceeded to explain to Edward that there were few difficulties in the way; and none but such as he could remove. But without making any pretence of gene- rosity or disinterestedness, Godwin stipulated for his own reward. King Edward was to be his friend. God- win and his sons were to retain all their honours; and Edward, by marrying Editha the Fair, the daughter of Godwin, was to become a member of his family. The earl, in this discourse, had artfully endeavoured to work upon the best feelings of Edward, in order to obtain the means of satisfying his own ambition. From what we know of Edward's character, we can ascertain that he cared as little for the pride and pleasures of royalty, as he was unfitted for its toils. Had he returned to Normandy, he would probably have secluded himself in the cloisters of Bec or Fécamp, without the slightest regret for the kingdom which he had abandoned. But Godwin represented the assumption of the royal dignity as a duty; and Edward, yielding to his arguments, assented to the conditions which were enjoined.

Within a few days after the body of Hardicanute had been consigned to the earth, the prelates and great men of the Anglo-Saxon realms assembled at London, and accepted Edward as their king. William, Duke of Normandy, aided Edward by his influence; and it was intimated to the English, that if they refused to recognise the son of Emma, they would experience the weight of the Norman power. Yet the act of recognition was mainly owing to the exertions of the Earl of Wessex, and to the consequence which he possessed in the assembly. Many of the members of the legislature yielded a blind assent to his influence—many were "persuaded by gifts," or, as we should say, were bribed—many yielded to Godwin's art and eloquence: he was a quick and fluent speaker, witty and clever, and wonderfully well calculated to please the giddy multitude. The more thinking and considerate voted for Edward, because they felt that he had the right: lastly, some opposed his accession, and voted against the prevailing party; and these, as the old chronicler tells us, were " carefully marked," and not long afterwards driven out of England.

I relate these particulars, because they are important in many points of view. It is interesting to observe how influential, even at this early period, the gift of popular eloquence had become in England, and we shall find that it has continued to possess this value during every portion of our history. And the detail of the motives which actuated the majority of the assembly, shows how little the prerogative possessed by the English witenagemot, of directing the succession of their monarchy, was attended with any real liberty of suffrage. For, as we have seen, one man was bought, another was intimidated, a third talked over, and a fourth sent out of the country as a troublesome fellow, because he would not vote against his inclination or his feelings.

There was no doubt, however, but that Edward was the true and lawful sovereign; and he was endeared by the amiability of his temper. So mild and humble was he, that no affront, no injury, could disturb his calm and placid mind. Just and merciful in his judgments, the promise to "observe the laws of good King Edward" was inserted in the coronation-oath of all his successors, until the revolution, when Parliament abrogated the ancient form. To Edward, also, the English owed the abolition of the Danegeld, which, as we have seen, had been levied with great rigour; and the whole tenor of his conduct deservedly recommended him to the body of the people; and in process of time, the memory of the "Confessor" was hallowed by the fond piety of his votaries. But, if we close the legend and open the chronicle, we shall find that he was a very erring mortal. In his own court and household there were great causes of dissension and discord. He evidently bore a grudge against all who had supported the Danish kings. So far did he carry this feeling, that even his own mother Emma was not spared; he deprived her of all her property, land, gold and silver; acting towards her with great harshness, if not with injustice.

As soon as Edward was settled upon the throne, he invited over from Normandy many of those who had been his friends during his exile; an act, plausible in

itself, inasmuch as he might allege that his conduct
proceeded from affection and gratitude, but which was
scarcely to be reconciled with his duties as a sovereign.
Amongst all the matters which aggrieve the nobles and
great men of any country, there is none which gives
such general cause of offence as favour shown to over-
weening foreigners, who, forming a little knot or cabal
about the person of the sovereign, are considered as the
possessors of his confidence, to the detriment of those
who claim this trust by reason of their station or their
services; and such precisely was the position of our
Anglo-Saxon king.   Edward, according to his covenant
with Godwin, had wedded the fair Editha; and her
brothers—Harold, Sweyne, Wulnoth, Tostig, Gurth, and
Leofwine, were all respectively advanced to honours and
dignities.   In the old English expression, they were
" the king's darlings;" they had the complete sway over
Edward; and, so far as they could make use of their
sovereign's authority, they ruled all England.   They
were bold and able men.   Harold, in particular, was
distinguished by his stature, his beauty, his engaging
manners, his wit, and his eloquence; and he held the
great earldoms of East Anglia, Essex, Cambridge, Hunt-
ingdon, and Middlesex.   Sweyne was Earl of Oxford,
Gloucester, Hereford, Somerset, and Berks; and Godwin himself, as Earl of Wessex and Kent, was in possession of all the remainder of the south of England.   If
you look upon the map,* you will see how much strength
they derived from the compactness and position of the dominions which they possessed; and gratitude, as well as
policy, might induce the king to favour those who had become his kindred, and who had placed him on the throne.

That a family thus circumstanced should so conduct themselves as to excite the ill-will of their equals, may be easily understood; and they bore the utmost hatred towards the Norman courtiers, alleging that it was a shameful thing that King Edward should encourage these strangers. Edward himself was not spared by the *Godwin-sons*; for they behaved with great insolence towards the king. Brilliant and clever, they troubled his quietness and simplicity. And we are literally told by one who derived his information from their contemporaries, that they made him their butt—the object against which they directed the shafts of their ridicule.

Edward was too placid to resent these affronts; but the Norman retainers considered themselves as offended in the person of their patron, and made his injuries the subject of a quarrel of their own. Leofric, the wise and wealthy Earl of Coventry, and Siward, the son of Beorn, whose earldom extended from the Humber to the Tweed, were opposed to the family of Godwin. The former, Leofric, appears to have headed a party in the witenage-mot against the Earl of Wessex—a fact which we ascertain from a debate upon a question of foreign policy, when it was proposed to grant an aid of naval force to Sweyne of Denmark. These earls sided with the Normans. Thus the actors in the drama of discord were prepared. On the one side of the scene is the king's party; while the other is occupied by the opposition, by Godwin, his adherents and followers.

It is certain that the Norman party began to conduct themselves in such a manner as to occasion much disgust amongst the nation at large. Edward, during his residence in Normandy, had become partial to the customs of that country, and introduced many such usages into England. The Norman hand-writing was thought handsomer, by Edward, than the Anglo-Saxon; and he established the mode of testifying his assent to official documents by adding an impression of his great seal, which was appended to the parchment, in addition to the mark of the cross, according to the Anglo-Saxon custom which I have before noticed.

Hitherto the Anglo-Saxon kings never used a seal for the purpose of authenticating their charters. But the custom had been long established in France. And from the Frankish monarchs Edward borrowed the practice, though the seal itself, exhibiting his effigy, surrounded by the legend " *Sigillum Eaduuardi Anglorum Basilei,*" * seems rather to have been copied from the patterns afforded by the Greek emperors.

It may appear that this innovation was no great grievance ; but, upon examining the matter, it will be found connected with more important consequences. The adoption of these forms gave the king an additional reason for retaining about his person the "clerks" whom he had brought from France, and by whom all his writing business was performed. They were his domestic chaplains, and the keepers of his conscience ; and, in addition to these influential functions, they were his law advisers, and also his secretaries of state ; and as such they seem to have formed a bench in the witen-agemot. The chief of these was his arch-chaplain or chancellor ; and through them, judging from the practice both of the French and English courts, it was the custom to prefer all petitions and requests to the king. One

---

* The crown is evidently an imperial crown. The bird surmounting the wand is a dove. On the reverse he is represented with the sceptre and the mound, or the globe surmounted by a cross.

suitor was desirous of obtaining a grant of land—
another, mayhap, required a "writ" to enable him to
recover amends for an injury; since no person could sue
in the king's court without a special permission—a
third wished to ask for leave to quarter himself and his
hounds and his horses on one of the king's manors—and,
in such cases, we cannot doubt but that Robert, the
Norman monk of Jumieges, or Giso the Fleming, or
Ernaldus the Frenchman, would have many means of
serving their own party and disappointing their adversaries; and many an honest Englishman was turned
away, with a hard word and a heavy heart, by these
Norman courtiers. The chaplains, or clerks of the
chancery, were particularly obnoxious: many of them
obtained the best pieces of preferment in the king's gift.
The bishoprics were filled by prelates who might be
good stout soldiers or clever lawyers, but who were
therefore eminently disqualified for the stations in the
church, which they had obtained merely by favour or
importunity.

The Normans had, by this time, adopted the use of the
French language, or, as it was then called, "Romance."
Edward had acquired a partiality for this dialect, which
had become familiar to him during his stay in Normandy,
and by his example it was becoming fashionable amongst
the higher classes, at least amongst the favourites of
Edward; and we cannot doubt but that this circumstance
tended to raise up a further cause of discontent. A nation
which loses its own speech is half conquered. If we
talk like another set of people, we are very apt to begin
to think and act also like them.

The first years of Edward's reign were not entirely
tranquil. An invasion was threatened from Norway (A.D.

1043-1050) ; and one band of pirates, under Lothen and Irling, landed in Kent and Essex, which countries they ravaged. Earl Sweyne occasioned much scandal and disturbance. He carried off the lady abbess of Leominster; and slew his kinsman, Beorn, for which last mentioned offence he was outlawed, but afterwards pardoned. Edward let the reins of government drop out of his hands; allowing matters to take their own course, he now appeared almost as a simpleton; and the defence and protection of the country depended entirely upon the great earls, amongst whom the territory of England was divided.

Whilst matters were in this state, an event occurred, which put the whole nation in confusion. Goda, the daughter of Ethelred, Edward's sister, had been twice married (A.D. 1051). Her first husband was Gauthier, Count of Mantes, by whom she had a son, called Ralph, much favoured by his uncle, the English king—Edward having bestowed upon him the earldom of Worcester. The second husband of Goda was also a foreign prince of great power—Eustace,* the Count of Boulogne, who repaired to England, to the court of his brother-in-law.

When Eustace and his retainers were passing through the town of Dover, they behaved with great insolence; and, without asking permission from any one, they determined to take free quarters in the town. Had they been in an enemy's country, they could not have acted more oppressively. The Kings of England themselves could not exercise such a right, except upon those domains which were in the nature of the private property of the crown. And so jealously did the Anglo-Saxon

* Eustace II., surnamed " Aux grenons," from the length and importance of his whiskers.

law guard against similar exactions, that, even after the conquest, a citizen of London had the right of killing any person who attempted to intrude into his dwelling, under the pretence of being the follower of king or baron.

The retainers of the Count of Boulogne dispersed themselves in the town of Dover, and a couple of them forcing their way into a house, a scuffle arose between them and the goodman who owned the dwelling. The Frenchmen drew their swords and wounded the Englishman, and the latter acting in self-defence, slew one of the foreigners. The alarm spread—Count Eustace and his retainers were armed and horsed in a moment; surrounding the house of the unfortunate Englishman, they forced their way in, and murdered him by his own fireside; then, scouring the streets of the borough, they killed several of the townsmen and wounded many more. However, the Englishmen rallied; and though a horseman in chain-armour was a most fearful adversary to such an array as that of the burghers, yet the latter defended themselves so stoutly, that Eustace was driven out of Dover, and almost all his men fell in the conflict.

Count Eustace hastened to the king and told his own story, laying all the blame upon the men of Dover. Edward, without any further examination, believed the accuser, and commanded Earl Godwin to proceed forthwith to Dover, and to punish the town by military execution. Nothing could be more severe than such an order, even had it been justified by law, since innocent and guilty were thereby involved in the same proscription. But in this instance the conduct of Edward was equally cruel and unjust; for according to all natural equity, he ought to have heard the townsmen in their defence; and he should have summoned them to appear before the witenagemot. Earl Godwin therefore refused to obey the order, at which, without doubt, he was rejoiced in his own heart. No adversary is so dangerous to a government as an ambitious agitator, who can unite himself to an honest cause, and thus gain a plausible pretence for the furtherance of his schemes : and Godwin, who could show right on his side, while he was treacherous in his heart, immediately attempted to avail himself of his advantage.

Earl Godwin gathered his forces far and wide, and so did his sons, Earl Sweyne and Earl Harold; and out they came in battle-array against the king, demanding that Count Eustace and the Frenchmen should be delivered up to their vengeance.

Edward, who was then at Gloucester, was greatly alarmed. Earl Godwin, his father-in-law, who had made him king, might have the inclination to deprive him of his kingdom; and Edward therefore instantly sent hasty and special messengers to Earl Leofric and Earl Siward, praying for their assistance in this hour of peril. These chieftains were at first but lukewarm in the king's cause: however, upon consideration, they assembled the " Fyrd" or militia of their earldoms, and marched to the aid of their sovereign, being joined also by Ralph, the Norman Earl of Worcestershire.

The best and noblest of England constituted the armies who were now opposed to each other. The northern earls were inveterate against Godwin ; but, much as the people had been wrought upon by the nobles, the Englishmen on either side felt that, conquer who might, the victory would be for the advantage of the foes of England. It is possible also, that the warriors of both parties were not heartily inclined towards their leaders. The king's party must have been aware that he had engaged in an unjust quarrel: the followers of Earl Godwin could not fail to distrust the motives of their superior, and peace was obviously the only object to be sought by the inhabitants of the kingdom. In ascribing these motives to the English forces, we must recollect that they were not hired or mercenary soldiers, but free men, performing a legal duty; and an independent army, thus composed, may, on some occasions, exercise a deliberate and useful check upon the conduct of their commanders.

The result was a compromise: a truce was negotiated. The king and the witan agreed that hostages should be given on either side; and that an assembly of the legislature should be held in the following autumn, in which the dissensions should be decided.

This witenagemot was accordingly held; but the interval of time had tended greatly to the disadvantage of Godwin (A.D. 1051-1052). His forces were melting away—many of his followers abandoned him. The king had been actively employed in raising the forces of such of the parts adjoining the Thames as were under his own actual control; and when the witan met, the first measure which they adopted was an adjudication that Sweyne should be outlawed. This was a heavy doom. An outlaw was said to bear a "wolf's head," that is to say, he was declared as much out of the protection of society as the savage animal; any one might slay him with impunity; and therefore sentence of death was virtually passed against the earl. Godwin and Harold were cited or summoned to appear, in order that they might justify themselves of those things which were

Great Seal of Edward the Confessor.
(From the Original in the British Museum.)

Silver Penny of Edward the Confessor.

Silver Coins of Edward the Confessor.

Westminster Abbey, Western Entrance.

laid to their charge.   But they were afraid of their
enemies, and demanded a reasonable security that they
might come and stay and depart in safety.   This request
was refused, and the refusal casts some suspicion upon
the king.   Indeed, the tide had turned, and Godwin's
adversaries were determined to push their advantage to
the uttermost.   Sentence of banishment was pronounced
against Godwin and Harold, and within five days they
were to depart out of England.   There was no appeal;
and so rapidly had their power declined, that they were
entirely unable to resist.   Godwin and his sons, so late
the "king's darlings," were now exiles; and, "wonderful would it have been thought," in the words of the
Saxon chronicle, "if any one had said before, that matters would have come to this pass."   The old earl and
his son Sweyne sailed to Flanders, to Earl Baldwin's
country; and they had a ship full of treasure with them,
to purchase a hearty and good welcome from the Flemings.   Harold crossed to Ireland, and he was so far
favoured, as to be allowed to remain in that country
under the king's protection.   This fact should be remarked, because it seems to show that he was not considered as being out of the king's dominions; or, in
other words, that the opposite coast of Ireland was part
of Edward's realm.   Editha the Fair shared in the disgrace of her father and family.   Her husband, the king,
did not spare her: all her riches, gold, silver, and jewels,
were taken from her by his command; she was stripped
to the last groat, and then sent to the monastery of
Wherwell in Hampshire, where, placed under the custody
of the abbess, King Edward's sister, she was kept in
cheerless captivity.

It may excite surprise, that the mild and humble-minded Edward should have been stimulated to such a succession of harsh, if not tyrannical acts, as those which I have narrated. But he was evidently of a timid and desponding character; and no one is more oppressive than a timid man, roused to vengeance by apprehension of danger. Towards the beginning of the reign, Godwin and his family considered that they had the king entirely in their grasp. That power they abused openly and grossly; and the bitterness of their tongues, without doubt, tended quite as much as any other cause to alienate the affections of Edward; affronts are more galling than injuries. Subsequent events also show that Edward dreaded their influence; and his marriage had not added to his comfort or security. Editha the Fair deserved this epithet. She was very beautiful; and the monkish chroniclers, according to their homely conceits, compare this daughter of Godwin to the rose springing from the thorn: but the lovely rose was a suspicious, and perhaps, as some historians insinuate, an unfaithful helpmate. Edward considered her as an enemy. He never loved her as a wife, nor had they any children; and when, to all the causes which tended to irritate the monarch, we add the influence exerted by the northern earls in the tumultuous assembly of the Anglo-Saxon nobles, we shall obtain an explanation of the apparent anomalies in the actions of the Confessor.

Robert, Duke of Normandy, had been succeeded by his base-born son, William (A.D. 1051). Herleva or Harlotta, the mother of this prince, is said by some to have been the daughter of a currier at Falaise. Other reports, however, tell us that the concubine was the child of Fulbert, the duke's chamberlain; and the English were even willing to believe that she was the granddaughter of Ironside.   William had fully established himself in the duchy, after encountering many difficulties.   He was a prince of extraordinary shrewdness and energy; and he now arrived from beyond the sea with a large and splendid train of Frenchmen, on a visit to his good cousin, Edward, King of England; cousins they certainly were; for, as you will recollect, Edward's mother, Emma, was own sister to Robert, the father of William; and even if the kindred had been more remote, it would still have afforded a ground for attention and civility.   Prosperity acts like a telescope, and often enables folks to bring distant relations much nearer than they would be without its aid.   And we shall not be guilty of any great breach of charity if we suppose that William, young, ambitious, and enterprising, did not undertake this journey purely out of natural love and affection towards his old aunt and kinsman.   Did he begin to form any plans for the invasion of England? Did he contemplate the possibility of wearing his kinsman's crown?   In our modern days it is not at all an unfrequent thing for a man to sit down and write his own memoirs; in which, with great ingenuity and accuracy, he tells you everything concerning his actions and intentions, or at least everything which he wishes you to believe.   In the eleventh century, however, these *asides* were not so common.   William the Conqueror neither wrote his autobiography, nor hinted to any good and serviceable friend that he had no objection to have his opinions reported for the amusement and instruction of the world; and his "correspondence" is not extant, therefore I cannot exactly tell you what he thought.   However, I can tell you what he saw, and then you may judge for yourself as to the sentiments

which possibly floated in the mind of the Norman
warrior.

King Edward was surrounded by Frenchmen and
foreigners, who filled his court, and were spread over
England.   Of the few castles and strongholds which
were in the realm, some, the most important, those
towards the Welsh marches, were garrisoned by French
and Norman soldiers, under the command of leaders of
their own nation.   In the great towns and cities, no
inconsiderable number of Frenchmen were to be found,
who, having settled there, enjoyed what we should now
call the freedom of the corporation, living in houses of
their own, and paying scot and lot, or taxes, like the
English burgesses.   The country itself invited the attacks of an enemy; the great towns, with few exceptions,
were either quite open, or fortified only by stoccades and
banks, or, perhaps, by a ruinous Roman wall; and the
Englishmen themselves, though very brave, were much
inferior to the continental nations in the art of war.   As
soldiers, they laboured under a still greater deficiency
than any which can result from the want of weapons or
of armour.   Stout, well-fed, and hale, the Anglo-Saxon,
when sober, was fully a match for any adversary who
might be brought from the banks of the Seine or the
Loire.   But the old English were shamefully addicted to
debauchery, and the wine-cup unnerves the stoutest arm.
The monkish chroniclers, as you will recollect, tell us
that we learnt this vice from the Danes—a sorry excuse;
and it is little to the credit of Englishmen, that drunken-
ness still continues to stain our national character.

The empire was distracted by factions.   The members
of a very powerful family, whose conduct had excited
the suspicions of the sovereign, had been deprived of

their possessions, but certainly not according to equity, so that they and their adherents had a double cause of hostility, disaffection, and the sense of the injury which they had sustained.

Edward was advancing in years, childless, and without hope of children. Upon his death, the royal line of Cerdic would be represented solely by Edward the "Outlaw," the only surviving son of Edmund Ironside, then a fugitive in a distant realm, far away in Hungary. Hardly did it seem probable that this prince, so estranged from England, could possibly assert his right to the succession; and, therefore, as soon as Edward should be stretched on the bier, the vacant throne might be ascended by any one who, whether by force or favour, could obtain the concurrence of any powerful partisans, or the sanction of the legislature.

Such then was the state of affairs when William, Duke of Normandy, afterwards the Conqueror, repaired to England. We have no positive evidence concerning what was said or done; and I am not prepared to relate the conversations between King Edward and his cousin, as if I had listened behind the tapestry. But the matters narrated by chroniclers I can repeat: and from their testimony we do know, that William was honourably received. He conducted himself with so much address as to acquire the confidence and good-will of Edward, who, by the expulsion of Godwin and his family, had obtained a temporary respite from uneasiness and disquietude. The country seemed to be cleared of these turbulent and dangerous chieftains. The whole of Harold's earldom had been granted to Algar, the son of Leofric. Devon, Somerset, Dorset, and West Wales, all parts of the earldom of Godwin, were transferred to

Odda, and the rest of Godwin's territories remained in the king's hands.

This calm did not last long—Godwin, as you will recollect, was in Flanders, with a ship full of treasure, and gathering together a fleet, he attacked the southern coast, and laid the country under contribution (A.D. 1052). King Edward was not unprepared; he and his witan apprehended that such an attack was meditated, and they had taken counsel how they might best avert the danger. They had, therefore, sent a fleet with orders to blockade the Flemish ports, and prevent the escape of Godwin. This naval force was placed under the command of Godwin's personal enemies: Earl Ralph, the Frenchman, and Earl Odda, who possessed the best portion of Godwin's dominions. But the Earl was on the alert; the weather favoured him; he outwitted his adversaries, and the king's affairs were so badly managed, that the fleet returned home, and the expedition was wholly dispersed.

Harold, on his part, was full of activity; he sailed from Ireland, and joining his forces to those of his father, they proceeded to rouse their adherents. The mariners belonging to Hastings appear to have been the first who joined them. Kent, Sussex, Surrey, and Essex followed the same example, besides many other districts and shires—all were for Godwin, and all declared that they would live and die in his cause. Godwin and Harold had their chief station off the Isle of Wight, and they now determined to sail to London. As they advanced up the river, their forces still continued increasing, both by land and water. The peasantry supplied them with provisions, and all the country seemed to be at their command.

When the "earls" arrived in the port of London they transmitted their demands to the king. In appearance, their requests were sufficiently reasonable and just, since they confined their petitions to the restoration of their former territories and dignities. If Godwin and his family had not been liable to suspicion, such a proceeding would have indicated great moderation. But Edward considered it as fraught with danger; for he gave a peremptory denial, and his refusal excited so bitter a feeling against him amongst the troops of Godwin, that the old earl had great difficulty in restraining them, though at the same time he steadily pursued his own purpose, and succeeded in gaining over the burgesses of London and Southwark to his party. When all Godwin's men were assembled, he put himself in motion; and whilst his vessels sailed up the river, his land army assembled on the "Strand," then, what its name implies, an open shore, without the walls of London, and extending along the northern bank of the river Thames.

The king's forces were considerable. But, as before, they were extremely averse to civil war. They were loth to fight with their own kinsmen; Englishmen only were engaged on either side. If Edward had been worsted in battle, a revolution was to be apprehended, and the crown might have been transferred to the house of Godwin. And, under these circumstances, King Edward, however unwillingly, was compelled to yield to the wishes of his subjects, and to agree to a compromise. Offers were made by the king, sufficient to appease the resentment, and satisfy the ambition of Godwin and Harold. Edward submitted to their preponderance, and the treaty was concluded, like all important transactions, by means of the witenagemot. Godwin appeared before the "earls, and the best men of the land," who were assembled, and declared that he and his sons were innocent of the crimes which had been laid to their charge.

The great council not only agreed that Godwin and his sons were innocent, but decreed the restoration of their earldoms; and such was the influence of the Earl of Wessex, that the witan adopted all the views of his party. All the French were declared outlaws, because it was said that they had given bad advice to the king, and brought unrighteous judgments into the land; a very few only, whose ignoble names have been preserved—Robert the Deacon, Richard the son of Scrub, Humphrey Cock's-foot, and the Groom of the stirrup,—were excepted from this proscription: obscure, mean men, whom Godwin could not fear. Robert, the monk of Jumieges, who had been promoted to the Archbishopric of Canterbury, was just able to escape with his life, so highly were the people incensed against him. He and Ulf, Bishop of Dorchester, after scouring the country, broke out through the east-gate of Canterbury, and killing and wounding those who attempted to stop them, they betook themselves to the coast, and got out to sea. Other of the Frenchmen retired to the castles of their countrymen, and the restoration of the queen to her former rank, completed the triumph of the Godwin family.

A very short time after these events, Godwin died (A.D. 1053). We are told, that when he was banqueting with Edward at Windsor, words arose between them. Edward still believed that Godwin had been the guilty cause of Alfred's murder. "May this morsel be my last," said Godwin, "if I committed the crime;" and this imprecation was followed by his death, he being choked by the bread which he had attempted to swallow. I do not vouch for these particulars. Tradition has been busy with his memory. The shoals called the "Godwin Sands," are popularly considered as his estates, which being overflowed by the sea, became and are the terror of the mariner. The exact circumstances of Godwin's death are doubtful; and the more authentic chroniclers, omitting the other details, only state that he was struck speechless, and that he died miserably within three days.

Harold, as the eldest son of Godwin, succeeded to his father's territories, and to his authority (A.D. 1053-1055). He vacated the earldom of East Anglia, which was bestowed upon Algar, son of Leofric, who had held the honour during Harold's outlawry. This appears to have been a device, enabling him to quiet his opponents until he should gain more power; and his influence rapidly increased. Upon the death of Siward, the doughty Earl of Northumbria, the king appointed Tostig, Harold's brother, as his successor; but with little justice, and contrary to the wishes of the people, and the right of Siward's heir. Harold gained much by the expulsion of Algar, who was outlawed by the "witenagemot," upon the accusation of treason, but unjustly, and without any real cause. Algar, trusting in the power of his father Leofric, who was still able to counterbalance the influence of Harold, was not to be easily disheartened. The stout exile imitated the example of Godwin and Harold under similar circumstances, and appealed to the sword. Retiring to the dominions of Griffith, King of Wales, who had espoused Algitha, his sister, and was then waging war against Harold, they collected a large force, and, advancing upon Hereford, burnt the city, and penetrated into Gloucestershire.

Here Algar and his allies were encountered by Harold; and after much bloodshed had been occasioned, peace was established between the competitors, the sentence of outlawry being reversed; and Algar was restored to his possessions and dignity. Some time afterwards, Leofric died, and the earldom of Cestrian-Mercia devolved upon Algar, who again falling under the displeasure of Edward, or rather of Harold, was outlawed and banished a second time. Algar was as bold as before; and, repairing to his old friends and allies, the Welsh, and assisted by a fleet of the Danes, he recovered possession of his earldom by main force, defying Edward and his power. A greater affront was offered to King Edward by the Northumbrians, who, rising against Tostig, slew his retainers, seized his treasure, and expelled him from the earldom, and, electing Morkar, a son of Algar, as their earl, demanded that assent from Edward which he could not refuse.

A kingdom in which such events could take place, was evidently on the verge of ruin. Neither confidence nor unanimity subsisted. Faction was contending against faction; and, like the Britons of the old time, every bystander must have seen that the realm was at the mercy of any invader. During these transactions, old age was rapidly advancing upon Edward. I have told you he was childless. He saw the increasing power of Harold, and that the kingdom which he had been called to govern, would be exposed to the greatest confusion. Upon the decease of Edward, the only representatives of the line of Cerdic would be found in the

descendants of Edmund Ironside (A.D. 1057). King
Edward had hitherto regarded his family with coldness, if
not with aversion. But the wish to ensure tranquillity
to his kingdom prevailed; and he recalled "Edward
the Outlaw" from his abode in Hungary, with the
intention of proclaiming him as heir to the crown.

Edmund Ironside had been much beloved, and greatly
did England rejoice when Edward, no longer the Outlaw,
but the Atheling, arrived here, accompanied by his wife
Agatha, the emperor's kinswoman, and his three fair
children, Edgar, Christina, and Margaret. But the
people's gladness was speedily turned to sorrow. Very
shortly after the Atheling arrived in London, he sick-
ened and died. He was buried in St. Paul's Cathedral;
and sad and ruthful were the forebodings of the English,
when they saw him borne to his grave. Harold gained
exceedingly by this event. Did the Atheling die a
natural death?—the lamentations of the chroniclers seem
to imply more than meets the ear.

Edward's design having thus been frustrated, he
determined that William of Normandy should succeed
him to the throne of England (A.D. 1058-1065), and he
executed, or, perhaps, re-executed a will to that effect,
bequeathing the crown to his good cousin. This choice,
disastrous as it afterwards appeared to be from its
consequences, was not devoid of foresight and prudence.
Edward, without doubt, viewed the nomination of the
Norman as the surest mode of averting from his subjects
the evils of foreign servitude or domestic war. The
Danish kings, the pirates of the north, were yearning to
regain the realm which their great Canute had ruled.
At the very outset of Edward's reign, Magnus, the successor of Hardicanute, had claimed the English crown.

A competitor at home had diverted Magnus from this enterprise ; but it might at any time be resumed. And how much better would the wise and valiant William be able to resist the Danish invasions, than the infant Edgar ? Harold was brave and experienced in war, but his elevation to the throne might be productive of the greatest evil. The grandsons of Leofric, who ruled half England, would scarcely submit to the dominion of an equal; the obstacle arising from Harold's ancestry was indeed insuperable. No individual, who was not of an ancient royal house, had ever been able to maintain himself upon an Anglo-Saxon throne.

William himself asserted, that Edward had acted with the advice and consent of the great Earls, Siward, Leofric, and Godwin himself; consequently the bequest was made before the arrival of Edward the Outlaw. The son and nephew of Godwin, who were then in Normandy, had also been sent to him, as he maintained, in the characters of pledges or hostages, that the will should be carried into effect; or, as is most probable, that no opposition should be raised by the powerful earl. The three earls thus vouched, were not living when William made this assertion ; but if we do not distrust his veracity and honour, we may suppose that Edward, in the first instance, appointed William as his heir. As the king grew older, his affection for his own kindred awakened, and he recalled the Atheling, revoking his devise to the stranger : to which, however, he seems to have returned again, when his kinsman died.

The messenger by whom the intelligence of the bequest, thus made by Edward, reached William, was no other than Harold. There is much contradiction as to the immediate cause of Harold's journey ; nor are we

less in doubt concerning the minor incidents.   Whether
accident or design conducted him to the court of the
Duke of Normandy, is uncertain; and the preceding account of the two wills in favour of William, is an hypothesis collected only from the general bearing of the
narrations.   William, well aware of Harold's influence,
used every endeavour to ensure his future aid; and in
return, William agreed to bestow upon Harold the hand
of his daughter, the fair Adela.   The English earl
promised that he would give up to the Norman duke
the castle of Dover, a fortress belonging to him as part
of the inheritance of Godwin, and considered as the key
of England.   He confirmed the engagement by oath,
and became the "man" or vassal of William, whom he
acknowledged as his future sovereign.

In the meanwhile, Harold was rising in repute.   He
invaded Wales, and desolated the country (A.D. 1063-
1064).   Griffith opposed him valiantly, but he was slain
by the treachery of his own countrymen.   His gory head
was sent to the Confessor as a trophy of victory; his
dominions were bestowed upon his brothers Blethyn and
Rhiwallon, who were accessary to the murder.   And
these princes became the vassals, not only of King Edward, but of Earl Harold, to whom they performed fealty
and homage.   As Earl of Wessex, Harold could have no
claim to this obedience, and if enforced by him, the act
can only be construed as an attempt to establish a
sovereign power.

Edward was now rapidly declining in health; he had
rebuilt the ancient abbey of Westminster, founded, as
you will recollect, by Sebert, but which had been ruined
during the Danish wars.   And, holding his court, according to the ancient custom, at Christmas, he caused

the new fabric to be consecrated, in the presence of the
nobles assembled during that solemn festival.

Edward felt that the hand of death was upon him. A
little while before he expired (Jan. 5, 1066), Harold and
his kinsmen forced their way into the chamber of the
monarch, and exhorted him to name a successor, by
whom the realm might be ruled in peace and security.
"Ye know full well, my lords," said Edward, "that I
have bequeathed my kingdom to the Duke of Normandy,
and are there not those here whose oaths have been
given to secure his succession?" Harold stepped nearer,
and interrupting the king, he asked of Edward, upon
whom the crown should be bestowed. "Harold! take
it, if such be thy wish; but the gift will be thy ruin.
Against the duke and his baronage, no power of thine
can avail thee." Harold replied, that he did not fear
the Norman, or any other enemy. The dying king,
wearied with importunity, turned himself upon his couch,
and faintly intimated that the English nation might
name as king, Harold, or whom they liked; and shortly
afterwards he breathed his last.

Harold afterwards founded his title upon Edward's
last will; many of our historians favour his claim, and
the different statements are difficult to be reconciled;
yet taken altogether, the circumstances are exactly such
as we meet with in private life. The childless owner of
a large estate, at first leaves his property to his cousin
on the mother's side, from whose connections he has
received much kindness. He advances in age, and alters
his intentions in favour of a nephew on his father's side
—an amiable young man, living abroad,—and from
whom he had been estranged in consequence of a family
quarrel of long standing. The young heir comes to the

Windsor Castle, temp. Edward III.

Harold's Stones, Trelech, Monmouthshire.

Coronation of Harold (Bayeux Tapestry).

testator's house—is received with great affection—and
is suddenly cut off by illness.   The testator then returns
to his will in favour of his cousin, who resides abroad.
His acute and active brother-in-law has taken the
management of his affairs, is well-informed of this will;
and, when the testator is on his death-bed, he contrives to
tease and persuade the dying man to alter the will again
in his favour.   This is exactly the state of the case; and
though considerable doubts have been raised relating to
the contradictory bequests of the Confessor, there can be
no difficulty in admitting that the conflicting pretensions
of William and Harold were grounded upon the act
emanating from a wavering and feeble mind.   If such
disputes take place between private individuals, they are
decided by a court of justice; but if they concern a kingdom, they can only be settled by the sword.

Our kings, in the castle of Windsor, live on the brink
of the grave, which opens to receive them.   The throne
of Edward was equally by the side of his sepulchre, for
he dwelt in the palace of Westminster, and on the festival of the Epiphany, the day after his decease, his ob-
sequies were solemnized in the adjoining abbey, then
connected with the royal abode by walls and towers.
Beneath the lofty windows of the southern transept of
the abbey, you may see the deep and blackened arches,
fragments of the edifice raised by Edward, supporting the
chaste and florid tracery of a more recent age.   Within
stands the shrine, once rich in gems and gold, raised
to the memory of the Confessor by the fond devotion of
his successors, despoiled indeed of all its ornaments,
neglected and crumbling to ruin, but still surmounted
by the massy iron-bound oaken coffin which contains the
ashes of the last legitimate Anglo-Saxon king.

Chapter XV.

Harold assumes the Crown — His authority not recognised throughout all the realm—William prepares to invade England—Assembly of the Norman Baronage at Lillebonne—the Pope sanctions William's enterprise—Equipment of the Norman Fleet—Harold marries Algitha, the Sister of Edwin and Morcar — Tostig incites Harold Harfager to attack Harold—the Norwegian Expedition — Battle of Stamford Bridge—Harfager and Tostig slain—Sailing of the Norman Fleet—Landing of the Norman Army—Harold marches to attack William — Preparations for the Conflict—Battle of Hastings—Tradition of the escape of Harold.

UPON the death of Edward the Confessor, there were three claimants to the crown, his good cousin, William of Normandy, and his good brother-in-law, Harold— each of whom respectively founded their pretensions upon the real or supposed devise of the late king—and Edgar Atheling, the son of Edward the Outlaw, who ought to have stood on firmer ground. If kindred had any weight, he was the real heir—the lineal descendant of Ironside—and the only male now left of the house of Cerdic ; and he also is said to have been nominated by Edward, as the successor to the throne.

Each of these competitors had his partisans : but, whilst William was absent, and Edward young and poor, perhaps timid and hesitating, Harold was on the spot ; a man of mature age, in full vigour of body and mind ; possessing great influence and great wealth. And on the very day that Edward was laid in his grave (Jan. 6,

1066), Harold prevailed upon, or compelled the prelates and nobles assembled at Westminster, to accept him as king. Some of our historians say, that he obtained the diadem by force. This is not to be understood as implying actual violence; but simply, that the greater part of those who recognised him, acted against their wishes and will. And if our authorities are correct, Stigand, Archbishop of Canterbury, but who had been suspended by the pope, was the only prelate who acknowledged his authority.

Some portions of the Anglo-Saxon dominions never seem to have submitted to Harold. In others, a sullen obedience was extorted from the people, merely because they had not power enough to raise any other king to the throne. Certainly the realm was not Harold's by any legal title. The son of Godwin could have no inherent right whatever to the inheritance of Edward; nor had the Anglo-Saxon crown ever been worn by an elective monarch. The constitutional rights of the nation extended, at farthest, to the selection of a king from the royal family; and if any kind of sanction was given by the witan to the intrusion of Harold, the act was as invalid as that by which they had renounced the children of Ethelred, and acknowledged the Danish line.

Harold is stated to have shewn both prudence and courage in the government of the kingdom; and he has been praised for his just and due administration of justice. At the same time he is, by other writers, reprobated as a tyrant; and he is particularly blamed for his oppressive enforcement of the forest-laws. Towards his own partisans, Harold may have been ostentatiously just, while the ordinary exercise of the royal

prerogative would appear tyrannical to those who
deemed him to be an usurper.

Harold, as the last Anglo-Saxon ruler, has often been
viewed with peculiar partiality; but it is perhaps
difficult to justify these feelings. He had no clear title
to the crown in any way whatever. Harold was certainly
not the heir: Edward's bequest in his favour was very
dubious; and he failed to obtain that degree of universal
consent to his accession, which, upon the ordinary
principles of political expediency, can alone legalize a
change of dynasty. The Anglo-Saxon power had been
fast verging to decay. As against their common sovereign, the earls were rising into petty kings. North of
the Humber, scarcely a shadow of regular government
existed; and even if the Norman had never trod the soil
of England, it would have been scarcely possible for the
son of Godwin to have maintained himself in possession
of the supreme authority. Any of the great nobles who
divided the territory of the realm might have preferred
as good a claim, and they probably would have been
easily incited to risk such an attempt. Hitherto, the
crown had been preserved from domestic invasion by
the belief that royalty belonged exclusively to the
children of Woden. Fluctuating as the rules of succession had been, the political faith in the " right royal
kindred " excluded all competition, except as amongst
the members of a particular caste or family; but the
charm was now broken—the mist which had hitherto
enveloped the sovereign magistracy was dispelled—and
the way to the throne was opened to any competitor.

William was hunting in the Park of Rouen, surrounded
by a noble train of knights, esquires, and damsels, when
a " serjeant," just arrived from England, hastened into

his presence, and related the events which had happened :
Edward's death and Harold's assumption of the crown.
The bow dropped out of the hand of the Norman, and he
was unnerved by anxiety and surprise. William fastened
and loosened his mantle, spake not, and looked so fierce
and fell, that no one ventured to address him. Entering
a skiff, he crossed the Seine, still silent ; stalked into the
great hall of his palace, threw himself into a seat, wrapped
his head in his mantle, and bent his body downwards,
apparently overwhelmed.   " Sirs," said William de
Breteuil the seneschal, to the inquiring crowd, " ye
will soon know the cause of our lord's anxiety;" and
then, approaching his master, he roused the duke by
telling him that everybody in the streets of Rouen would
soon hear of the death of Edward, and of his claims to
the succession.   William instantly recovered from his
reverie ; and upon the advice of a Norman baron, Fitz-
Osbern the Bold, it was determined that he should forthwith require Harold, the sworn liegeman of William, to
surrender the inheritance, and to perform the engagements which he had contracted with the Norman sovereign.

Harold answered, that the kingdom was not his to
bestow : implying, no doubt, that he could not make the
transfer without the consent of the witenagemot. He
also alleged distinctly, that he could not marry Adela
without the advice of the nobility of his realm. If this
assertion be taken in its strict sense, we must suppose
that, as the queen had some, though a very undefined,
share in the royal authority, she could not be raised to
that rank without the assent of the legislature.   But
perhaps we must receive the expressions according to a
more qualified construction ; and suppose that Harold

merely meant to say, that it was not expedient for an
English king to choose a wife in such a manner as
might render him unpopular. But these excuses need not
be weighed very accurately. Other parts of Harold's
reply were scurrilous and insulting; and the whole is only
to be considered as an intimation that the son of Godwin
defied the power of William, the Bastard of Normandy.

Harold did not feel his own weakness, and he scarcely
knew the resources of his adversary. Normandy, at this
period, was in the height of its prosperity. Under the prudent government of the late dukes, Richard and Robert,
there had arisen a race of wise, active, and loyal nobility.
The heads of the great houses of Beaumont, Montgomery,
Fitz-Osbern, Mortimer, and Giffard, were stout of heart
and strong of hand: they could give the best counsel,
and execute the counsel which they gave; and in the
great parliament assembled at Lillebonne, the barons
determined to assist their sovereign in his contest with
the English usurper, the perjured Harold.

In this memorable meeting, there was at first much
diversity of opinion. The duke could not command his
vassals to cross the sea; their tenures did not compel
them to such a service. William could only request
their aid, to fight his battles in England: many refused
to engage in this dangerous expedition, and great debates arose. Fitz-Osbern exhorted his peers to obey the
wishes of their liege lord. After some discussion, they
allowed the intrepid baron to be their spokesman; and
in their name did he engage that each feudatory should
render double the service to which he was bound by his
tenure; and, moreover, he, Fitz-Osbern, promised to fit
out, at his own expense, sixty vessels, all filled with
chosen warriors.

Fitz-Osbern might make any promise on his own part, to which he was stimulated by his loyalty.   But the other barons had not empowered him to assent on their behalf to bind them to similar exertions; and whilst he was speaking, such an outcry of disapprobation arose, that it seemed as if the very roof of the hall would be rent asunder.   William, who could not restore order, withdrew into another apartment: and, calling the barons to him one by one, he argued and reasoned with each of these sturdy vassals separately, and apart from the others. He exhausted all the arts of persuasion; their present courtesy, he engaged, should not be turned into a precedent; the troops now granted as a favour should never be demanded as a right by himself or his successors; and the fertile fields of England should be the recompense of their fidelity.   Upon this prospect of remuneration, the barons assented; and, that they might not retract, the ready clerk wrote down in his roll, the number of knights and vassals which each prelate and baron would furnish to this expedition.

William did not confine himself to his own subjects. All the adventurers and adventurous spirits of the neighbouring states were invited to join his standard. Armorica, now called Britanny, had become a fief of Normandy; and though the duke could not compel the baronage of that country to serve in his army, still they willingly yielded to his influence.   Alan Fergant, and Bryan, the two sons of Eudo, Count of Britanny, came with a numerous train of Breton knights, all ready for the conflict — perhaps eager to avenge the wrongs of Arthur upon the Saxons, who had usurped the land of their ancestors.   Others poured in from Poitou and Maine; from Flanders and Anjou; and to all, such promises were made as should best incite them to the enterprise—lands, liveries, money, according to their rank and degree; and the port of St. Pierre sur Dive was appointed as the place where all the forces should assemble.

William had discovered four most valid reasons for the prosecution of his offensive warfare against a neighbouring people: the bequest made by his cousin; the perjury of Harold; the expulsion of the Normans, at the instigation, as he alleged, of Godwin; and lastly, the massacre of the Danes by Ethelred on St. Brice's day. The alleged perjury of Harold enabled William to obtain the sanction of the papal see. Alexander, the Roman pontiff, allowed, nay, even urged him to punish the crime, provided England, when conquered, should be held as the fief of St. Peter. In this proceeding, his holiness took upon himself to act judicially, and in solemn consistory; not, however, without opposition,— but the measure was carried: and Hildebrand, Archdeacon of the Church of Rome, afterwards the celebrated Pope Gregory VII., greatly assisted, by the support which he gave to the decree.

As a visible token of protection, the pope transmitted to William the consecrated banner, the Gonfanon of St. Peter, and a precious ring, in which a relic of the chief of the apostles was enclosed. Nothing could be more futile than the pretext that the war was undertaken for the purpose of redressing the wrongs sustained by Archbishop Robert and his companions, or of avenging the slaughter committed by Ethelred; and the sanction given by the pope was in itself an attack upon the temporal authority. Yet the colour of right, which William endeavoured to obtain, shows a degree of deference to public opinion; he was anxious to prove that his attempt was not prompted by mere ambition or avarice; and that, at all events, supposing Edward's bequest might be disputed, he was justified in his attempt by good conscience and honour.

There was little regular communication between England and the continent; but it was impossible that the extensive preparations of William should remain unknown to Harold; and he immediately began to provide for defence. He mustered his forces at Sandwich, and then he took his station at the Isle of Wight, during the whole of the summer and part of the autumn. Such a navy as he could assemble guarded the coast, while his land forces were encamped on the shore. During this period, he transmitted a spy to procure further particulars of the forces which the Normans had raised. The agent was discovered, and carried to William, by whom he was received without either harshness or affectation of concealment, and dismissed without harm. The spy was informed by the duke, that Harold need not take any trouble or incur any expense for the purpose of ascertaining the Norman strength; for he would see it, aye, and feel it too, within the year.

The computation of the navy assembled by William has varied exceedingly. Master Wace, to whose poetical chronicle we are so largely indebted, relates, that he often heard his father say, that the number of vessels amounted to six hundred and ninety-six; but that he found it stated in writing, that upwards of three thousand had been assembled. This latter computation, probably, included all the smaller barks; but, be that as it may, the fleet was the largest which had ever been seen. William's own vessel, which had been given to

him by his wife Matilda, was distinguished above the
rest; at night, by the cresset which flamed on the top-
mast; and in the day, by its resplendent ornaments and
decorations. The crimson sails swelled to the wind, the
gilded vanes glittered in the sun, and at the head of the
ship was the effigy of a child, armed with a bow and
arrow, and ready to discharge his shaft against the
hostile land.

The gathering of the fleet at the mouth of the Dive
had been delayed by contrary gales, and other mischances. The ships sailed to the Somme, but the winds
were still unfavourable. The relics of St. Valery were
brought forth from their shrine. On the eve of St.
Michael, the patron of Normandy, a prosperous gale
arose, and the whole armament was wafted in safety
across the waves (Sept. 28, 1066). Want of provisions,
and other circumstances, had compelled Harold to draw
off his forces from the coast, which was entirely unpro-
tected; and when the Norman armada approached the
shore of England, between Hastings and Pevensey
(Sept. 29, 1066), not the slightest opposition could be
offered to the invaders. As the vessels approached, and
as the masts rose higher and higher on the horizon, the
peasantry who dwelt on the coast, and who had con-
gregated on the cliffs, gazed with the utmost alarm at
the hostile vessels, which, as they well knew, were drawing near for the conquest of England; portended by the
fearful comet blazing in the sky. The alarm spread—
and one of the few thanes who were left in the shire of
the South Saxons—for the greater part, as you will
shortly hear, were on duty in the north—galloped up to
a rising ground to survey the operations of the enemy.

The thane saw the boats pushing through the surf,

glistening with shields and spears; in others, stood the war-horses, neighing and pawing at the prospect of release from their irksome captivity. Now followed the archers, closely shorn, arrayed in a light and unincumbering garb; each held his long bow, strung for the fight, in his hand, and by his side hung the quiver, filled with those cloth-yard shafts, which, in process of time, became the favourite and national weapon of the yeomanry of England.

The archers leap out of the boats, disperse themselves on the shore, and station themselves in the out-posts, so as to protect, if necessary, the heavy armed troops who are about to disembark. The knights are now seen, carefully and heavily treading along the planks, each covered with his haubergeon of mail, his helmet laced, the shield well strengthened with radiating bars of iron, depending from his neck, his sword borne by his attendant esquire. The gleaming steel-clad multitude cover the shingly beach in apparent disorder, but they rapidly separate, and, in a few moments, each warrior is mounted upon his steed. Banners, pennons, and pennoncels are raised; the troops form into squadrons, and advance upon the land, which they already claim as their possession.

Boat after boat poured out the soldiery of the various nations and races assembled under the banner of William; and lastly came the pioneers, with their sharp axes, well trained and taught, and prepared to labour for the defence of the army which they had accompanied.

The quick eye of the leader selected the spot for the stockades and entrenchments. The timbers and pavoises, and other materials, were floated from the store-ships, and dragged to the position which had been pointed out.

The work began with the utmost skill and energy, and the thane plainly saw that, before night-fall, the Norman chief would be entirely secured from surprise. He waited no more, but he instantly determined to bear the ill news to Harold. He turned his horse's head towards the north, and riding night and day, he neither tarried nor rested, until he reached the city of York, where, rushing into the hall, he found Harold, banqueting in festal triumph, with hands embrued in the blood of a brother.

The historians indicate, as I have observed, that many parts of England were opposed to the accession of Harold. I cannot find any evidence that his authority was ever formally and legally recognized in Mercia; and we are assured it was wholly rejected in Northumbria. The Anglo-Saxon States had begun to coalesce, but there was no legislative union between them; and still less was there any union of feeling. On every revolution, the three leading kingdoms of Wessex, Mercia, and Northumbria, had acted as distinct communities, not necessarily bound by the resolutions of the other, or others of them. Admitting that the prelates, earls, aldermen, and thanes of Wessex and East Anglia had sanctioned the accession of Harold, their decision could not have been obligatory upon the other kingdoms; and the very short interval elapsing between the death of Edward and the recognition of Harold, utterly precludes the supposition that their consent was even asked.

Harold's first endeavour appears to have been to secure the friendship of the rival family of Leofric. Edwin's earldom included great part of Mercia. Morcar held Northumbria; and Harold's marriage with their sister Algitha, the widow of Griffith, late King of

Wales, seemed to create a powerful connexion against
the Norman power. But it may be doubted whether
any real strength was gained by this alliance. Harold
gave his hand to the dowager queen of Wales, to her
whose husband he had murdered; but his affections
were placed upon Editha the Fair—" the Swan's Neck "
—as she was called from her beauty; and the existence
of such an attachment negatives the idea of any real
union between Harold and the princess whom he had
espoused. Nor could the political influence of his
brothers-in-law greatly avail him. Edwin might persuade the thanes of Mercia, he could not compel them,
to submit to Harold. The population of Northumbria,
ever impatient of government, wholly refused obedience,
and were ready to find any pretence for attacking the
southron king, whom they had never acknowledged as
their sovereign; and Harold's nearest kinsman was
preparing to assail his authority.

From their earliest youth, nay, even from their baby-
hood, a bitter spirit of rivalry had subsisted between
Tostig and his brother Harold. When Tostig, who had
taken refuge in Flanders after his expulsion from Northumbria, was informed of his brother's accession, he
instantly determined to supplant him, or to drive him
from the throne. Tostig began by machinating with
William; and the Duke of Normandy supplied this
recreant with a force for attempting the invasion of
England. Supported by the foreigner, Tostig ravaged
the Isle of Wight and the neighbourhood of Sandwich;
and it was for the purpose of repelling this invasion,
that the forces of Harold, to which I have before alluded,
were assembled on the southern coast and shores. Tostig did not await the conflict, but pressing some of the

mariners of Sandwich into his service, and persuading others to follow him, he sailed to the coast of Lincolnshire, where he did much harm.

The rapid advance of Edwin and Morcar compelled Tostig to delay the execution of his enterprise. He directed his course towards the north, and repaired to Malcolm, King of Scots, in whose dominions he continued, until towards the close of the summer season, when the fleet of Harfager, King of Norway, suddenly sailed up the Tyne. There is no doubt but that this invasion was undertaken at the instigation of Tostig. The Norman and Norwegian historians inform us, that having first applied to Sweyn of Denmark, he then visited Norway, and persuaded Harfager to the enterprise; and, during his stay in Scotland, Harfager had joined him, and he became the man, or vassal, of the Norwegian king.

The fleet was exceedingly formidable—one half of the Norwegian population fit to bear arms, had been summoned to form the army, which five hundred vessels of the largest burthen had borne across the sea. The fleet touched first at the Shetland Isles, then at the Orkneys, where they received reinforcements. Harfager then coasted along, until he arrived off the shore of Cleveland, where he landed, and compelled the inhabitants to submit to him. Scarborough, after a stubborn, but unavailing defence, was also compelled to yield; and having effected this partial occupation of the country, Harfager seems to have sailed again to the north, and to have been joined by Tostig and his fleet in the Tyne. The combined fleets now entered the Humber, and landed their forces at Riccall, within a short distance from the city of York.

Harfager unfurled his banner, named " landeyda," or
" the desolation of the country" (Aug. 1066).   Tostig's
friends and retainers rallied with ardour, and joined
Harfager in great numbers, adding strength, and imparting confidence to his army.   Edwin and Morcar
issued forth from York with all the forces which they
could assemble : but after a desperate conflict (Sept. 20,
1066), they were put to flight, and in such confusion,
that more men were drowned in the river than slain in
the field.   A great portion of the thanes of the adjoining
wapentakes adhered to Harfager ; those who did not,
fled ; so that he had the entire command of the country ;
and the citizens of York, either believing opposition to
be hopeless, or not choosing to resist, opened their gates
to the Norwegian conqueror.   Harfager proceeded to
establish his authority according to the forms of the
constitution.   He held a court without the walls of the
city, and all the inhabitants being summoned thereto,
they performed homage to the victor.   And, furthermore,
Harfager proclaimed " full peace" to all who would
proceed to the south with him, and enable him to win
the land.   This proceeding discloses the plan of Harfager and Tostig.   They did not seek a military
possession of Northumbria, but they intended to acquire
the lawful dominion of Anglo-Saxon Britain.

As soon as Harold heard the news of the landing of
Harfager and Tostig, he rallied all his forces, and
marched with the utmost expedition to the seat of war,
where he arrived four or five days after the surrender
of York (Sept. 25, 1066).   Harold endeavoured to detach Tostig from his ally, by offering him the earldom
of Northumbria.   Tostig replied, by asking the thane
who bore the message,—Would Harold make any grant

of land to his coadjutor, Harfager? " Seven feet of land
for a grave." " Ride back again," exclaimed Tostig,
displaying a spirit worthy of a better cause, " and desire
King Harold to gird himself for the fight; for never
shall it be told in Norway that Earl Tostig abandoned
Harfager, the son of Sigurd, and went over to his foes."

Harfager had encamped at Stamford Bridge, long
afterwards known as " Pons Belli," or "the Bridge of
Battle." The firm array of the Norwegians, who, ranging target close to target, had formed what they called a
skiold-borg, or "fortress of shields," bristled with spears,
could not be broken by the English, and the latter retreated. The Norwegians, thinking that their adversaries
were about to fly, opened their ranks and began a pursuit. The English instantly wheeled round, and attacked
the enemy (Oct. 7, 1066). Harfager struck around him
as if he were frantic; neither shield nor hauberk could
resist his blow; but an arrow brought him to the ground,
and a pause ensued. Tostig seized the banner and assumed the command. Harold sent a herald to offer
peace to him, and to all the Norwegians who were yet
alive. But they answered with one voice that they
would not take quarter. The war-cry rose again, and
in this conflict Tostig fell. The " landeyda," the fatal
banner, was now seized by a warrior named " Eysteynn
Orri," and a third onslaught began. The Northmen
fought with the utmost desperation; whether their
bodies were protected by their shields or not, they did not
heed;—all they sought, was to give and receive a mortal
wound. In this conflict many of the English fell, but
they ultimately maintained their ground. Late in the
evening the battle was terminated by the death of almost
every Norwegian, and the heaps of unburied bones,

blanched by the sun and rain, long continued to remind the passer-by of the fatal day.

It was on the morrow of the battle, that the Thane of Sussex came to Harold, and apprised him of the arrival of his most dreaded enemy. Harold immediately marched south, and halted at London, where he prepared to attack the invader. The best part of his troops had fallen; few others joined him, either as volunteers, or by virtue of their tenures or of their allegiance. Edwin and Morcar stood aloof; they did not support their brother-in-law; Algitha, his wife, also quitted him, and abandoned him to his fate. Harold's army too plainly testified the danger of his cause; his ranks were imperfectly filled by hired soldiers, who served him merely for their pay; and whatever force he had, was raised from the south of the Humber; not a man came from the north. Githa, his mother, sad and weeping for the loss of her son Tostig, earnestly dissuaded Harold from attempting to give battle to William; his other friends and relations joined her in such entreaties, none so earnestly as Gurth, Earl of Suffolk, Harold's brother, praised for his singular merit and virtue. Gurth pointed out to him, that his troops were wearied and exhausted, the Normans fresh and confident; and furthermore, the Earl of Suffolk represented to Harold that the violation of his oath would lie heavy upon his soul in the field of battle. If Harold would send his troops against William, Gurth solicited that he, who was unfettered by any such obligation, might take the command; for it appears that the oath was considered as binding merely upon the individual Harold, and that it did not restrain him from sanctioning hostility in others. But Harold was influenced by that obstinate, self-willed determination, which leads the sinner on to his fate ; and he persevered, and prepared to encounter his enemy.

Near London, at Waltham, there was a monastery, founded for regular or conventual canons of the order of St. Augustine, and containing a crucifix, supposed to be endued with miraculous power. The abbey of the "holy rood" had been richly endowed by Harold, and before he set out against the enemy, he offered up his orisons at the altar. Whilst Harold was in prayer, in the darkness and gloom of the choir, we are told that the crucifix bowed its head. The portent may have been fancied, but there was a presentiment of evil abroad. It was one of those periods when men's minds are oppressed by the lowering of impending danger, and the brethren of Waltham determined that two members of the convent, Osgod and Ailric, should accompany their benefactor on his march. Harold, having arrayed his forces to the best of his power, directed his course to the shore of Sussex. At Senlac, now better known as Battle, he halted. His camp was surrounded by entrenchments, and on the spot where the high altar of the abbey was afterwards placed, he planted his royal standard.

William had been most actively employed. As a preliminary to further proceedings, he had caused all the vessels to be drawn on shore and rendered unserviceable. He told his men, that they must prepare to conquer or to die—flight was impossible. He had occupied the Roman castle of Pevensey, whose walls are yet existing, flanked by Anglo-Norman towers, and he had personally surveyed all the adjoining country, for he never trusted this part of a general's duty to any eyes but his own. One Robert, a Norman thane, who was settled in the neighbourhood, advised him to cast up entrenchments

Supposed Saxon Keep, Pevensey.

Walls, Pevensey.

Waltham Abbey.

for the purpose of resisting Harold. William replied, that his best defence was in the valour of his army and the goodness of his cause ; and throughout the whole of this expedition, the cool good sense by which he increased the moral courage of his followers is singularly remarkable.

In compliance with the opinions of the age, William had an astrologer in his train. An oriental monarch, at the present time, never engages in battle without a previous horoscope, and this superstition was universally adopted in Europe during the middle ages. But William's "clerk" was not merely a star-gazer. He had graduated in all the occult sciences—he was a necromancer ; or, as the word was often spelt, in order to accommodate it to the supposed etymology, a *nigro-mancer*—a "sortilegus"—and a soothsayer. These accomplishments in the sixteenth century, would have assuredly brought the "clerk" to the stake. But in the eleventh, although they were highly illegal according to the strict letter of the ecclesiastical law, yet they were studied as eagerly as any other branch of metaphysics, of which they were supposed to form a part. The *sorcerer*, or "sortilegus," by casting "*sortes*," or lots, had ascertained that the duke would succeed, and that Harold would surrender without a battle, upon which assurance the Normans entirely relied. After the landing, William inquired for his conjurer. A pilot came forward, and told him that the unlucky wight had been drowned in the passage. William then immediately pointed out the folly of trusting to the predictions of one who was utterly unable to tell what would happen unto himself. When William first set foot on shore, he had shown the same spirit. He stumbled, and fell

forward on the palms of his hands. " *Mal signe est çi !* "
exclaimed his troops, affrighted at the omen. " No,"
answered William, as he rose ; " I have taken seizin of
the country," showing the clod of earth which he had
grasped. One of his soldiers, with the quickness of a
modern Frenchman, instantly followed up the idea—he
ran to a cottage, and pulled out a bundle of reeds from
the thatch, telling him to receive that symbol also, as
the seizin of the realm with which he was invested.
These little anecdotes display the turn and temper of the
Normans, and the alacrity by which the army was pervaded.

Some fruitless attempts are said to have been made at
negociation. Harold despatched a monk to the enemy's
camp, who was to exhort William to abandon his
enterprise. The duke insisted on his right ; but, as
some historians relate, he offered to submit his claim to
a legal decision, to be pronounced by the pope, either
according to the law of Normandy, or according to the
law of England ; or, if this mode of adjustment did not
please Harold, that the question should be decided by
single combat, the crown becoming the meed of the
victor. The propositions of William are stated, by other
authorities, to have contained a proposition for a compromise, namely, that Harold should take Northumbria,
and William the rest of the Anglo-Saxon dominions.
All or any of these proposals are such as may very
probably have been made. But they were not minuted
down in formal protocols, or couched in diplomatic
notes—they were verbal messages, sent to and fro on
the eve of a bloody battle, whereof the particulars were
not related by historians until many years had elapsed ;
and therefore we have no reason to be surprised at the

diversity of such narratives, nor is it at all necessary to attempt to reconcile them.   The general truth is easily understood.   It was evident to each of the chieftains, that they had respectively ventured their whole fortunes on the cast of the die ; and before engaging in a conflict which must prove fatal to one of them, they made an attempt to avoid the danger.

Fear prevailed in both camps. The English, in addition to the apprehensions which even the most stout-hearted feel on the eve of a morrow whose close they may never see, dreaded the papal excommunication, the curse encountered in support of the unlawful authority of a usurper. When they were informed that battle had been decided upon, they stormed and swore; and now the cowardice of conscience spurred them on to riot and revelry.   The whole night was passed in debauch. " *Wæs-heal*" and " *drink-heal*" resounded from the tents ; the wine cups passed gaily round and round by the smoky blaze of the red watch-fires, while the ballad of ribald mirth was loudly sung by the carousers.

In the Norman leaguer, far otherwise had the dread of the approaching morn affected the hearts of William's soldiery.   No voice was heard excepting the solemn response of the litany and the chaunt of the psalm. The penitents confessed their sins—the masses were said— and the sense of the imminent peril of the morrow was tranquillized by penance and prayer.   Each of the nations, as we are told by one of our most trustworthy English historians, acted according to their "national custom ;" and severe is the censure which the English thus receive.

The English were strongly fortified in their position by lines of trenches and palisadoes ; and within these defences they were marshalled according to the Danish fashion, shield against shield, presenting an impenetrable front to the enemy. The men of Kent formed the vanguard, for it was their privilege to be the first in the strife. The burgesses of London, in like manner, claimed and obtained the honour of being the royal body-guard, and they were drawn up around the standard. At the foot of this banner stood Harold, with his brothers, Leofwin and Gurth, and a chosen body of the bravest thanes, all anxiously gazing on that quarter from whence they expected the advance of the enemy.

Before the Normans began their march, and very early in the morning of the feast of St. Calixtus (Oct.14, 1066), William had assembled his barons around him, and exhorted them to maintain his righteous cause. As the invaders drew nigh, Harold saw a division advancing, composed of the volunteers from the county of Boulogne and from the Amiennois, under the command of William Fitz-Osbern and Roger Montgomery. "It is the duke," exclaimed Harold, "and little shall I fear him. By my forces will his be four times outnumbered!" Gurth shook his head, and expatiated on the strength of the Norman cavalry, as opposed to the foot soldiers of England; but their discourse was stopped by the appearance of the combined cohorts, under Aimeric, Viscount of Thouars, and Alan Fergant of Brittany. Harold's heart sank at the sight, and he broke out into passionate exclamations of fear and dismay. But now the third and last division of Norman army was drawing nigh. The consecrated Gonfanon floats amidst the forest of spears; and Harold is now too well aware that he beholds the ranks which are commanded in person by the Duke of Normandy.

As the Normans were marshalled in three divisions, so they began the battle by simultaneous attacks upon three points of the English forces.   Immediately before the duke rode Taillefer, the minstrel, singing, with a loud and clear voice, the lay of Charlemagne and Roland, and the emprizes of the Paladins who had fallen in the dolorous pass of Roncevaux.   Taillefer, as his guerdon, had craved permission to strike the first blow, for he was a valiant warrior, emulating the deeds which he sung : his appellation, *Taille-fer,* is probably to be considered not as his real name, but as an epithet derived from his strength and prowess ; and he fully justified his demand, by transfixing the first Englishman whom he attacked, and by felling the second to the ground. The battle now became general, and raged with the greatest fury.   The Normans advanced beyond the English lines, but they were driven back, and forced into a trench, where horses and riders fell upon each other in fearful confusion.   More Normans were slain here than in any other part of the field.   The alarm spread ; the light troops left in charge of the baggage and the stores thought that all was lost, and were about to take flight, but the fierce Odo, Bishop of Bayeux, the duke's half-brother, and who was better fitted for the shield than for the mitre, succeeded in reassuring them, and then, returning to the field, and rushing into that part where the battle was hottest, he fought as the stoutest of the warriors engaged in the conflict, directing their movements, and inciting them to slaughter.

From nine in the morning till three in the afternoon, the successes on either side were nearly balanced.   The charges of the Norman cavalry gave them great advantage, but the English phalanx repelled their enemies ;

and the soldiers were so well protected by their targets, that the artillery of the Normans was long discharged in vain. The bowmen, seeing that they had failed to make any impression, altered the direction of their shafts, and, instead of shooting point-blank, the flights of arrows were directed upwards, so that the points came down upon the heads of the men of England, and the iron shower fell with murderous effect. The English ranks were exceedingly distressed by the vollies, yet they still stood firm; and the Normans now employed a stratagem to decoy their opponents out of their entrenchments. A feigned retreat on their part, induced the English to pursue them with great heat. The Normans suddenly wheeled about, and a new and fiercer battle was urged. The field was covered with separate bands of foemen, each engaged with one another. Here, the English yielded — there, they conquered. One English thane, armed with a battleaxe, spread dismay amongst the Frenchmen. He was cut down by Roger de Montgomery. The Normans have preserved the name of the Norman baron, but that of the Englishman is lost in oblivion. Some other English thanes are also praised, as having singly, and by their personal prowess, delayed the ruin of their countrymen and country.

At one period of the battle, the Normans were nearly routed. The cry was raised, that the duke was slain, and they began to fly in every direction. William threw off his helmet, and galloping through the squadrons, rallied his barons, though not without great difficulty. Harold, on his part, used every possible exertion, and was distinguished as the most active and bravest amongst the soldiers in the host which he led on to destruction. A Norman arrow wounded him in the left eye; he

Battle of Hastings.

Battle Abbey.

dropped from his steed in agony, and was borne to the foot of the standard. The English began to give way, or rather, to retreat to the standard as their rallying point. The Normans encircled them, and fought desperately to reach this goal. Robert Fitz-Ernest had almost seized the banner, but he was killed in the attempt. William led his troops on, with the intention, it is said, of measuring his sword with Harold. He did encounter an English horseman, from whom he received such a stroke upon his helmet that he was nearly brought to the ground. The Normans flew to the aid of their sovereign, and the bold Englishman was pierced by their lances. About the same time, the tide of battle took a momentary turn. The Kentish men and East Saxons rallied, and repelled the Norman barons; but Harold was not amongst them; and William led on his troops with desperate intrepidity. In the thick crowd of the assailants and the assailed, the hoofs of the horses were plunged deep into the gore of the dead and the dying. Gurth was at the foot of the standard, without hope, but without fear—he fell by the falchion of William. The English banner was cast down, and the Gonfanon planted in its place, announced that William of Normandy was the conqueror.

It was now late in the evening. The English troops were entirely broken, yet no Englishman would surrender. The conflict continued in many parts of the bloody field, long after dark. The fugitives spread themselves over the adjoining country, then covered with wood and forest. Wherever the English could make a stand, they resisted; and the Normans confess that the great preponderance of their force alone enabled them to obtain the victory.

By William's orders, a spot close to the Gonfanon was cleared, and he caused his pavilion to be pitched among the corpses which were heaped around. He there supped with his barons; and they feasted among the dead. But when he contemplated the fearful slaughter, a natural feeling of pity, perhaps allied to repentance, arose in his stern mind; and the Abbey of Battle, in which the prayer was to be offered up perpetually for the repose of the souls of all who had fallen in the conflict, was at once the monument of his triumph and the token of his piety. The abbey was most richly endowed : and all the land, for one league round about, was annexed to the Battle franchise. The abbot was freed from the authority of the metropolitan of Canterbury, and invested with archiepiscopal jurisdiction. The high altar was erected on the very spot where Harold's standard had waved; and the roll, deposited in the archives of the monastery, recorded the names of those who had fought with the conqueror, and amongst whom the lands of broad England were divided. But all this pomp and solemnity has passed away like a dream. The perpetual prayer has ceased for ever—the roll of Battle is rent. The shields of the Norman lineages are trodden in the dust. The abbey is levelled with the ground—and a dank and reedy pool fills the spot where the foundations of the quire have been uncovered, merely for the gaze of the idle visitor, or the instruction of the moping antiquary.

The victor is now installed; but what has become of the mortal spoils of his competitor? If we ask the monk of Malmesbury, we are told that William surrendered the body to Harold's mother, Githa, by whose directions the corpse of the last surviving of her children

Porch of Malmesbury Abbey.

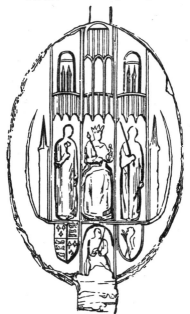

Arms of Malmesbury.

Porch of Malmesbury Abbey

Arms of Malmesbury

was buried in the abbey of the Holy Cross. Those who lived nearer the time, however, relate in explicit terms that William refused the rites of sepulture to his excommunicated enemy. Guillielmus Pictavensis, the chaplain of the conqueror, a most trustworthy and competent witness, informs us that a body of which the features were undistinguishable, but supposed, from certain tokens, to be that of Harold, was found between the corpses of his brothers, Gurth and Leofwine, and that William caused this corpse to be interred in the sands of the sea-shore. " Let him guard the coast," said William, " which he so madly occupied;" and though Githa had offered to purchase the body by its weight in gold, yet William was not to be tempted by the gift of the sorrowing mother, or touched by her tears.

In the abbey of Waltham, they knew nothing of Githa. According to the annals of the convent, the two brethren who had accompanied Harold, hovered as nearly as possible to the scene of war, watching the event of the battle : and afterwards, when the strife was quiet in death, they humbly approached William, and solicited his permission to seek the corpse.

The conqueror refused a purse, containing ten marks of gold, which they offered as the tribute of their gratitude ; and permitted them to proceed to the field, and to bear away not only the remains of Harold, but of all who, when living, had chosen the abbey of Waltham as their place of sepulture.

Amongst the loathsome heaps of the unburied, they sought for Harold, but sought in vain,—Harold could not possibly be discovered—no trace of Harold was to be found ; and as the last hope of identifying his remains, they suggested that possibly his beloved Editha might

be able to recognise the features so familiar to her
affections. Algitha, the wife of Harold, was not to be
asked to perform this sorrowful duty. Osgood went
back to Waltham, and returned with Editha, and the
two canons and the weeping woman resumed their
miserable task in the charnel field. A ghastly, decom-
posing, and mutilated corpse was selected by Editha,
and conveyed to Waltham as the body of Harold; and
there entombed at the east end of the choir, with great
honour and solemnity, many Norman nobles assisting in
the requiem.

Years afterwards, when the Norman yoke pressed
heavily upon the English, and the battle of Hastings
had become a tale of sorrow, which old men narrated
by the light of the embers, until warned to silence by
the sullen tolling of the curfew, there was a decrepit
anchorite, who inhabited a cell near the abbey of St.
John at Chester, where Edgar celebrated his triumph.
This recluse, deeply scarred, and blinded in his left eye,
lived in strict penitence and seclusion. Henry I. once
visited the aged hermit, and had a long private discourse
with him; and, on his death-bed, he declared to the
attendant monks that he was Harold. As the story is
transmitted to us, he had been secretly conveyed from
the field to a castle, probably of Dover, where he continued concealed until he had the means of reaching the
sanctuary where he expired..

The monks of Waltham loudly exclaimed against this
rumour. They maintained most resolutely, that Harold
was buried in their abbey: they pointed to the tomb,
sustaining his effigies, and inscribed with the simple and
pathetic epitaph, "*Hic jacet Harold infelix;*" and they
appealed to the mouldering skeleton, whose bones, as

they declared, showed, when disinterred, the impress of the wounds which he had received.   But may it not still be doubted whether Osgood and Ailric, who followed their benefactor to the fatal field, did not aid his escape? They may have discovered him at the last gasp; restored him to animation by their care; and the artifice of declaring to William, that they had not been able to recover the object of their search, would readily suggest itself as the means of rescuing Harold from the power of the conqueror.   The demand of Editha's testimony would confirm their assertion, and enable them to gain time to arrange for Harold's security; and whilst the litter, which bore the corpse, was slowly advancing to the abbey of Waltham, the living Harold, under the tender care of Editha, might be safely proceeding to the distant fane, his haven of refuge.

If we compare the different narratives concerning the inhumation of Harold, we shall find the most remarkable discrepancies.   It is evident that the circumstances were not accurately known; and since those ancient writers who were best informed cannot be reconciled to each other, the escape of Harold, if admitted, would solve the difficulty.   I am not prepared to maintain that the authenticity of this story cannot be impugned; but it may be remarked that the tale, though romantic, is not incredible, and that the circumstances may be easily reconciled to probability.   There were no walls to be scaled, no fosse to be crossed, no warder to be eluded; and the examples of those who have survived after encountering much greater perils, are so very numerous and familiar, that the incidents which I have narrated would hardly give rise to a doubt, if they referred to any other personage than a king.

In this case we cannot find any reason for supposing that the belief in Harold's escape was connected with any political artifice or feeling. No hopes were fixed upon the usurping son of Godwin. No recollection dwelt upon his name, as the hero who would sally forth from his seclusion, the restorer of the Anglo-Saxon power. That power had wholly fallen,—and if the humbled Englishman, as he paced the aisles of Waltham, looked around, and having assured himself that no Norman was near, whispered to his son, that the tomb which they saw before them was raised only in mockery, and that Harold still breathed the vital air—he yet knew too well that the spot where Harold's standard had been cast down, was the grave of the pride and glory of England.

THE END.